DIGGER
OR
GEORDIE?

John Simpson Kirkpatrick, the 'Man with the Donkey' – the untold story of his family history

By

Kelso McEwan Yuill

First Edition   February 2015

Copyright

ISBN 978-0-9571257-3-5

Published by Relativity

Printed by B&B Press (Parkgate) Ltd.,
Aldwarke Road,
Rotherham, S62 6DY

This book is dedicated to Ned Parnell,

an 'Aussie' with an enquiring mind

who introduced me to John Simpson Kirkpatrick.

Further copies of this book may be obtained from the author.

Front cover illustration, statue of John Simpson Kirkpatrick, South Shields, England.

Back cover illustration, ANZAC Memorial at Blackboy Camp, Western Australia.

Contents

Simpson Family headstone at Craigton Cemetery, Glasgow.

Image KY Collection

Transcription for Simpson Gravestone in

Craigton Cemetery, Glasgow

ERECTED BY

JAMES SIMPSON
IN
LOVING MEMORY
OF HIS WIFE

ANN HOSGOOD
Died 22nd October 1887, aged 64 Years

ALSO OF THEIR CHILDREN

SEBASTIAN, Died at Fernando Po
13TH May 1873, Aged 21 Years
JULIA Died 11TH February 1878
Aged 17 Years
SAMUEL Lost at Sea in 1880
Aged 21 Years
CHRISTIAN WHITE Their Eldest Daughter
Died 11TH February 1882 Aged 35 Years

THE ABOVE
JAMES SIMPSON
Died 19TH June, 1897, Aged 80 Years

JAMES Their Eldest Son
Died 18TH May 1915 Aged 64 Years
MARTHA SIMPSON, Their Daughter
Died 30TH May 1946, Aged 87 Years
JANE JAMES SIMPSON, Their Daughter
Died 22ND September 1946, Aged 96 Years
HELEN SIMPSON, Their Daughter
Died 11TH May 1958 Aged 92 Years

Introduction

Over the last decade, there has been an ever increasing groundswell of interest in family history. Archivists around the English speaking world have been digitising their records feverishly and making them available on the internet. Genealogy is big business. Television companies have responded to the interest with programmes such as "Who Do You Think You Are", in which celebrities are conducted through a search of their family history with deceptive ease. The search usually starts with the celebrity visiting an elderly relative, grandparent, uncle or aunt etc., who provides a starting point for the metaphorical journey through the records.

If John Simpson Kirkpatrick, known as Jack, 'the Man with the Donkey' had been asked "Who Do You Think You Are"? he would have been flummoxed. Neither Jack nor his sister Annie, who was interviewed by Sir Irving Benson, author of the 1965 biography 'The Man with the Donkey', appeared to know anything of their ancestry other than their mother was from Glasgow, a Scot and proud of it and their father was a master mariner from Leith in Scotland. In 1994, Tom Curran produced a more lengthy biography, titled 'Across the Bar'. Curran had the advantage of meeting the descendants of Jack's sisters, Maggie married to Will Balneaves and Sarah married to Sam Christie who settled in Australia after WWI. He also had extensive correspondence with Jack Parkin, son of Jack's sister Annie and her first husband Francis Parkin, but in spite of picking up a few family stories about the Simpson Kirkpatricks, he added not one jot about kinsfolk or ancestors. Moreover, family stories although usually containing an element of truth are often prone to a bit of spin, a little bit of exaggeration, or dramatization here and there, when passed by word of mouth from one generation to the next. A family with no known relatives whomsoever is very rare. Did Jack's parents, Sarah and Robert Kirkpatrick conceal their family history from their children and if so why?

One Australian with the perspicacity to look beyond the published biographies is Ned Parnell from Western Australia, the man to whom this book is dedicated. In 2005, following a report he had commissioned from a professional genealogist in Scotland, Ned phoned me and introduced himself with the words, "I think you might be related to one of Australia's heroes. Have you heard of the "Man with the Donkey?"

Living in North East England, only 30 miles from South Shields, I had a vague recollection of reading the story in our local newspaper, 'The Northern Echo'. The genealogist's report received by Ned linked 'Sarah Simpson', Jack's mother to my family tree, though I had never known of any connection to the 'Man with the Donkey'. Before delving into the records at Scotland's People, I quickly acquired a copy of Sir Irving Benson's book 'The Man with the Donkey' but this told me little, only that Sarah Simpson came from Glasgow, was a Scot and proud of it (as I am). It did not take long to find my great grandmother's sister Sarah Simpson in the Scottish records, and she seemed at first sight to be quite prolific. It soon became clear there were two Sarah Simpsons living in the same area of Scotland at the same time and giving birth to numerous children. Clearly there was more than one Sarah Simpson and my Sarah Simpson, it transpired was not the hero's mother. The research by the professional genealogist was flawed.

By this time I had also acquired and read Tom Curran's book 'Across the Bar', published in 1994 which aroused my interest still further. I was intrigued by the fact that the Simpson Kirkpatricks had no relatives. Were there skeletons in the cupboard?

Unearthing the story was a challenge that could not be resisted. The resultant search for Jack's ancestors has taken me on many journeys: in Australia to Newcastle, Corrimal, Blackboy Camp near Perth, and to Canberra; to Anzac Cove in Gallipoli; to Malaga in Spain; to Valparaiso in Chile, sailing round Cape Horn; and through the back streets of Glasgow, Leith and South Shields. My knowledge of geography and 19th century political, social and military history has improved dramatically.

Along the way, I have been in regular contact with Ned Parnell who has continued his quest to track down living descendants of Jack Simpson Kirkpatrick. We have shared the results of our researches as new information has come to light. This book traces the story of Jack's missing grandparents, uncles and aunts. Ned has gone further in tracing family roots to the coal mines and iron works of the Welsh Valleys in the turbulent early years of Britain's Industrial Revolution. It is to be hoped Ned will soon publish the wealth of data he has amassed concerning the Simpson/Hosgood family.

The story of the Simpsons, Kirkpatricks and Hosgoods follows the fortunes and misfortunes of a family during the reign of Queen Victoria; during the incredible growth in Britain's Empire, with its concomitant growth in her wealth and prosperity; it embraces success and failure, fornication and adultery; sudden death and tragedy; insanity and sorrow; a family feud and bitter estrangement; shipwreck and drowning. It spans the globe. The story has all the ingredients of a Victorian saga necessary for a TV costume drama or film.

Jack had no knowledge of his ancestral history it seems, but how much did his inherited DNA contribute to his heroic conduct at Gallipoli? The personalities in "Who Do You Think You Are" often find ancestors with whom they can empathise. What resonances would Jack have felt with the characters revealed in his family tree? Would he have thought of himself as a Digger or a Geordie?

Kelso McEwan Yuill

ACKNOWLEDGEMENTS AND THANKS

Northern Hemisphere

As the author of this book, I have received a high level of support from many people and am very grateful to them all. These include:

David Bradley and Tanya McDonald of the Maritime History Archives at the Memorial University of Newfoundland, who have been tremendously helpful over several years in finding and supplying Crew Agreements, or telling where they might be found. I regard them as old friends and still hope to meet them someday.

The staff at the National Archives, Kew, and especially the official who unearthed the Consular Register for Malaga 1837 – 1891; this was a real breakthrough.

Catrin Galt and the ever obliging and knowledgeable staff of South Shield's Central Library. I am especially grateful for permission to use the illustrations from the 'South Tyneside Images' website.

Sunderland Library which holds a good run of 19th century Lloyds Shipping Lists and the staff of Bishop Auckland Library who procured out-of-print books for me on the history of Spain and Malaga.

The technician of Photos4U, Bishop Auckland, who reduced outsized Newspaper Illustrations to manageable proportions and restored old photographs.

The National Maritime Museum, Greenwich who made available Masters', Mates' and Engineers certificates.

Jean Crawford at the National Archives of Scotland, for records of the London and Edinburgh Shipping Company. Others for access to Wills and the Records of Trinity House.

Lorna Hunter and the Northern Lighthouse Board, for the photograph of John Kirkpatrick, Master of the North Carr Lightship.

Edinburgh Central Library who produced newspaper archives for Leith and have given permission to use images from their 'Capital Collections'.

Edinburgh University Library who supplied the records of Edinburgh Royal Maternity Hospital, 1873.

Glasgow University Library who supplied committal documents and case notes from the records of the Royal Glasgow Mental Asylum, Gartnavel.

The Mitchell Library who supplied extracts from Glasgow's Education Department records, gave permission for the use of photographic images, and found for me the burial records for Craigton Cemetery.

The Foreman and groundsmen at Craigton Cemetery, who hacked their way through the decades of undergrowth to locate the Simpson Family Gravestone. Standing before that monument was a pivotal and emotional moment. So much was learned from reading those brief inscriptions carved in stone so long ago.

Southern Hemisphere

So much of the archival material relating to John Simpson Kirkpatrick rests in Australian Archives making life difficult for a researcher on the other side of the world. As a result, I have been heavily dependent on a few friends, cousins and a number of archivists. I wish to acknowledge their help and express my deepest gratitude to;

Ned Parnell of Western Australia, who set me off on the trail of John Simpson Kirkpatrick. We have shared information, ideas, theories and opinions (not always agreeing) and have remained firm friends. On route to visit cousins on the east side of Australia, my wife and I spent a few days in Perth in 2011. Ned and his wife Joanne could not have been more hospitable, and the highlight was a visit to the site of Blackboy Camp.

Grant Malcolm of Western Australia. I have yet to meet Grant but he has very generously allowed me to use the fruits of his research into the Gallipoli Campaign and also transcriptions of correspondence between Jack's sister Annie Pearson and the Australian High Commissioners around the time of the 50th Anniversary Celebrations in 1965.

Alan Williams of Perth, Western Australia. While in Perth we met up with an old friend from England who took us to visit the State Memorial in Kings Park and to Fremantle from where the First Contingent A.I.F. set off for the Great War in 1914.

My cousins, Mary and Bill Chapman, Wollongong, New South Wales, who have been our hosts on three visits to Australia. In 2008, they took us to the Australian War Memorial at Canberra. Bill has kept me up to date with press cuttings from the Australian newspapers concerning Simpson Kirkpatrick and the campaign to win him a Victoria Cross, as well as supplying the occasional relevant photograph.

John and Fay Reay of Corrimal, New South Wales whom we met almost by chance. While in Wollongong, we visited John and Fay to deliver a calendar from a friend in Durham. John, we discovered has a wonderful library of local history photographs. He readily contributed photographs of the mines in which Kirkpatrick worked and the ships in which he sailed. We look forward to Fay's delicious home baking on our next visit.

Jim Hunter, a cousin from Cove Boulevard, New South Wales, who loaned me the books 'GALLIPOLI ' by L.A. Carlyon and 'ANZAC TO AMIENS' by C.E.W. Bean. I shall return these books next time we visit though we would be equally delighted if you Jim and Steph could come to Durham to collect them.

Paul Heiser and Pat Coomber of Queensland for images and information about the Kirkpatrick descendants in Queensland.

Staff at various state libraries and archives for copies of documents and photographs: the Australian War Memorial at Canberra for photographs and information from the Annie Pearson archive; the State Library of South Australia for the photograph of the Scythia; the State Library of Victoria for two prints of the hurricane at the Lacepede Islands, in Western Australia; and the State Library of Western Australia and the Royal Western Historical Society for joint permission to use the image of Bullfinch Store in 1910.

Finally, a huge thank you to my typist, photographer, computer expert and travel organiser who has been with me on every step on the trail of John Simpson Kirkpatrick and his family – my wife Anne, without whom this book might never have seen the light of day.

Chapter 1

ROBERT KIRKPATRICK: BACHELOR DAYS

JOHN SIMPSON KIRKPATRICK'S FATHER

On the 20th June 1837, Queen Victoria came to the throne of Great Britain, a nation on the verge of an industrial and social revolution. She would reign for sixty four years and would preside over a period of undreamed-of technological advances, economic growth, and colonial expansion. Empire, trade, invention, manufacturing and commerce brought great wealth to the nation, though this prosperity was not shared equitably among Victoria's subjects. During her reign, Britain's social fabric changed utterly. Agricultural communities were decimated as people flocked from the country to the cities to work in the mills and factories. Cities like Manchester and Glasgow mushroomed at a squalourous rate. In Scotland thousands of families, displaced by the Highland Clearances braved long, perilous sea voyages in small wooden ships to the new colonies in Canada, Australia, New Zealand, and to the Americas in search of a better life. By the time of her jubilee in 1897, Victoria's vast empire on which it was said the sun never set, stretched around the globe.

Five months after she ascended the throne, Victoria had another addition to her subjects. On the 26th November Robert Kilpatrick, seaman Queen Street, Leith and Margaret Low, his spouse had a lawful son named Robert. The baptism was recorded in Leith South, and the parish clerk inscribed the name in the parish register as 'Kilpatrick'. The parents, Robert and Margaret, daughter of the late John Low, cooper, had been married in Leith on 25th June 1830 by the Rev. James Grant. Before Robert junior arrived the Kilpatricks had two other children, Isabella born 27th July 1831 and Elizabeth born 18th June 1833.

Leith harbour 1842 – earliest known photograph using the Calotype process.
A two masted brigantine drawn up on the shore at Leith for maintenance.
Robert was 5 at this time and could be one of the children in the fore ground.
The brig is typical of the ships in which Robert first went to sea. They were all
purpose, sailed surprisingly long distances, were the fore runner of the tramp
steamer.

Ref. Scran ID: 000-000-145-175-C Glasgow University Library

The young Robert went to sea at the age of 12 and by the time he himself
got married, he had seen most of Victoria's empire in both hemispheres.

At the time of the 1841 census, the family were living in the parish of St
Clements, Aberdeen, on Scotland's North East coast, but only Margaret,
and two children are listed, Robert age 3, and Elizabeth 7. Robert senior was
presumably at sea, and it looks as though Isabella had died. By 1844, the
Kilpatricks who became known as Kirkpatrick were back in Queen Street,
Leith where Maggie gave birth to another son, John on 17th April and by this
time Robert senior was a *Ship Master*. The spelling of the family name
varied between Kilpatrick and Kirkpatrick.

When the 1851 census was taken the family's fortunes had taken a few
twists. Margaret was head of the house, described as a 'Seaman's Wife',
living with a daughter Margaret, age 9, born since the previous census, son

John age 6, and a daughter Elizabeth age 1. Had the first Elizabeth died? Neither Robert, senior or junior, were accounted for in the census, both being away at sea.

The Shore, Leith circa 1850. Robert's career began as an ordinary seaman, age 13 years in small sailing ships like these.
Image courtesy of Capital Collections, Edinburgh City Libraries

Leith, the principal seaport on Scotland's east coast, and also the port for Edinburgh, would be Robert Kirkpatrick's home for 49 years, before his move to South Shields. Born into a seafaring family it was inevitable he would also go to sea. The year after his birth, an early paddle steamer built in Leith, the SIRIUS made the first ever east to west Atlantic crossing powered entirely by steam. She left Cork on 4th April 1838 and anchored in New York harbour on the 22nd April, beating Isambard Kingdom Brunel's GREAT BRITAIN by a day. The SIRIUS did have a four day start on the GREAT BRITAIN, however, delayed at the outset by technical problems. By the time Robert's maritime career ended after fifty five years, he would witness the launch of the MAURETANIA, on the Tyne in 1906, a 32,000 ton luxury liner, powered by steam turbines and capable of crossing the Atlantic with 2,000 passengers in six days.

Leith's docks and harbour was Robert's playground. He grew up amongst cordage and creels, amongst bales and barrels; amidst the smell of tar and timber, amidst the rattle of rigging and the screech of pulley blocks; amidst

3

the babble of accents and foreign tongues. He saw emigrants' sorrowful and hopeful, leave for the colonies; he saw coals and whisky leave for London. Coming in he saw cargoes of wine from France, ore from Sweden, timber from Canada, grain from the Baltic and by the age of 12 he was completely familiar with the rigs of schooners, smacks and luggers; with barques, brigs, brigantines and clippers. Then there was the newer heady smell of oil, smoke and steam mingling in the air. Leith was an exciting place for a boy and the sea was surely in Robert's blood, a legacy to be inherited by two of his sons.

Robert's school days ended at the age of twelve, the age when any lad in good health was expected to start making his own way in the world. By the time the official census was taken in April 1851 he had been at sea since the age of 13 and was already earning his living as an ordinary seaman on board a Leith schooner called the GLANCE. This little sailing ship built in 1845, was owned by the London & Edinburgh Shipping Company. She was 114 tons burden, measured 74.5 feet in length, 18.4 feet beam and 11.4 feet in depth. The Crew Agreement for January to July 1852 shows the names, ages, place of birth, previous ship and rate of pay for each crew member. The master was William Cousins and he had a mate, seven seamen and three ordinary seamen to handle the ship. Ordinary seaman Robert Kilpatrick, age 14 and the youngest on board, signed on 1st January 1852 for a wage of '£1 per month, Share or Voyage', giving his previous ship also as "GLANCE OF LEITH". The merchant navy was regulated by Act of Parliament. The opening paragraph of the crew agreement, an official Board of Trade document and a legal contract between the master and each crew member, reads:

> "And the said Crew agree to conduct themselves in an orderly, faithful, honest, and sober manner, and to be at all times diligent in their respective duties, and to be obedient to the lawful commands of their said master...etc."

The Whitehall lawyer who drafted this clause must have lived in an ivory tower or been a supreme optimist. For merchant seamen life was hazardous and hard. The men were hard – they had to be. It seems to be asking a lot, particularly that they 'be of a sober manner'. At this time the Royal Navy still press ganged men and flogged defaulters, but such sanctions were not available to masters of merchant ships, but some masters were not averse to applying fists and boots to enforce discipline. The GLANCE was 'Employed in Trade betwixt Leith and Hull (8 voyages)'.

On 15th February 1852 Robert, now age 15, transferred from the GLANCE to the SWIFT, also a schooner belonging to the London & Edinburgh Shipping Company. She was a little larger than GLANCE, being a net tonnage of 184 tons, and crewed by a master, mate, carpenter, 6 seamen and 4 ordinary seamen including Robert whose wage was now £1.10/- *'per Month, Share, or Voyage'.* The SWIFT afforded young Robert a chance to extend his horizons as she traded from Leith to London and back. On return from London on the 10th June 1852 Robert was discharged. His young eyes must have boggled at the sight of London and the Thames, the biggest and busiest port in the world, crammed with sailing ships of all sizes, trading with every corner of the world. It seems his imagination may also have been fired with tales of gold and the vast fortunes to be made in the newly discovered goldfields in Australia.

The next extant crew list on which Robert is recorded is for the VALERIA, a small sail ship, 113 tons registered in Yarmouth. On 1st January 1853, the master James Wright signed up a crew of eight men for the first half of the year, amongst whom was a Mate Robert Kilpatrick, aged 44 from Leith and an Ordinary Seaman, Robert Kilpatrick aged 16 also from Leith. Father and son were serving on the same ship. Moreover both gave their previous ship as REGENT of Leith, for the second half of 1852, so we may take it father and son had an amicable working relationship. No crew list for the REGENT has been found. The VALERIA sailed from Leith 20th January for Honfleur in France, thence to Poole in Dorset and from Poole to Newcastle where both Robert Kilpatricks left the ship the reason being given by the Master as "their own wish".

Note: When Robert applied to take the exam for his mate's certificate he had to include a "*statement of service from first going to sea*". The Crew Agreements for his first two ships were traced from this information. The Crew List for the VALERIA was traced through the application for a Master's Certificate by Robert Kilpatrick Senior. After 13th March 1853 there is a gap in the service record of Robert Junior until 17th December 1856 when he joined a Liverpool ship, THE BRITISH LION in Melbourne. He may well have been prospecting in Victoria's goldfields.

List D.
No.

PORT OF

ACCOUNT OF VOYAGES AND CREW OF HOME TRADE SHIP, TO BE DELIVERED
HALF-YEARLY TO THE SHIPPING MASTER AT THE ABOVE PORT.

ACCOUNT OF THE CREW AND OF OTHER PARTICULARS REQUIRED BY LAW, IN RESPECT OF THE ABOVE-MENTIONED VOYAGES OR EMPLOYMENT OF THE SAID SHIP.

Crew list of the VALERIA in 1853 with Robert Kirkpatrick senior and his son Robert both serving on the same ship.

Photo courtesy of National Archives, Kew

When he joined the BRITISH LION in Melbourne he gave his previous ship as the WILLING LASS. Two ships of this name have been traced, one registered in Melbourne and one in Greenock. Alas no crew agreements have been found for either ship in the Melbourne archives or at National Archives, Kew. Thanks to the requirement to state 'previous ship' when signing on it is possible to trace a seaman's service retrospectively. However there is no way of working forward in time from an agreement. Other evidence is needed. There is no doubt Robert was a precocious and adventurous lad. He was not afraid of the perils of the sea, and was undeterred by the hardships of life on board ship. For a bold teenager it was an exciting life. The tantalising gap of three and a half years in his record of service is so far unexplained. It is highly probable however that, like every other sailor arriving in Melbourne at that time, he deserted and headed for the gold diggings. One visitor arriving at Melbourne in 1853 described the port as crammed with ships but deserted by sailors.

In 1856, Robert, aged 16 years reached Melbourne, deserted his ship and tried his luck in the goldfields. The image shows an interesting cross section of Melbourne's citizens greeting the arrival of a primrose from the 'Old Country'.

Illustrated London News, 1858. KY Collection

Interestingly when Robert rejoined the mercantile service, the BRITISH LION, on 17th December 1856, he was one of 20 men taken on as replacements. When the ship arrived from England earlier that month, no fewer than 21 men deserted, including the boatswain, sailmaker, two apprentices, and almost the entire crew, like the rest of their contemporaries fired with dreams of gold and untold riches.

The master of the BRITISH LION, Fred Harrington had a major headache. He desperately needed a crew for the return voyage, for apart from normal freight he had a contract to carry a rather special cargo back to England. When the time came for his ship to sail Harrington may have had to rely on one of the notorious boarding masters to find him a crew, Robert Kirkpatrick included. It is rather odd that the list of new crewmen signing-on is written entirely by one hand. None of the new crewmen actually signed for himself. Whether Robert filled one of the vacancies by coercion or willingly we may never know. When he signed on the BRITISH LION, he may have been disillusioned by three years of hard digging with 'nowt to show for it'; he may simply have felt it was time to go home, having been away for nearly four years from the age of 15 to 19. When he signed on his age was entered as 21. Whether this was a careless mistake or deliberate, there is no way of telling, but it would not be the last time he would give a false age. The BRITISH LION was a large sailing ship of 1369 tons, built in Quebec 1853. Her owners were Moore & Company of Liverpool where she was registered. She had left her home port on 25th July 1856. Before clearing out of Melbourne 20th December 1856, bound for England via Bombay, she took on board an unusually valuable cargo, 1001 ¾ ounces of gold, a product of Victoria's gold rush. Did the crew know what they were carrying? Details of a number of gold shipments were published for all to see in the Sydney Morning Herald of Friday 26th December 1856. At Bombay she lay from the 18th February to the 21st March 1857. During this lay-up, 10 of her crew took their discharge and 2 died of cholera – not a happy or a healthy ship it seems. The ship's log records that, on the return voyage two crewmen "came aft" to complain to the master that the pork had so much fat that they could not eat it. They wanted an issue of beef instead. Mr Harrington recorded the complaint in the log as he was obliged to do by law, and bluntly refused their request for beef. They could take the pork or leave it.

More crew members were recruited in Bombay and Mr. Harrington duly brought his ship safely back to Liverpool where Robert, having survived the bad food and the cholera, signed off on 25th July 1857. His ability as a seaman was recorded as only 'G' and his conduct as 'VG'. How did he get back to Leith from Liverpool? His mate's exam application lists his next ship as the PRINCESS ROYAL of Leith, from March 23 to June 11 1859, with no explanation of what he was doing since his return via Liverpool. The crew agreement for this ship gives his previous ship as the ESK of Leith but the agreement has not been found for this vessel. The agreement for the PRINCESS ROYAL gives an interesting glimpse of a seaman's working life at that time. She was a schooner, built in Aberdeen 1850, not a very big vessel with a registered tonnage of 158 tons, crewed by a master, James Burrell and eight men, a First Mate, a Boatswain, 3 Able Seamen, 2 Ordinary Seamen and a cook. When signing on, Robert gave his age as 22, and his wage was £2-15/- per month. The agreement shows how a seaman could provide for his next of kin while away from home for months at a stretch. The following clause was added to the pre-printed agreement by hand:

> ".... that an advance of wages will be made to the seaman for the amount stated against their respective names and payable to his order three days after the Vessel leaves Dysart, by Mr. John Gilchrist, the Owner, 52 Giles Street, Leith, provided the seaman sails in the said vessel from Dysart aforesaid and is then duly earning his wages, or without fault on his part is duly discharged with the consent of the master."

This modest little schooner with a regal name worked in "the foreign trade" as distinct from the 'home trade', and her voyage commenced from Dysart on March 28th 1859, her destination being Charante on France's SW Atlantic coast. Dysart is a harbour on the north side of the Firth of Forth opposite Leith and three miles east of the larger port of Kirkcaldy. It served as an outlet for coal mined a few miles inland in the Fife coalfield, so the PRINCESS ROYAL's cargo on the outward journey was most likely "black diamonds". The schooner's course took her south down the east coast of England, west through the English Channel then south east across the notoriously rough seas of the Bay of Biscay. The River Charente flows into the sea at Rochefort and the Charente region is famous for its cognac and pineau wine, so the returning cargo of the PRINCESS ROYAL was most probably barrels and a heady aroma in the hold.

The voyage of the PRINCESS ROYAL terminated in Dublin 13th June 1859 and there the crew were discharged. The terms of the Agreement allowed the master to discharge the crew in any port in the British Isles, leaving them to find their own way home, which seems a bit unjust to modern ways of thinking. For many merchant seamen however this was simply a way of life. They found a boarding house, indulged in the pleasures afforded by every port around the world, and when the money was gone, signed on another ship, heedless of destination. Robert however was more conscientious and must have worked his passage back to Leith, for within a month, he signed on his next ship in Alloa, another of the little coal ports on the north shore of the river Forth.

He joined the THAMES, registered in Alloa, on July 14th. She was probably the oldest ship Robert ever sailed in, being a Brig, of 371 tons, built in 1794 in Quebec, at the time of the French Revolutionary wars. His wage as an Able Seaman for this trip was £3.7/6 out of which he made a monthly allotment of £1.10/-, presumably payable to his mother. The crew numbered 15: Master, Mate, Carpenter, Boatswain, 10 Able Seamen, and a Cook, William Wright, a native of Alloa and the oldest man on board at 64 years of age. One voyage was enough for Robert, it seems. Having joined July 14th, he took his discharge on November 26th 1859 when the ship returned to the Forth. However, the THAMES had taken him in a completely new direction, westwards across the north Atlantic for the first time, to Canada. He had sailed up the St Lawrence to Quebec, more than likely to deliver another load of coal. The return cargo was probably grain or timber.

Having experienced the cold airs of the North Atlantic, and after spending Christmas and the New Year in Leith, Robert was lured to the South Pacific once more and joined the BEN NEVIS of Kincardine for a voyage to New Zealand. This was a time when the infant colonies of Australia and New Zealand were growing rapidly and were eager to attract immigrants.

It was also a time of social upheaval in Scotland when many Highland landlords were evicting tenants from their crofts to make way for sheep, deemed by landlords to be a more profitable use of the land. Displaced Scots were emigrating by the ship load to the new colonies. Canada and South Island in New Zealand still reflect this demographic movement in its place names and in its electoral rolls.

EX "BEN NEVIS."

3 CASES PARAFFIN LAMPS, great variety of patterns

ALSO,

400 gallons Oil for ditto

JAS. PATERSON & CO.

Just Landing ex "Ben Nevis,"

1 CASE BEST ASSORTED CUTLERY, consisting of

Table Knives and Forks, Dessert do., Carving do., Butcher's do., Hacking do.

Scissors, best plated Spokeshaves

C. S. Hand Saws, Spirit Levels, do. with cross sights

Telescopes, Spectacles with cases, Corkscrews assorted

1 cask Ornamental Brackets, Barrow Wheels

1 case,—1 complete Flour Mill, for producing at one operation 1st, 2nd, and 3rd flour and bran ; 2 steel do., No. 3, with fly wheel ; 1 pair Cart Springs, 1 set Fanner Mounting, Patent Scythes

1 case Turpentine in quart bottles

1 case—Avery's Weighing Machine with folding wings and hooks, Bushel Measures, Hearth Brushes, Japanned do., Gilt do., Banister do., Sash Tools, Painters' Brushes, Shoe do., Scrubbing and Dandy do., Sea-weed Brooms, Whitening Brushes, Broom Heads, Graining Brushes, Tin Scoops and fillers, Black Lead, Lustre

1 crate Kitchen and Parlour Fenders

1 case do., do., superior

1 case Kitchen Shovels, Pokers, and Tongs

1 case Wrought-iron Fireproof Safe

1 case Hand, Jack, and Plough Planes, C. S. Trowels assorted, Bastard, Cross-cut, and Hand Saw Files, Cross-cut Saws, and Splitting Wedges, Imperial Measuring Chains

1 Case—Wrought Iron Book Safe, School Slates, Pencils, Jack Chain, Tape Lines, Whipcord, Emery Cloth and Glass Paper

1 Case—1 Carron Money Chest, 1 do. Book do., Britannia Metal Tea Pots

1 Case—Mason's C.S. Irons, assorted Hammers, Coopers' Rivets, Lead Ladles, Glue, Blacking, &c.

1 Case—Cross-Cut, Frame, and Pit Saws, C.S. Hand Saws, Jack do., Sash do., Butchers' do., Trowels, Stubbs' Files, Stable Latches, Shoe Knives, Horse Syringe, Garden Shears, Norfolk and Suffolk Latches, Rim, Mortice, Stock, and Banbury Locks, Cart and Gig Whips

Black's Spades, Shovels (round and square) Potato and Manure, Hay and Pitch Forks

Patent Diagonal Iron Harrows

Diamond do. Ploughs

Fencing Wire Straitener, Straining Screw and Vice for do.

Patent Fuse for blasting, Folding Camp Beds

Annealed Fencing Wire

Lion Iron, Blister and Shear Steel, Hoop Iron, Kent Grates, Gothic Hall Stoves, Register do., Kitchen Ranges, Newcastle Ranges, Door Scrapers, Garden do., Skylights, Truck Wheels, Garden Seats, &c., &c.

Camp Ovens

Girdles and Frying Pans

JAS. PATERSON & CO.

By 1859/60, Robert was sailing for the antipodes again in an immigrant ship, the BEN NEVIS, arriving in Otago, New Zealand, July 1860.

Image Illustrated London News Sept 1852. KY Collection

This advert appeared in the Otago Witness dated 1 September 1860. Jas. Patterson was evidently a hardware merchant. His advert shows the huge range of merchandise being shipped in for a new colony but his was not the only advert. Turnbull, Bing & Co. of Stafford Street, were also advertising their merchandise unloaded from the same ship, and others were selling boots , shoes clothing, drapery and almost everything you could think of.

Robert joined the ship as bos'un, an appointment which says a lot about his character. Still only 22 he must have been a skilful seaman, physically robust, mentally tough and self-assured (qualities which his more famous son seems to have inherited). The bosun was responsible for maintenance of the sails and rigging. He was the senior man in the foc'sle and the link in the chain of command between the officers and the crew. It was his duty to ensure sails were set as needed with every change of the wind. Seamen of the day were no angels and it says much for Robert at a comparatively youthful age that he could command men and carry such responsibility. The crew agreement for the voyage has not been found but much information has been preserved in contemporary newspapers in New Zealand's archives.

The BEN NEVIS, 270 ton brig, built in Sunderland the previous year, sailed from Leith on Feb 2nd 1860, Mr J Turcan, Master. She was described by the agent as a "New fast-sailing Brig".....with "very superior accommodation for passengers". The BEN NEVIS called at London to embark additional passengers and cargo. This "new fast sailing ship" reached Otago, New Zealand, on 7th July, 155 days after departing from Leith.

Thanks to the website compiled by New Zealand's national library entitled "Papers Past", references to the BEN NEVIS's voyage and cargo are available to posterity. These give tantalising glimpses of life in the twenty year old colony in 1860, and the cargo advertised for sale by Otago's merchants says much about the life and times of the early settlers. Only 12 years earlier two ships, the John Wickliffe and the Philip Laing arrived at Otago, 1848, loaded with Scottish immigrants who established the new town of Dunedin (the Gaelic name for Edinburgh). The leaders of the new community were Captain William Cargill, a veteran of the Peninsular War, when Britain fought Napoleon's French Army in Spain and Portugal, forty years earlier, and the Rev. Thomas Burns, a nephew of Robert Burns, Scotland's famous poet. They established a staunchly Presbyterian society. When Robert Kirkpatrick landed in July 1860, he was amongst very familiar accents.

Trade in 1860 for the merchants of Otago was in the doldrums. The following report appeared in the Otago Witness on 5th May;

> "Of late several forced sales by auction of soft goods and
> miscellaneous articles have taken place, at which prices obtained
> have not been satisfactory to the vendors. This must be looked for in

an overstocked market; and the limited nature of our market is such as to make it extremely difficult to force sales, especially of soft goods and general merchandise. The "Clontarff," "Elizabeth" and "Ben Nevis" from London are shortly expected with general cargoes for this place, which will in all probability amply stock the market during the dull winter season."

The BEN NEVIS duly arrived on the 7th July and discharged her cargo into the warehouses of several merchants who immediately took advertising space in the Otago Witness. The variety of wares for sale is fascinating, everything a new community might need, even school slates, an article which the author remembers from his own school days during World War II.

The BEN NEVIS however did not unload her entire cargo. By early August the local shipping agents, John Jones & Company were announcing that she would shortly be sailing for Wellington and that she had "very superior accommodation for passengers". The Otago Witness of 25th August reported she had "CLEARED OUT – August 22nd", but she cleared out without Robert Kirkpatrick. He took his discharge on 10th July, just 3 days after the ship arrived. How he spent the next three months is not recorded. He may have found casual employment on local trading vessels, or simply lived on his earnings from the outward journey on the BEN NEVIS. He may even have stayed with Scottish immigrant friends.

On October 22nd 1860, Robert headed once more for deep waters, signing on as an Able Seaman on the WILLIAM MILES, a modern clipper ship "with great advantages for passengers", claimed the adverts belonging to Miles Brothers of Bristol. The ship had reached Otago via Lyttleton.

On leaving England the WILLIAM MILES was towed out of Cumberland basin, Bristol, 4th May 1860, and anchored in Kingroad where the steamer OSCAR (a ship which will re- enter Robert's story later) came alongside and transferred a number of passengers from Glasgow. Under the command of Captain W. Lilley, the WILLIAM MILES 1103 tons, was expecting to make the passage to New Zealand in 90 days. The ship as well as carrying a miscellaneous cargo of wines, spirits, silver plate, haberdashery, general ironmongery, and a large quantity of agricultural implements, carried 332 passengers. The emigrants represented a microcosm of Victorian society and the allocation of accommodation on board throws light on the Victorian class system. The Otago Witness of Saturday 25th August, 1860, reporting the arrival of the WILLIAM MILES, gives an analysis of the passenger list.

Destination	Lyttleton	Otago
Saloon	10	10
Second Cabin	10	2
Third Cabin	30	20
Steerage	200	50

The paper remarks that the preference of the English was for Canterbury and the 'Scotch' for Otago. About 200 of the passengers consisted of emigrants selected by Mr J.E. Fitzgerald, the representative in the U.K. for the Government of Canterbury, and were despatched under a contract between the Government and Messrs Miles Brothers & Company of Bristol.

The outward journey took 107 days rather than the expected 90, and was not without controversy. The Lyttleton Times of 25th August reported:

> "We have received communication from the saloon passengers of the William Miles reflecting on the conduct of the Captain, and expressing dissatisfaction with the general treatment they experienced on the voyage,"

The paper remained impartial and also reported:

> "We understand the captain has received a testimonial, signed by 150 of the steerage passengers."

The Otago Witness also ran with the story and their issue of October 13th carried an open letter with 31 signatures, including that of the surgeon:

> "Dear Sir, - We the undersigned, cabin passengers by the above ship, under your command, beg most sincerely to thank you for your kind and gentlemanly conduct to us during our voyage from our native land to this port; we exonerate you from a charge which one or two malicious persons were vile enough to accuse you of, on account of your having refused to let them have liquors in wholesale quantities, when you saw the improper use they made of them." Etc.

Was this a case of upper class bon-viveurs versus working class Presbyterian tee-totallers, with Captain Willey caught in the middle? If Robert Kirkpatrick read these accounts in the local newspapers or heard the gossip in the dockside taverns, he was not deterred from joining the WILLIAM MILES on October 22nd. Here was a chance to serve on one of the new top flight clipper ships. Sadly the crew agreements for the WILLIAM MILES are missing. Robert's Statement of Service says he served 9 months and 1 day on the WILLIAM MILES, quitting on the 20th July 1861 after working his passage back to England on this ship.

A month later, 19th August 1861, he joined the STIRLING, a ship registered in Leith, and trading with Pillau in the Baltic. For the first time, Robert sailed in a steamship. The STIRLING illustrates well the advances in ship design and construction during Robert's brief life of 24 years. The SIRIUS of 1837 had been wooden hulled, propelled by paddles, and powered by a simple steam engine operating at low pressure. The STIRLING still carried masts and sails, but was registered at Lloyd's as a screw steamer – a barque with an iron hull. She was built by J & G Thomson of Glasgow, leaders in ship building technology, and was fitted with a compound engine greatly improving efficiency and coal consumption, making steam a viable alternative to sail over long distance voyages. She could economise in the use of coal when the winds were favourable or use her auxiliary engine rated at 120 horsepower when winds were against her. The transition from sail to steam, however, would be a long one. Sail would still have a part to play in long distance commerce and the romance of the clipper ships such as Cuttysark and Thermopylae was still to come. Also the smaller ports and harbours which could not take the steamers continued to be served by the brigs and brigantines up to the Edwardian era. During World War I sailing ships were still numerous on the high seas and provided easy targets for German U-boats.

The year 1861 was one of unbearable sadness for Queen Victoria, who lost her beloved husband Prince Albert and, inconsolable with grief, withdrew from public life and entered ten years of mourning. On the other side of the Atlantic, the Confederate States seceded from the union to preserve their own way of life, based on a slave economy. Abraham Lincoln, president of the U.S.A. was determined to preserve the Union and to see slavery abolished. The result was a bitter civil war ending in defeat for the South with its plantations ruined, its cities devastated, its people humiliated and its way of life gone forever. The American Civil War had global repercussions. The cotton mills of Lancashire and Lanarkshire, starved of raw materials, fell silent for four years causing prolonged unemployment and extreme hardship for thousands of families. On the other hand, the war boosted the demand for ships, especially blockade runners for the Confederate Government, as a consequence of which the ship yards of Liverpool, Bristol, the Thames and the Clyde thrived; and the linen mills in Scotland's eastern counties also enjoyed a boom period as the dearth of cotton fabrics created an increased demand for linen goods. Dundee a major port on Scotland's east coast, enjoyed its most prosperous decade of the century from 1861 to1871, with imports of raw materials and export of finished goods expanding to fill the void caused by the shortage of cotton. Leith, Dundee and the smaller seaports on the east coast of Scotland also thrived on the increase in trade. 1861 was also a landmark year for Robert whose domestic circumstances were about to change irrevocably. Since his return from the Antipodes he had met a fisherman's daughter from North Berwick a few miles east of Leith on the south shore of the River Forth and he had proposed to her.

Primary Reference Sources.

Scotland's People; Old Parish Records for Leith pre 1855, Births and Marriages
Scotland's People; Old Parish Records for Aberdeen pre 1855, Births Births, Marriages and Deaths from 1855 onwards for Leith, Census Returns, 1841, 1851 and 1861.

National Archives (Kew) (BT 98 Series)
1852 January	*Crew Agreement – GLANCE*
1852 January – June	*Crew Agreement – SWIFT*
1856 Dec - !857 July	*Crew Agreement – BRITISH LION*
1859 March – June	*Crew Agreement – PRINCESS ROYAL*
1859 July – November	*Crew Agreement - THAMES*
1860 February – July	*Crew Agreement- BEN NEVIS*

Secondary Sources.

New Zealand Newspapers
Otago Witness:	*31st July, 25th, 1860 August, 6th October, 1860 27th October, 1860*
Taranaki Herald:	*26th May 1860*
Nelson Examiner:	*14th November 1860*
Wellington Independent:	*9th November 1860*

Australian Newspapers
Sydney Morning Herald:	*26th December 1856*

Chapter 2

ROBERT KIRKPATRICK: MARRIAGE, FAMILY AND CAREER 1861 TO 1880

JOHN SIMPSON KIRKPATRICK'S FATHER

At North Berwick, on 31st December 1861, after banns according to the forms of the Church of Scotland, Robert Kirkpatrick age 24, a seaman in the Foreign Trade, married Mary McLean age 23, a domestic servant. The groom's parents were given as Robert Kirkpatrick, North Sea Pilot and Margaret Kirkpatrick, maiden surname Low. The bride's parents were Andrew McLean, fisherman and Mary McLean, maiden name Knox. The marriage was witnessed by William McLean, brother of the bride and Thomas C. Brown, Robert's brother-in-law, the husband of his sister Margaret.

GRANTON HARBOUR AND PIER.

Granton Harbour c1860 was next door to Leith and was home to Robert and Mary Kirkpatrick for a time. Note passenger trains bringing clients for the regular services to London and the continent. Coal for shipment is in evidence and paddle steam tugs are towing ships in and out of the harbour.

Image KY Collection

At the time of the wedding Robert had not been to sea since signing off from the STIRLING on 5th November, and he did not join another ship until 27th

March 1862, a period of nearly 5 months. This seems a long time to be earning no wages, especially when embarking on married life and setting up a new home. Old prints and paintings of the Firth of Forth show dozens of small ships bustling to and fro. The small ports ferried their wares to their bigger neighbours for transhipment to London and around the globe. Ships were often moved in ballast, or were sold and moved to new ports. Single ship movements, known as 'runners', were plentiful and did not require an official crew agreement to cover their short trips. This may be how Robert kept himself in employment during the months before and after his wedding.

Robert's days of circumnavigating the globe were over. Never again did he cross the equator or navigate by the Southern Cross, but he still had time for one or two more voyages in the 'Foreign Trade' and on March 27th he joined the WANDERER, 686 ton Sail Schooner, owned by A. Thomson of Leith. Built in Quebec in 1847, she departed from Alloa, another of the coal ports on the north side of the Forth, destined for the place of her birth Quebec.

Quebec and shipping in the St Lawrence River as Robert may have seen it.
Image London Illustrated News, 1852, KY Collection

When Robert returned to Leith on June 15th he was greeted by a radiant Mary who informed him he was going to be a father next October. A fortnight later Robert booked a berth in the WANDERER for another trip across the Atlantic, returning home 2 ½ months later on September 10th, in good time for the birth of his first child. On the 16th October around 10pm, at 18 Coupar Street, Leith, Mary gave birth to Robert Kirkpatrick junior and a proud father duly registered the birth of his son in the Parish of North Leith.

Robert, not wishing to be apart from his wife and young son, now sought employment in the home trade and went to work for the London & Edinburgh Shipping Company with whom his career would be closely, though not continuously, linked over the next twenty four years. The London & Edinburgh had been running a fast passenger service between the two capital cities since the days of the Napoleonic wars and had an excellent reputation. Initially the service was provided by fast sailing smacks, armed with light cannon to deter French privateers. When Robert was born in 1837 the company was replacing Aberdeen built clippers with paddle steamships. As a boy Robert grew up with the rapid changes. When he himself went to sea at the age of 12, the London & Edinburgh's premier service was being run with two 'modern' paddle steamers, still schooner rigged, the ROYAL VICTORIA named after the young Queen and the ROYAL WILLIAM, named after her late uncle. In the summer months the ROYAL VICTORIA left Granton on Wednesdays and Leith on Saturdays at 3 o'clock, returning from St. Catherine's Wharf, London, on Wednesdays at 5 o'clock and Saturdays at 10 o'clock. The ROYAL WILLIAM sailed to a similar timetable in the reverse direction. The arrival and departure of these ships and their posh passengers was an event of great interest to the laddies playing around the docks.

When Robert joined the London & Edinburgh in 1862 the company followed a progressive policy of buying the most modern ships available. In November he signed on as a seaman on the OSCAR, a screw steamer, built in 1861 by Pile & Co of West Hartlepool and described in The Illustrated London News thus:

> *"She is of 1050 tons burden, and 200 horse power, carries a full poop and forecastle, and has accommodation for 100 first and 60 second class passengers. Her cabins are fitted in the most magnificent style and her average speed is thirteen knots per hour."*

At this speed she could cover the distance between Leith and Gravesend in 32 hours which meant Robert could be home with Mary and his son for a few nights each week. Robert seems to have been a steady employee. He stayed with the OSCAR for almost two years during which time he prepared to take the exam for his 2nd Mate's Certificate. On a crew agreement for the OSCAR in 1863 Robert is listed with the note against his name, *"Volunteer, 14795."* At this time diplomatic relations with France were strained and rising tensions on the continent, with the threat of war, gave rise to a rapid growth in the formation of volunteer military forces across Great Britain.

Apparently a naval volunteer reserve was formed at the same time as a volunteer army, but no evidence of Robert being called to do service has been found. Perhaps he was hoping to make some extra money from part-time earnings, just like his son Jack fifty years later when he joined the Royal Garrison Artillery Volunteers in South Shields. On the 31st July 1864 Robert was given another incentive to seek promotion and to further his prospects. Mary presented him with a second son, Andrew, born at 11 am in the family home, this time in Admiralty Street, Leith.

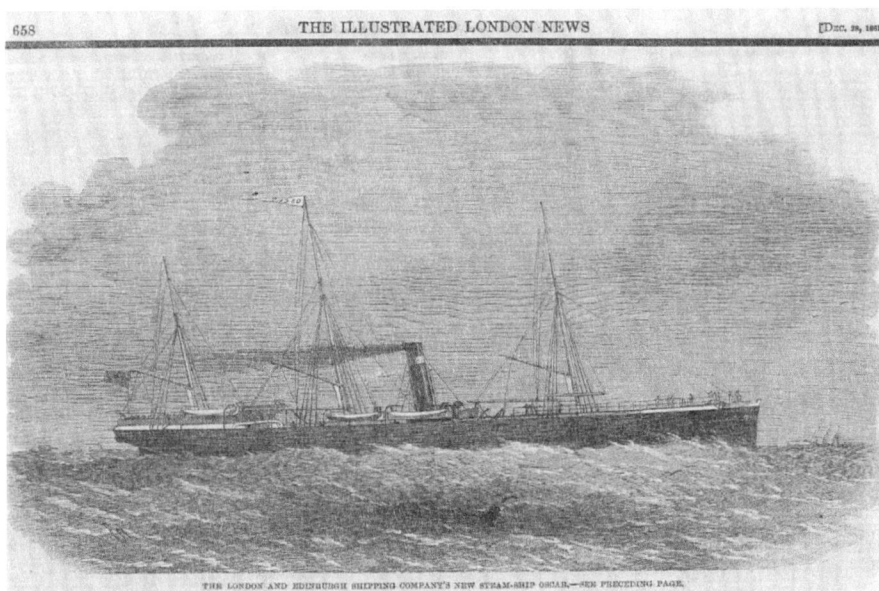

THE ILLUSTRATED LONDON NEWS

In November 1862, Robert made the transition from sail to steam. He began his first stint with the London and Edinburgh Shipping company on board their new steam ship, the OSCAR, making two trips a week between Leith and London.
Image Illustrated London News, 1861, KY Collection

Robert left the OSCAR on September 11th and entered service on the OSBORNE on September 13th. This ship ostensibly belonged to George Gibson of Leith but he may well have been acting as shipping agent for the London & Edinburgh. The handwriting on the crew agreements for the OSCAR and the OSBORNE is identical. The OSBORNE worked the run from Leith to Rotterdam and back. Somehow in between trips Robert managed to take his Second Mate's exam successfully, on 26th September 1864, passing in navigation and seamanship. He received his Certificate of Competency on 30th September. His exam application, for which he paid £1, included a "*Statement of Service since First Going to Sea*". Although there are time gaps in the list of ships, this document was a breakthrough in the search for Robert's early career.

After returning from a trip to Rotterdam on the Osborne Robert took his discharge in Leith on October 16th. Three days later, armed with his new certificate, he went to work for a new employer, D R McGregor, of Leith as a Second Mate. The rewards of promotion were not only monetary but a significant advance in status. Robert now enjoyed the luxury of a small cabin and a vastly improved diet, very different from the salt beef and pork served in the foc'sle. When he said farewell to Mary, wearing his new officer's uniform on October 19th to join his new ship, she must have been very proud of him and it was a happy occasion for both of them. His new ship was the MARIE STUART, a three masted screw steamer, 565 gross tons, built in Newcastle that year by Leslie, and equipped with a 130 horsepower engine. She was registered in Leith, her owner being D McGregor. Robert worked on this ship until April 11th the following year when he transferred to the PARIS, another McGregor ship, brand new from Barclay's yard on the Clyde. Like MARIE STUART, she was a three masted iron screw steamer with an auxiliary engine rated at 114 horsepower, but somewhat larger at 708 gross tons. McGregor was not involved in passenger services, but in freight only. His was the tramp steamer business and he was dependent on agents in the ports where his ships traded to find return cargoes. He traded mainly with the Baltic, Holland and France and his vessels would pick up and discharge wherever necessary around the coasts of the United Kingdom. Destinations where Robert called during this period of his career were Riga, Kronstadt, Stettin, Pillau, Kotka, Arborg (Iceland), Hudiksval in the Baltic states; on the west coast of Europe Bremerhaven, Rotterdam, Amsterdam, Dunkirk, le Havre, Rouen, Honfleur, St. Malo, Cherbourg; further afield Bilbao, Algiers, Canaries, Azores and even as far as Montreal; around the British Isles Dundee, South Shields, Hull, Portsmouth, Newport, Penarth, Dublin; and thankfully for the crew their home ports of Granton and Leith. The crew of the PARIS numbered 31, comprising a Master, First Mate, Second Mate (Robert Kirkpatrick), Third Mate, carpenter, lamp trimmer, cook, 11 able seamen, First Engineer, assistant engineer, and 11 firemen.

Foreign countries held little interest for the ordinary seaman. Be it Rotterdam, Pillau, Riga or Kronstadt the ports were all much the same to him. The streets around the docks could meet his needs. He did not need to be a linguist to satisfy his thirst and to find female companionship. Kronstadt, however, guarding the approach to the Russian capital of Saint Petersburg, did have a peculiarity which rankled especially with the crews of sailing ships. A local by-law prohibited them from lighting their galley fires while in harbour. Instead each ship's cook was obliged "to do their cooking at a filthy cook shed" on the pier. The food had to be carried in "leaking lurkies which were made of a few planks roughly nailed together in the form of a boat." The result at best was cold food for the crew: at worst a cook drowned by a capsizing lurkie. Masters in port congregated at Jack the Blaster's, a notoriously uninviting Schnapps shop. Sir Walter Runciman, who had risen from apprentice, to able seaman, to mate, to master and to owner, in his book "Collier Brigs and their Sailors" described the scene in Jack's when a Captain Belaney "*who was not a slave to abstinence*", was proposing a deputation to the Tsar to have this injustice remedied. The injustice was all the more irksome to the sail men since steamships were permitted to have their boilers lit to operate winches and more galling still, to have their galley fires lit. The more vodka consumed, the more raucous became the banter between masters of the steamers and the sailing ships. The officers had their favourite haunts just as the foc'sle had theirs. This was the familiar world in which Robert Kirkpatrick was at home and earned his living.

Kronstadt in the Baltic. Robert made many trips to the Baltic in the 1860s and 1870s, taking coal outwards and bringing grain back to Leith's granaries and flour mills. Steamers were jostling more and more with sailing ships at this time.

Image KY Collection

Countries across the globe were hungry for coal to feed their own industrial revolutions. Outward cargoes consisted mainly of coal and manufactured goods. Return cargoes from the Baltic were mostly grain, flax, ore and timber. It is no coincidence that Leith port still has grain elevators and has had flour mills nearby since the mid-19th century. Scotland's population expanded from 1.4 million in 1801 to 2.6 million in 1851 in spite of the migration to the colonies and America, and she could no longer grow enough grain to provide her people with their daily bread. Return cargoes from France on the other hand reflected the increasingly sophisticated tastes of Scotland's prosperous middle classes for wine, brandy and fashions.

On 1st July 1866, while serving on the PARIS, Robert had further cause for celebration when Mary presented him with a third son, John, born at 8 Cromwell Street, Leith. Did Robert bring home a special bottle or two from one of his trips to celebrate with, or did he repair to the King's Wark, Leith's oldest inn on the waterfront, with male family and friends to 'wet the baby's head' in the traditional Scottish manner- with a dram or two?

A view of Leith circa 1860 at the time Robert married Mary McLean. Leith not only traded but built and repaired ships. Indeed the first ever ship to cross the Atlantic east to west entirely under steam was the SIRIUS, built in Leith, beating Brunel's GREAT BRITAIN by two days in 1837. Note steam locomotive bottom left bringing coal into the docks.

Image: Edinburgh City Libraries Capital Collections

Sadly Robert never really got to know his newest son. On June 9th 1867 baby John just 11 months old, died of Bronchitis at 43 Bridge Street, Leith. Robert in between voyages to the Baltic, was present and registered little John's death the following day. Robert continued to work as 2nd Mate on board the PARIS until 1870, trading mainly to the ports in the Baltic and

Scandinavia, picking up outward cargoes in Leith, Granton, Dundee and Newport.

On 28th June 1870, still serving on the PARIS, his career advanced another step when, after examination, he was awarded his First Mate's Certificate. His first appointment in his new rank was on board a ship he had already sailed in 1864-65, the MARIE STEWART. The Crew Agreement shows Robert's wage increasing to £2.10/- per week as 1st Mate (£1.15/- on the Paris as 2nd Mate). This Crew Agreement is a bit unusual in that the personnel log has survived with it, revealing an aspect of life at sea which is mind boggling to modern minds. Small tramp steamers did not carry a doctor on board, nor even a trained first aider. Board of Trade regulations however did require the Captain of each ship to carry a medicine chest containing a prescribed list of drugs. The Captain also had to carry a Medical Handbook published by the Board of Trade. The Captain thus became his own Medical Officer dealing with illness and accidents, making his own diagnoses, administering his own medicines, and in extreme cases carrying out surgery as prescribed in his handbook. Captain John Drysdale of the MARIE STUART made the following entries in his logbook for the voyage commencing 4th August 1870.

"August 5th. at sea, Lat 56'26'N, L 2' 00 W.

Duncan McGregor Fireman laid off sick, complaining of pains in his chest and Stomack, gave him a dose of castor oil and applied a Mustard plaster to his Stomack.

6th Still no better, gave him another dose of castor oil and applied another plaster to his chest.

7th Getting more ease in his chest.

8th Complaining of looseness in his bowels, gave him 30 drops of laudanum with one glass of brandy.

9th Looseness stopped, feeling much better.

10th Still weak with little pain, giving him every attendance.

13th Finding him getting no better sent him to hospital at Kronstadt.

Obliged to discharge Duncan McGregor, fireman, as the doctor would not allow him to return to the ship."

The British Consul in Kronstadt ensured that McGregor was paid the wages due to him and his personal effects and belongings (in his sea chest) were landed and stored for him while in hospital. What became of the unfortunate Duncan McGregor? Who paid his medical bill? Did he return to good health and the seafaring profession? Did he recuperate in one of the Seamen's missions located in almost every large port? Did the Consul arrange his repatriation when he was well enough? The MARIE STEWART sailed without him and on her return to Leith, Robert Kirkpatrick parted company with her owner, co-incidentally a D R McGregor and entered the employ of William Laing, also of Leith. D R McGregor went on to become MP for Leith.

From October 17th 1870 to June 13 1871 Robert served as 1st Mate on board the GARRISON, an iron hulled, three masted, screw steamer built in 1867 by Aitken in Glasgow with a registered 550 tons. Typical of ships of that date, in the transition from sail to steam, she was driven by both forces, her engines being described as 'auxiliary' and rated at 95 horsepower. Engines were not yet reliable enough, nor powerful enough to enable masts, spars and sails to be dispensed with. There were no conversion courses for mariners, so seamen like Robert, raised initially on sail, had to adapt and learn by their native wit. His first stint on the GARRISON commenced in Leith and ended in South Shields after voyages to the Azores, Stettin, Riga and Bremerhaven. When the census was taken on 10th April 1871 Robert was home on leave spending the night in Granton with Mary who it would seem had made a bit of space for themselves. On the night of the census their two boys Robert and Andrew had been sent to stay with their grandparents Andrew and Mary McLean at Canty Bay, North Berwick.

On the 11th November Robert and the GARRISON were sailing from Riga to Stettin. That day, at 7 Summerfield Houses in Leith his mother Maggie died of apoplexy (stroke) after a short illness of five days. She was 61. The 1871 census in April the following year shows Robert senior, a widower, still living a 7 Summerfield with his married daughter Margaret and her husband Thomas Brown, a watchmaker.

Kirkpatrick's second stint on the GARRISON started in South Shields, and after voyages to the Baltic ports ended in Hull. Shields and Hull were not ideal home ports for a seaman with a home and family in Leith, which may be the reason why Robert transferred to another Laing ship, the HEADQUARTERS. She was built a year after GARRISON with a similar configuration but larger at 819 tons, also iron hulled, three masted and with a 94 horsepower auxiliary engine. Although she also traded with the Baltic and the continent her home port, more conveniently for Robert and his family, was Granton next door to Leith. His final voyage on the HEADQUARTERS was *"from Granton to Newcastle on Tyne and from thence to Montreal in Canada"*. As 1st Mate Robert was paid £8 per month from which he made an allotment of £1 per week (presumably to his wife Mary). At the end of the voyage he was discharged on Nov. 27th in Leith and the balance of wages paid on discharge was £8.8/11. At this time he took his leave of William Laing.

LEITH PIER ON FIRE.

The price of progress. Steam ships emitting burning embers set fire to Leith's wooden pier. Paddle tug boats fight the fire as spectators watch. 1871
Image KY collection

When Robert arrived home he was greeted by Mary with the sad news that his father, a North Sea Pilot, had drowned the previous month, 14th October, while working off the Isle of May. His father was 62 years of age and had held a Trinity House pilot license for 13 years. A local weekly newspaper *'The Leith Burghs' Pilot'* of Saturday, October 21, 1871 gave a brief report.

> *"**PILOT LOST AT SEA** – On Saturday afternoon last the Steam Yacht Wasp of Dunkirk, left Leith for that port, having Robert*

*Kilpatrick, a deep sea pilot on board to direct the vessel's course.
About twelve o'clock at night, when the vessel was off the Isle of
May, the cry of "Pilot overboard" was raised. The Wasp's engines
were immediately stopped, several pieces of timber were thrown
overboard, and lights shown, but nothing could be seen or heard of
the unfortunate man. A search was kept up for two hours but no
trace of him was seen. The Wasp was then anchored under
the lee of the island all night, during which one of her anchors was
lost and the vessel damaged. She returned to Leith on Sunday
afternoon. Mr Kilpatrick was long and favourably known in Leith. He
was a widower well advanced in life. It is not known how the
accident happened, but it is supposed that Mr Kilpatrick had
stumbled and been pitched over the low bulwarks by the heavy swell
which was on the sea at the time."*

In less than a year Robert had lost both parents.

In 1872 and '73 Robert sailed on the MIDLOTHIAN, another 3 masted screw
steamer owned by C. Salvesen & Company of Leith. This ship was quite
large for her day, registered at 832 tons, with a 2 cylinder compound engine
rated at 135 horsepower. The crew agreements for this ship have not been
traced but it appears she traded across the Atlantic between Liverpool and
the U.S.A. In the latter part of 1873 Robert returned to the London and
Edinburgh Shipping Company serving for a time on the IONA, built by
Thomson in Glasgow, 1866. Again the crew agreement is missing but it is a
reasonable assumption that Robert served as 1st Mate on both these ships.
He took his discharge in Granton, August 5th 1873.

Kirkcaldy (pronounced 'Kirrcoddy') on the north shore of the Forth in the
Kingdom of Fife lies opposite Leith. Since the 1860's the towns linen
manufactories had thrived and in 1873 a group of local business men set up
a company to transport their goods direct to London instead of sending them
by pinnace to Leith for onward shipment, thus making obvious savings in
time and money. At the start the Kirkcaldy and London Steam Shipping
Company chartered ships while the company's first vessel, the FIFESHIRE,
was being built nearby at Kinghorn. The new company needed seamen and
opportunities opened up for the men from the other side of the water, Leith
and Granton. On August 1st 1873 Robert Kirkpatrick signed on as First Mate
on the FIFESHIRE, but his first trip was not to London but to Stettin and
Kronstadt to bring home cargoes of flax. Thereafter Robert sailed regularly in
the London trade until March 1876.

In the meantime Mary now age 35, presented him with another son on 29th September 1873, named William who would be the last of their children.

Robert's final voyage for this company was in their newest ship the CALCIUM. The company appears to have been wound up and Robert returned to employment in Leith with James Cormack sailing as First Mate in the GLENROSA from March to October 1876 and following familiar routes to the Baltic and to Dunkirk.

The Kirkcaldy and London Shipping Company was acquired by an enterprising linen manufacturer Mr. J.T. Stocks who revived the London traffic with a new ship the ADAM SMITH, named after Kirkcaldy's most famous son, the author of 'Wealth of Nations' and founding father of modern economic science. J.T. Stocks was the archetypal Victorian businessman. He inherited his father's linen mill; improved and expanded it; was a Harbour Commissioner; became Provost of the town and in his spare time was Colonel of the local Volunteer Artillery. He campaigned throughout his life to have the old harbour which had a bad entrance and was too small, replaced by a new harbour.

GRANDFATHER

CAPT. R. KIRKPATRICK

A & G TAYLOR. 2 BROWN BUILDINGS, QUEEN VICTORIA ST

Photograph of Captain Robert Kirkpatrick, the only photograph found so far of Robert. The photographer, A&G Taylor worked at 2 Brown's Buildings, Queen Victoria Street, London between 1872 and 1875. Robert worked for the Kirkcaldy and London Shipping Company during this period, later winning his first command as 'Master' of their ship the ADAM SMITH.
Image courtesy of Ned Parnell W.A.

His new ship the ADAM SMITH was only 293 gross tons and she needed a master. Although Robert Kirkpatrick only held a First Mate's certificate Stocks took a chance and gave Robert his first appointment as Captain.

Lloyd's Register for 1877 clearly shows to the world that Robert Kirkpatrick was master of the ADAM SMITH and gives us details of his first command. Built the previous year in Glasgow she was a schooner rigged steamer, with a registered tonnage of 183, gross tonnage of 293. She was 150.3 ft. long, 22.2 ft. Beam, 12 ft. deep and was powered by a 2 cylinder compound engine rated at 60 horse power and working at 65lb boiler pressure. She

was built of iron, with 4 bulkheads and a raised quarter deck, a sturdy fast, modern little ship.

The Crew Agreement for the first half of 1877 records she was in the coastal trade and was manned by just 11 men in addition to the master; a mate, a second mate, 4 seamen, a first and a second engineer and 3 firemen. Note there was no cook on board. The Agreement states *"Crew to find their own Provisions"* an arrangement customary in the coastal trade. From Jan 2nd to June 30th the ADAM SMITH and her busy crew traded almost nonstop between Kirkcaldy and London making 23 round trips in 26 weeks. One has to admire the stamina of the small crew, especially the three firemen who must have sweated round the clock shovelling coal while she was at sea. They enjoyed only two 5 day respites during the six months.

As master Robert was paid £3 2/6 per week. During his service with the Kirkcaldy Shipping Company, Robert lived at Victoria Road, Kirkcaldy. When he left the company on 27/10/1877 his discharge certificate shows "VG" for both general conduct and for seamanship. Having tasted the power of command Robert returned to Leith intent on furthering his career with a more prestigious company.

In November 1877 Robert rejoined the long established London Leith & Edinburgh Shipping Company.   He had first served in their newly commissioned screw steamer Oscar as a seaman from 1862 to 1864. Now in 1877 Robert rejoined the London & Edinburgh as First Mate, his experience with the Kirkcaldy & London of navigating from the Forth to the Thames along England's eastern seaboard standing him in good stead.

He enlisted first on the MORNA, an older 1862 built screw steamer, contemporaneous with the OSCAR, but within weeks transferred on December 15th 1877 to one of the company's modern vessels the MALVINA, a 300 horsepower steamer, 260 ft long with two decks and 669 registered tons. His position was 2nd mate on a weekly wage of £1.18/- only half his earnings on the ADAM SMITH but he must have been promised better things to come. Just over two weeks later, 5th January 1878, he was appointed 1st mate on the MORNA his wage being £2.8/-, giving Mary a bit more leeway with the weekly housekeeping.

At the beginning of 1879 Robert's career had reached a high point. Age 40 he had been at sea since the age of 12. He had sailed to the farthest corners of Victoria's empire, Australia, New Zealand, India and Canada. He had progressed from two masted brigs, to full rigged sail ships to hybrid sail and steam ships, to tramp steamers and to the latest fast screw steamers driven by compound engines. He had risen from seaman to bos'un, to second mate, to first mate and now had the imminent prospect of winning his master's ticket. He was working for the London & Edinburgh Shipping Company, a line with a prestigious history and an enviable reputation, which prospered by providing a top class service for its clientele. He had been married to Mary for 19 years and three of his four sons had survived infancy and were thriving, Robert age 16, Andrew 14 and William 5. The weather seemed set fair for the Kirkpatricks but as every seaman knows storms can blow up without warning from unexpected quarters.

The Crew Agreement for the London & Edinburgh steamer IONA for the first half of 1879 records Robert signing on 7/1/79. The same agreement shows a 24 year old stewardess signing on 19/3/79; her name – Sarah Simpson. Stewardess Sarah took her leave of the IONA on August 14th while Robert Kirkpatrick carried on to the end of the year, but their fortunes were by then irrevocably linked. Troubled waters lay ahead.

Primary Reference Sources.

Edinburgh Central Library; Newspaper the Leith Burghs' Pilot (on microfilm).
Lloyd's Shipping Registers.
Maritime History Archives, Newfoundland; Crew Agreements post 1860.
National Archives, Kew; Crew Agreements prior to 1860.
National Maritime Museum, Greenwich; Mates Certificates and related papers.
New Zealand National Library; Papers past.
Scotland's People; Old Parish Records pre 1855, Births, Marriages and Deaths from 1855 onwards, Census Returns, 1841, 1851, 1861, and 1871.

Secondary Sources.

Bone, Alexander; **Bowsprit Ashore**, *Jonathan Cape, London 1932.*
Gee, Marjory; **Captain Fraser's Voyages**, *Stanford Maritime Ltd. London 1979.*
Graham, Eric J; **Clyde Built,** *Birlinn Ltd. Edinburgh, 2006 (an enthralling account of blockade runners in the American Civil War – highly recommended)*
McNeill, Carol; **Round the World Flying**, *published privately, a Scottish emigrant's voyage to Melbourne on a clipper ship 1869.*
Sullivan, Tom AB, **Escape to the Sea**, *edited Mike Clarke; Whittles Publishing, Caithness 2008.*

Websites.
www.edinphoto.org.uk Photos, maps, time-lines and history of Leith – an invaluable resource.
www.electricscotland.com/history/leith. The Story of Leith, XXX1 The Commerce of Leith.
www.leithhistory.co.uk/2004/04/24/shipping-in-the-past

Chapter 3

THE HOSGOOD FAMILY

This chapter steps back in time to look at the family tree of Sarah Simpson, the young stewardess, mentioned at the end of the previous chapter, who joined the IONA in March 1879.

Sarah , the mother of the 'man with the donkey' has been portrayed in 20th century biographies and in a recent play staged in South Shields as very much a working class woman of humble origins. Benson described her as a proud Scot, born in Glasgow. Every writer since had plagiarised these errors. Nothing could be further from the truth. Sarah was born in Malaga in Spain, her father being Scottish and her mother Ann Hosgood being Welsh. Sarah was born into a privileged upper middle class society in Malaga's English speaking community. However a series of family misfortunes, some of her own making, saw Sarah slide down the social ladder, living the latter half of her life in the working class streets of Tyne Dock, South Shields, a far cry from the sunny villas of Malaga.

Ann Hosgood, Sarah's mother and John Simpson Kirkpatrick's grandmother, was christened at Cadoxton Juxta Neath, Glamorgan, Wales on 31st December 1822, her father being Sebastian Bond Hosgood, and her mother Jane James – a name Ann would later bestow on one of her own daughters. Sadly for Ann, her mother died in childbirth on 12th June 1825. Ann's father Sebastian remarried seven months later on 21st January 1826, his new wife being Martha Everson. Martha bore him 12 children of whom only five survived beyond infancy. The Hosgood family came from a strong Quaker tradition though sometime in the 1840 period; Sebastian exchanged the quiet meditative atmosphere of a Quaker Meeting House for the powerful oratory and rousing singing of the Methodist Chapel. The Methodism preaching of John Wesley had deep roots in the Welsh Valleys. For certain Ann Hosgood had a strict religious upbringing, which in later years would cause an irreconcilable rift between her and her daughter Sarah.

Sebastian Hosgood followed his father's footsteps into employment with the Neath Abbey Iron and Coal Company, owned by Joseph Price, a prominent Quaker, an enlightened employer, and a humanitarian – a rarity in the early years of the Industrial Revolution. Sebastian's father Samuel had risen from the bottom of the ladder to become Land and Mineral Surveyor for the Neath Abbey Iron and Coal Company. When he died in 1852, the local paper published the following obituary.

> *"…death of Mr Samuel Hosgood, a Member of the Society of Friends and for many years in the employ of the Neath Abbey Iron and Coal Company as Mineral and Land Surveyor. He was esteemed by his employers and respected by his neighbours as a worthy and ingenious man, steadily fulfilling his duties and living in peace with all men."*

Sebastian started as an apprentice in the Neath Abbey Iron Works which was in the forefront of the blast furnace technology at that time and he quickly mastered the skills of iron manufacturing. By 1836 he had been promoted to Furnace Manager at the Neath Abbey Works. Two years later he moved to the Ystalyfera Iron and Tin Plate Works in the upper Swansea Valley, one of the largest tin plate manufactories in the world with 16 tin mills and 40 furnaces for puddling and balling. Sebastian's expertise was earning him an international reputation. On 25th August 1842, Sebastian accompanied by his family arrived in Malaga on Spain's Mediterranean coast. He had been engaged by Malaga's leading industrialist, Manuel Augustin Heredia, to install new blast furnaces at the Ferreria de la Constancia Ironworks. Malaga at that time was in the forefront of Spain's industrial revolution thanks to Heredia and a handful of like-minded entrepreneurs. Sabastian aided by his engineer son Thomas Hopkin Hosgood, completed his assignment in Malaga in 1848, at which time he returned with his family to Wales. He did however leave one member of his family behind in Malaga, his eldest daughter Ann, who had tied the marital knot with a young Scottish engineer, manager of the Angel Iron Works on the eastern side of Malaga's picturesque bay – his name James Simpson.

Sebastian Hosgood described in one newspaper report as "a man remarkable for his activity", remained at the top of his profession in the Welsh iron industry throughout his life and was still working as a consultant until his death on the 21st February 1875. He enjoyed a most successful career thanks to hard work and natural genius. What would Sebastian have thought of his great grandson who showed little signs of natural genius, but nevertheless became an Australian hero at the age of 22 as 'the man with the donkey' at Gallipoli? He would have frowned at Jack's views of the class system, at his lack of religion and at his tobacco habit, but he would probably have been proud. Jack, though not a pacifist was at least a non-combatant helping to save lives.

The life of Ann Hosgood and James Simpson, Jack's grandparents unfolds in the next chapter.

Primary Reference Sources.

International Genealogical Index (Latter Day Saints) CO56832 Christening of Ann Hosgood
FO 927 Registers of Malaga Consulate 1837 – 1891 - National Archives (Kew)

Secondary Sources.

Information has been culled from extensive research by Ned Parnell, Western Australia, into the history of the Hosgood Family in the context of the Industrial Revolution in Wales in the 19th Century. Apart from the link with John Simpson Kirkpatrick, this work deserves publication in its own right. I am grateful to Ned with whom I have exchanged research findings over a number of years.

Chapter 4

THE SIMPSON FAMILY IN MALAGA: 1840 - 1869

MALAGA: THE ARRIVAL

In October 1842 a British merchant ship arrived in the harbour at Malaga on Spain's southern Mediterranean coast. The harbour was crowded and the master unable to find a berth immediately had to back sail and drop anchor in the outer harbour. His passengers, eager to see their destination, had been lining the rails for some hours as the ship approached. Even in the early nineteenth century, Malaga was a popular destination for British visitors. One such visitor to Malaga in 1836 was an artist, David Roberts, who later made an engraving of Malaga and left the following description to accompany his print.

> "The approach to the ancient city of Malaga from the sea has something noble and striking, which at once rivets the eye and the imagination of the traveller. Rising from the bosom of its spacious bay, flanked by lofty mountains stretching far beyond, with its time worn bulwarks and antique castle, the ruins of which spread along its eastern hill, it bears the aspect of a fallen capital and of a dominion passed away. The impression of its general appearance in the distance is stern and melancholy; as one draws nearer; the town assumes a more pleasing and animated, though less imposing air. The sudden contrast of the rich gardens, grounds, fields, teeming with fruit and grain, studded with villages, convents, and smiling villas, and ranges of wildly broken mountains appearing only in the distance, must be seen to be appreciated, affording a rich draught of pleasure etc."

Two of the passengers studying Malaga from the rails of their ship were not conventional tourists and probably took a more prosaic view of the prospect before them. James Simpson, a 25 year old engineer from Scotland was accompanied by an elder sister Jean. Both had been born in Kirkcaldy in Fife into a working class family, their parents being James Simpson, a tailor and his spouse Christian White. James was carrying in his pocket a letter appointing him engineering manager in one of Europe's most modern iron works, El Angel, built the previous year 1841, by an industrialist and entrepreneur, Juan Giro, and equipped with the most modern machinery and technology available from the workshops of Britain, then world leader in the industrial revolution. While Jean may have been enamoured with the scenery and the 'smiling villas', James was much more interested in the red brick chimneys belching smoke on either side of the bay. To the west of the bay where the deep water quays were crowded with shipping, a number of tall chimneys proclaimed the presence of numerous factories. On the east side of the bay a short spit of land stretched into the sea providing shelter for a fleet of smaller vessels and fishing boats. At the end of this promontory stood a lighthouse and behind it James could see a complex of factory buildings with two more handsome chimneys. He may not have known at that moment, but those chimneys belonged to El Angel Ironworks and a villa on the site would be his home for the next 25 years. There he would raise a family with all the happiness and occasional tears that ensue.

Arriving at Malaga circa 1840. Note upper class passengers (men in top hats) being rowed ashore, perhaps the Hosgood Family or James Simpson, engineer. At the extreme right behind the lighthouse is the chimney of the Angel Ironworks where James Simpson was Manager. The Simpson home was attached to the works.   *Image: KY Collection*

Pending docking the master of the ship arranged for his cabin passengers to be ferried ashore. The ladies carrying their hand luggage and the gentlemen wearing frock coats and Brunel style top hats, as was the fashion for engineers, took their places in the cutter and were rowed to the jetty to be met by the shipping agent. After completing immigration formalities they were probably conducted to La Fonda de la Alameda, or L'Hotel d'Orient, both well patronised by British visitors, to spend the night while they waited for their trunks to be disembarked. Wherever they stayed, James and Jean would have been taken aback by the warmth of their welcome. Richard Ford, another visitor around this time states in his book 'Gatherings from Spain':

> "English Agents and Engineers were received with almost divine honours, so incensed were they with flattery and cigars"

The Rev Thomas Debary, on a visit in 1848, reported:

> "I found the magnificent Fonda de la Alameda filled with my countrymen and countrywomen; and a table d'hote of some thirty people, without a single Spaniard present…… a magnificent establishment managed by a gentlemanly Englishman named Mr Hudson………you could have Harvey's sauce, pale ale, and Stilton cheese for the asking."

Even though flattered and incensed by the cigars, James Simpson would have been eager to take up the reins of his new position and to start making his mark on the factory. Before long, however, he was invited to meet the British Consul, William Penrose Mark at the Consulate in Calle Del Peligro (since renamed Calle Trinidad Grund). W P Mark had assumed the role of Consul in 1836 on the retirement of his father the redoubtable William Mark who still lived in Malaga. The Consul no doubt gave James a wide ranging briefing on the political, social and economic situation in Malaga and in Spain. He also impressed on James the need to maintain close contact with the consulate. Although there was no legal obligation to register arrivals, or the births, marriages and deaths of expatriates, the Consul was emphatic that he should be informed so that he could safeguard the interests of his community. Registration of the births of children born to the exiles ensured their British nationality. He also invited James and Jean to attend Sunday Service held every week, over which he presided in person. There was no permanent chaplain in Malaga but visiting clergy did occasionally conduct services. Between sixty and one hundred people attended weekly and the occasion gave newcomers a chance to make friends and to settle into the English speaking community.

A consular clerk took notes of James Simpson's details and, in copper plate script, duly made an entry in a double page ledger.

> *"292 James Simpson, Engineer, Angel Iron Works, 27 Octr. 1842, Native of (Kircaldy) Scotland"*

Jean's arrival in Malaga was not recorded, nor was any other member of the female community. Victorian male chauvinism prevailed in Malaga.

James learned a lot from his conversation with the consul. He learned that Malaga was one of two leading regions in Spain's embrace of the 19th century industrial revolution, in spite of lacking the main basic mineral resource, coal. Asturias in North West Spain had coal deposits, but could not supply sufficient for Malaga's needs. She did however have an excellent harbour and a trading tradition that stretched back to Phoenician times. Much of the fuel for Malaga's foundries and furnaces came from Britain's coalfields, at a cost. Above all, however, Malaga was blessed with a group of extraordinary merchants who had become entrepreneurs and industrialists within the first quarter of the century. Their names and monuments are in evidence today around the city: Huelin, Reissig, Larios and Heredia. The factories and chimneys which James had observed to the west of the bay, as his ship approached were in the Huelin district. There orchards, gardens and vineyards had given way to sugar manufacture, cotton and linen textiles; soap and chemical works; tobacco factories; flour mills, iron foundries, metal working and railway workshops. Pre-eminent among these entrepreneurs, was Manuel Augustin Heredia.

Heredia, born 1786, began working life age 15, in a small trading company at Velez- Malaga and succeeded in turning it into a profitable business. During the Napoleonic wars he traded successfully with the British base at Gibraltar delivering essential supplies for Nelson's navy and Wellington's army. At the end of the war in 1815 his ships were free to trade across the Atlantic bringing home tobacco and cotton. His ships could now trade around the coast of Europe, exporting wine, raisins, oil, nuts and agricultural products in exchange for manufactured goods. An Anglophile and a man of vision he was determined Malaga would play its part in Spain's industrial development. In the second quarter of the 19th century railway mania was rampant in Spain. Also, a liberalisation of land laws in Spain had precipitated an agrarian revolution giving a boost to agriculture, wine and oil production and creating a demand for implements and machinery. Heredia foresaw that Spain would need its own iron production to support the new developments and boldly re-invested the surplus from his trading activities into industrial manufacturing.

Heredia established his first iron foundry, la Conception, at Marbella in 1826. Iron ore was available from Orjen, charcoal for fuel came from local forests and a nearby river supplied ample water for the process. Demand for iron rapidly outstripped the capacity of la Conception, and Heredia was soon contemplating the construction of a new factory. He opted to use the latest 'English' technology. For this however he needed massive supplies of coking coal which would have to be imported , partly from Asturias in North West Spain, but mostly from Britain. On the beach of San Andres at Malaga, close to Heredia's quays, la Constancia forge began to produce iron in 1833, employing 5 modern blast furnaces, 20 puddling furnaces and 28 steam engines and boilers to power the factory.

Manuel Augustin Heredia, trader, entrepreneur, industrialist, was the prime mover in taking Malaga into the Industrial Revolution. In 1842, Welsh engineer Sebastian Hosgood (accompanied by daughter Ann) later to become Mrs James Simpson, was hired by Heredia to install the most modern blast furnace technology in the Constancia Ironworks.

Image: KY Collection

Later in 1841, an associate of Heredia, Juan Giro, built another factory, El Angel, on the east side of Malaga's port. The technical expertise needed to make these developments happen did not exist in Spain. Heredia, using his numerous contacts in Britain had no qualms about importing engineers and technicians, together with their families, from all over Britain. The consul's ledger on one page records an engineer from Exeter, a bundler from Bristol, a roller from Merthyr, a puddler from Staffordshire, another roller from Merthyr, and a baller from Pontypool, all arriving in Malaga between 25th

August and 4th September 1842. Heredia was not content to rely entirely on foreign expertise and sent groups of his own employees to work and learn in English factories. Some of these were Romanies who had no official Spanish papers. Undeterred Heredia gave them papers using his own surname, as a result of which there are many 'Heredias' in Malaga today, though with no direct blood ties to Manuel Augustin himself. He was a remarkable man! Age 56 he was still managing his diverse commercial empire when James Simpson arrived at El Angel.

The consul estimated the permanent population of English speaking residents to be around 120. In addition approximately 300 visitors arrived each year, many of them spending the winter in Malaga's temperate climate. The Malaguenos claim they have only three seasons; spring, summer and autumn. The number of Brits was further enhanced by around 800 transient merchant seamen.

Nothing is known about James Simpson's working life prior to Malaga, but at the end of his time in Spain he returned to Govan, Glasgow where he had a number of connections. It is likely he gained his professional engineering skills in the workshops of Govan. Wherever he trained he now found himself enjoying his new status in a very different social climate. At just 25 the lad from Kirkcaldy had made it onto the ladder of success.

MALAGA – THE BOOM YEARS

James and Jean had been raised in the Scottish Presbyterian tradition and had no hesitation in taking up the Consul's invitation to attend his Sunday services in a warehouse rented for that purpose in the Calle del Peligro. They would have felt very much at home with the service, which the Rev. Debary, an Anglican, described rather ungenerously as,

> ".. tinctured by Calvinistic extravagances of the Scotch Theology, many of them being of Scottish Origin."

Calvin would have raised his eyebrows at the use of the word 'extravagances'. He and John Knox his disciple in Scotland had reformed their churches to get rid of what they deemed to be the patent extravagances of the established church of their day. Perhaps Debary was just making a gentle jibe to annoy the Scots, as is the wont of Englishmen.

After the service James and Jane would have been flattered to be introduced by the Consul to everybody who was anybody, including his father William Mark who had played a major part in fostering good relations between Britain and Malaga's entrepreneurs. The new arrivals also met another British family who had arrived just two months earlier. The Consul in the usual male chauvinistic fashion had recorded only male arrivals, namely:

> "Sebastian Bond Hosgood Engineer   Ferreria de la Constancia 25th August 1842 Native of (Exeter) England
>
> Thomas Hopkin Hosgood do   25th August 1842 Native of (Neath Abbey) Wales"

Thomas was age 15, having been born 20th July 1827 at Cadoxton juxta Neath, Glamorgan, Wales to Martha Everson, Sebastian's second wife. Although only the two male Hosgoods are listed in the Consul's ledger, Sebastian had brought at least one other member of his family, a daughter Ann, age 19, by his first wife, Jane James. Thomas apparently had come as apprentice and assistant to his father and Ann fulfilled the role of housekeeper. Sebastian had arrived in Malaga August 1842, and his wife gave birth to another son, William Alexander, less than eight months later in Cadoxton, Wales. Perhaps she remained in the family home in Wales with the younger members of the family. A further six years elapsed before Sebastian and Martha had another child, Joseph born in Neath 1849, suggesting Sebastian may have terminated his contract with Heredia, and said farewell to his married daughter Ann sometime in 1848. The six year gap between William and Joseph suggests their parents may have been separated by Sebastian's work commitment in Malaga.

James Simpson was delighted to meet Sebastian Hosgood. Here was a man after his own heart, an engineer age 42, who already had an impressive curriculum vitae. Here was a role model for the younger man. Sebastian had left Neath Abbey Iron Works where he had been furnace manager in 1838 to take up a similar position at the new Ystalfera Iron and Tinplate Works in the upper Swansea Valley, and after setting up the new furnaces there, he was now in Malaga, contracted to do the same for Heredia's Constancia Iron Works. Not only that, Mr Hosgood had an attractive 19 year old daughter with him, though there does not appear to have been a whirlwind courtship.

The date of the marriage between James and Ann is not recorded in the consular register. A best guess of the date is sometime in 1845 or around the beginning of 1846, as their first child was born 8th December 1846. The timing may have depended on a fortuitous visit by a passing clergyman from the U.K. as Malaga did not have a resident English speaking chaplain. Alternatively the couple might have travelled to Gibraltar, a day's sail away, in order to have the nuptials performed by a non-conformist minister. The Hosgoods came from a background of Quakers, Methodists and Baptists.

In 1847, one of the 19th century's greatest inventions arrived in Malaga – photography. A Polish exile called Ludwik Tarszenski established a photographic studio using and selling the latest equipment from Paris, the Daguerrotype process named after its inventor, Louis Daguerre. Tarszenski was a colourful character. After taking part in an abortive rebellion in Poland he fled to Spain, set up his photography studio in Segovia, aided Queen Isabella II's forces to defend the city against an uprising and was rewarded with a title, Conde de Lipa. Initially the process was complicated and expensive. Studio photographs were not for the masses but did appeal to the upwardly mobile middle classes like the Simpsons. No photographs of the Simpsons in Malaga have been found so far, but one daughter would bequeath a photograph of her mother Ann to a friend in the next century. It is tantalising to think there may be some unidentified family photographs lying in an album somewhere.

On 19th December 1848, James, mindful of his responsibilities as a family man, took out a life insurance policy with the Scottish Equitable Life Insurance Society. He evidently kept up his links with home.

In spite of the Consul's exhortations to keep in touch it was almost ten years before James Simpson got round to informing him of the events occurring in his family. Then on 1st July 1854 the consular clerk made seven entries in the consular ledger, all in the same copper plate writing as before.

Entry No.
550 Ann Simpson (formerly Hosgood)
551 Christian White Simpson Born at Malaga 8th December 1846
552 Jane James Simpson   Born at Malaga 28th January 1848
553 James Simpson, junior   Born at Malaga 30th May 1849
554 Sebastian Simpson   Born at Malaga 7th August 1851
555 Ann Simpson   Born at Malaga 15th September 1852
556 Jean Simpson   (native of Scotland)

All lived at the same address, Ferreria del Angel, Camino de Reding, and the children were described as either a *'daughter or son of a Native of Scotland'*.

During the decade recorded above, the passage of time inevitably called some of Malaga's citizens to meet their maker. Most notable was Manuel Augustin Heredia, Malaga's arch entrepreneur who died in 1846. The English speaking community lost its much loved former Consul, William Mark who died on 13th January 1849. Perhaps William Mark's greatest and long lasting achievement was the establishment in 1830 of a cemetery to the east of the town for the Protestant community. Prior to that Mark had been horrified at the barbaric funeral ritual forced on the non-Catholic community, of burying their dead at night on the beach by torchlight, outside the city. The bodies had to be buried in an upright position, but even then they were not to enjoy any rest. Superstitious fishermen were believed to resurrect the corpses and throw them back on land so that they would not bring bad luck to the fishing harvest. Mark fought a vigorous campaign lobbying the Foreign Office, the Government in Madrid and the Ayuntiamento (governing council) of Malaga to have a grant of land for a cemetery where members of his parish might be buried with Christian dignity and his efforts were rewarded in 1830 when King Ferdinand VII, bowing to British diplomatic pressure, gave permission for Protestant cemeteries to be established in every town where a British Consul resided. Mark obtained a plot of land about a mile to the east of the town, above the level of the beach and not far from the site of the Angel Ironworks.

When Mark died in January 1849 he was buried in his own cemetery. The hearse proceeded to the cemetery followed by a procession of three or four hundred people, including vice consuls from around the region in full dress uniform; and no doubt also including the Simpson family in full mourning. Half the citizens of Malaga, it was estimated, lined the route and watched the cortege pass, paying their own silent respects to the man whom they affectionately called 'il Pomposo' (he was notorious for long winded speeches). The Rev. Thomas Debary, who happened to be in Malaga at the time, conducted the burial service, wearing a surplice that had been hastily stitched together for him at short notice. The ceremony passed off with a dignity and decorum that would have pleased the old man's heart and which no doubt left a lasting impression on the minds of the young Simpsons.

THE 1850s
The year 1850 was one of great optimism among the industrial nations.

> *"Nobody will doubt for a minute that we are living at a period of most wonderful transition, which tends rapidly to accomplish that great end*

to which, indeed, all history points – the realisation of the unity of all mankind .The distances which separated the different nations and parts of the globe, are rapidly vanishing before the achievements of modern invention, and we can traverse them with remarkable ease; the languages of all nations are known and their acquirement placed within the reach of everybody; thought is communicated with the rapidity, even by the power of lightning. On the other hand, the great principle of division of labour, which may be called the moving power of civilisation, is being extended to all branches of science, industry and art."

Many of the sentiments expressed above are equally relevant in the 21st century – the vanishing of distance, the knowledge of languages, the speed of communication and the division of labour – yet this speech was made in the Mansion House, London in 1850. The address was made by none other than Prince Albert, Queen Victoria's consort. The audience comprised ambassadors and foreign diplomats from many of the world's leading nations. Albert was speaking in his role as head of a Royal Commission established in order to stage a '**Great Exhibition of the Works of Industry of all Nations**'. Thanks in no small measure to Albert's zeal, enthusiasm and influence the Commission succeeded and on 1st May 1851 Queen Victoria declared the exhibition officially open in the Crystal Palace in Hyde Park.

The Crystal Palace Exhibition in London 1851. Malaga exhibited examples of her produce and manufactured articles in the Spanish Pavilion. The judges were favourably impressed by the quality of goods from James Simpson's Angel Ironworks.

Image: KY Collection

This remarkable building made of wood, glass, cast and wrought iron was planned and erected in just nine months. More than 100,000 exhibits, provided by 14,000 exhibitors from as far apart as America and India were on display. The planning, logistics and project management that made this happen, without the power of the computer and electronic communications, are almost impossible to comprehend. The exhibition was an unparalleled success and set the standard for subsequent international exhibitions. It ran for six months and six million visitors passed through the doors.

Spain made a very modest contribution to the event, sending 247 exhibits, displaying them in replicas of three courtyards of the Alhambra Palace. Spain also provided four judges for the Juries judging the various categories of products on display, one being Manuel Heredia from Malaga who had to judge 'General Hardware, including Locks and Grates'. The merchants from Malaga exhibited varieties of grain, nuts, dried fruit, olive oil, olives, wine etc. Her manufacturers sent refined sugar, optical instruments, guitars and harps. Don Juan Giro submitted 'variegated soaps' from one of his factories and from another, **the Angel Ironworks**, 'specimens of iron'. The exhibition ran for six months and it is almost unthinkable that James Simpson, the English speaking chief engineer of the Angel Ironworks would not have been in attendance at the company stand for some of the time at least. Moreover from his own professional stance, James would have been keen to see the latest technology on display from Britain's factories and to mix with the world's leading engineers. Both Robert Stephenson and Isambard Kingdom Brunel had been involved to some degree in the organisation of the event, and no doubt James' father in law, Sebastian Hosgood, a leading figure in Wales' iron industry, would have been one of the six million visitors. After nine years in Malaga, James could also afford to bring Ann and the family back to Britain for a holiday. However Ann was six months pregnant when the exhibition opened and gave birth to a son in August in Malaga. Would she have risked a 2/3 week sea voyage from Malaga to England?

One comment on Malaga's entries has been found:

> "The specimens of iron and copper, in ore and manufactured state, are numerous. The iron, some of which is of very fine quality, is a matter of interest to us."

James Simpson was evidently part of a successful management team at the Angel Ironworks.

The Spanish display which attracted the greatest interest was the Queen of Spain's jewels, and on the first 'shilling day', when the general public were admitted, an extra force of Peelers was stationed on guard beside this exhibit but nothing untoward occurred,

The doors of the Crystal Palace closed on the 15th October 1851. Don Juan Giro and Engineer James Simpson returned to the Angel Ironworks. The Crystal Palace had been a triumph. Britain had shown that she 'held the lead in almost every field where strength, durability, utility and quality were concerned, whether in iron and steel, machinery or textiles.' Albert and his Royal Commission achieved most of their aims. One objective, however, eluded the naive Royal Prince. The 'brotherhood of nations' which he hoped to promote, was not so easily won. Within two years, four of the exhibitors, France, Britain, Turkey and Russia were fighting a bitter war in the Crimea. The next one hundred years would prove that technological progress was as much on the side of the war mongers as the peacemakers.

When James Simpson registered the additions to his family on 1st July 1854, Great Britain, allied with France, had declared war on Russia in support of the Turkish Ottoman Empire. With bands playing, crowds cheering, the British expeditionary force had marched from their barracks to the docks, resplendent in scarlet tunics, the guards wearing lofty bearskin hats, the infantry wearing totally impractical shakos specially designed for them by Prince Albert himself. This army was a magnificent sight on the parade ground. Unfortunately the British Army had not fought a major war since the battle of Waterloo which brought to an end the Napoleonic War forty years earlier. Sadly the British genius which had organised the 1851 Exhibition so brilliantly was conspicuously lacking in Horseguards (the office responsible for running the army). The force was sent first to Varna in Bulgaria and then to the Crimea to capture the Russian Black Sea naval base at Sevastopol. Troop ships and supply vessels passed through the Mediterranean using Gibraltar and Malta as staging posts. As they had done in the Napoleonic war, the merchants of Malaga were back in business supplying the British bases with provisions and victuals. Thanks to maladministration the British army lost far more men to disease than to war. Malnutrition, cold, dysentery, typhus, typhoid and cholera, etc. accounted for around 16,000 fatalities compared with 5,000 men died of wounds and killed in battle. One positive to come out of the Crimean war was the inauguration of a new award for conspicuous gallantry to be named after Her Majesty the Queen. The Victoria Cross, which is still made from the metal of Russian guns captured in the Crimea, would become a controversial issue sixty years later. Many people today believe James Simpson's grandson deservedly earned a piece of this gun metal at Gallipoli in 1915 and has been wrongfully denied proper recognition of his bravery.

Grave of Jane (or Jean) Simpson in the English cemetery, Malaga. Jane, sister of James Simpson seems to have settled in Malaga as James's housekeeper and remained in the household after his marriage to Ann Hosgood circa 1849. She died unmarried in Malaga, March 1855.

Image: KY Collection

Cholera epidemics were common in the Mediterranean in the 19th century and Malaga was not exempt. On 6th March 1855 the Simpson family suffered its first bereavement, when Jean Simpson, age 43, Spinster, died at the Angel Ironworks. The cause of death is not given in the Consul's burial register, but a number of deaths due to cholera were registered that spring. Jean was buried in the tranquillity of the English cemetery two days later. Her brother James had a gravestone erected in her memory, although, curiously, her first name is inscribed as ' Jane'. Perhaps she preferred 'Jane', or perhaps a local monumental sculptor unfamiliar with English names misread it.

Spain's industrial revolution rolled onwards and Malaga continued to prosper throughout the decade. The Simpson family also thrived and continued to grow in numbers as the Consul's register reveals.

Entry in the Malaga Consular Register for the birth of Sarah Simpson

Image courtesy of National Archives, Kew

583 Sarah Simpson,	Camino de Reding	Born at Malaga	28th Decr. 1854
593 Samuel Simpson,	Camino de Reding	Born in Malaga	2nd Feby 1857
621 Martha Simpson,	Camino de Reding	Born at Malaga	11th Septr 1858
622 William Simpson,	Camino de Reding	Born at Malaga	17th Octr 1859
*** Julia Simpson (1)	do.	do.	do
633 Julia Simpson(2)	Camino de Reding	Born in Malaga	4th Jany 1861

Children's Grave, English Cemetery, Malaga. Infant mortality was common in large families, even well off families. James and Ann Simpson lost twins born on the 17th October 1859. Julia surviving for 2 months and William, 10 months.

Image: KY Collection

Sadly the first baby Julia had a very short life, and died of 'Inflammation of the Lungs' on 3rd December 1859. Her twin brother William had only a slightly longer life of ten months, succumbing to 'Gastric Fever' on 6th September 1860. Both are interred in a section of the English cemetery set aside for children where the small graves are decorated with sea shells. The twins share a common headstone with the following inscription.

"NO SIN, NO SORROW, NO COMPLAINTS,
OUR PLEASURES HERE DESTROY.
WE LIVE WITH GOD AND ALL HIS SAINTS,
AND ENDLESS IS OUR JOY.

In Victorian times infant mortality was accepted as part and parcel of having a large family and it was not uncommon to re-use the name of a deceased child, hence the birth of a second Julia in January 1861. The religious faith of the Victorians may have made it easier to bear the loss of a child.

Gates to the English Cemetery, Malaga

English Cemetery, Malaga. The cemetery, close to the Angel Ironworks, was a botanical garden and meeting place for English speaking residents to socialise. Hans Christian Anderson on a visit to Malaga in 1862 commented on the 'pretty children' (possibly Simpson children) playing there.

A major concern for the English speaking community in Malaga, especially families like the Simpsons with several children of varying ages, must have been education. No mention of an English school or of members of the teaching profession in Malaga has been found. The nearest schools appear to be in Gibraltar where both Anglican and non-conformist schools operated. It is possible the young Simpsons attended boarding school at Gibraltar or they may have been educated by a private tutor or governess. Judging by their subsequent careers they all had a sound basic education, could pass themselves off in the higher echelons of polite Victorian society and were very capable of progressing in professional careers. Sarah Simpson had a better start in life both in education and etiquette, than her working class contemporaries.

RUNNING OUT OF STEAM?

In 1860 at the start of a new decade, Queen Victoria's Prime Minister, Lord Palmerston made a confident announcement to an audience in London:

> *"Wealth is within the reach of all", he said, and almost all believed him. There seemed no reason to doubt that the prosperity generated by the industrial revolution, the growth of trade and the expansion of empire would continue unabated and this optimism was universal, being as addictive in Madrid as in London, New York and Paris. Railway mania was rampant everywhere. Developers and speculators floated companies, raised capital by share issues, borrowed money and invested in new projects with reckless abandon. However, storms were brewing on the other side of the Atlantic which would profoundly affect the lives of people of every rank not only in America but all round the globe – even in sunny Malaga."*

On November 6th 1860, Abraham Lincoln was elected President of the United States. He was committed to the abolition of slavery but equally committed to the preservation of the Union. The Southern States, with an agrarian economy and a way of life dependant on slave labour, began to secede one after another, eventually forming the Confederate States of America. When Confederate troops fired on a Federal garrison in Fort Sumter, on 12th April 1861, it signalled not only the start of a bitter bloody civil war, but the start of a global trade war. The South began to print its own currency, but this was worthless outside its own borders. The only currency of any value with which the South could trade for the arms and materials needed for her war effort was cotton. The North was soon blockading the southern ports in an effort to stop the South from exporting cotton and from importing materials of war which included cloth for uniforms, buttons, belts, printing presses, as well as the more obvious guns and ammunition. In consequence supplies of raw cotton to the mills in Lancashire and Malaga dwindled and the cost rocketed. Fortunately the economy of Malaga, unlike the mill towns of Lancashire, was not reliant solely on one product and could weather the downturn without suffering serious destitution.

On December 14th 1861 Victoria's beloved husband Albert died of typhoid fever. Prostrate with grief Victoria withdrew from public life for several years, and mourned Albert for the rest of her life, making the wearing of black and of jet jewellery fashionable for the rest of her reign.

In Andalusia the warmth, the wine, the historic cities of past civilisations and the incomparable scenery continued to attract visitors from around Europe and Malaga in spite of the factories on her outskirts was still a place of beauty, regarded by many as a health resort. One of the most distinguished visitors in 1862 was the author Hans Andersen who was particularly enamoured of the English cemetery which he visited on a number of occasions during his stay. He wrote of it:

> "I wandered in a little paradise, this charming garden. Here were myrtle hedges, covered with flowers sufficient for a thousand bridal wreaths............ pretty children with laughing eyes were playing there. The whole cemetery was encircled by a hedge of wild cacti, over which one beheld the wide, heaving ocean."

This idyllic scene is only a stone's throw from the Simpson villa at the Angel Ironworks. The 'laughing' children almost certainly included the Simpsons, amongst whom was seven year old Sarah, all of them still happy in the innocence of childhood.

In spite of his fame Hans Andersen was not the most exalted visitor to Malaga in 1862. That year Malaga staged its own International Trade Fair which was honoured by a visit from her Majesty Queen Isabella II, the only female monarch in Spain's modern history. Her predecessor Isabella I was the monarch who financed the Columbus expedition to the New World in 1492. One enterprising wine grower, Jose de la Guardia named a new wine after the Queen, 'Moscatel Isabella II', and he made such a good impression that he was appointed governor of Segovia two years later. On a more serious note the Queen inaugurated the building of a new railway between Malaga and Cordoba. On 27th August a share issue was launched in Malaga to raise the capital for the Cordoba – Malaga Railway. Did James Simpson buy some shares? No doubt the Simpsons joined the throng lining the route and the children waved and cheered as the Queen processed along the main Avenidas.

The importance of this railway to the region and to Malaga can be gauged from the following statistics; length of track 192 kilometres; tunnels 17; bridges 8; viaducts 18; and stations for 13 major towns along the route. This specification needed an awful lot of iron, both cast and wrought. However Malaga's foundries could not supply iron in the quantities needed. Construction of the railway was contracted to overseas suppliers, mainly French, who were granted tax exemptions on iron and other materials imported for the new railway.

By 1864 the Civil War in America was having a major impact on the world's iron industries. Fortunes were being made by blockade runners who could evade the Union's ships, running arms and luxury goods into Savannah and Charleston, and bringing cotton out. While soldiers in grey and blue were dying in tens of thousands on battlefields like Antietam and Gettysburg, speculators, such as the fictional Rhett Butler in Margaret Mitchell's novel 'Gone with The Wind', found that just two successful round trips could pay for the cost of building a suitable ship, one that was fast and of shallow draft for working in estuaries. Ship builders in France and Britain were working at a frantic pace. An acute shortage of iron fuelled sharp increases in price, bad news for manufacturers working on fixed price contracts. In April 1864 the *Dumbarton Herald* reported that no fewer than 42 blockade runners were under construction in Clyde shipyards, even though Britain was officially neutral. Perhaps James Simpson should have returned to Clydeside at this juncture in his career.

Malaga's ironmasters were left with the domestic market only. From about 1830 onwards Spain had followed a policy of 'disentailing' land, as a result of which church lands, common lands, and state owned land were sold off. Most of the redistributed land was turned over to wheat production and wine growing, creating a boom in agriculture lasting through to the 1860s. While the French were building the railways, James Simpson in the Angel Ironworks was producing plough shares and wine presses, nails and barrel hoops, kettles and textile machines, and perhaps the ornamental wrought iron that graces Malaga's elegant 19th century buildings and parks.

The Angel Ironworks, post 1873. The bullring at Malaga was built in 1873, using slag form the Angel Ironworks for its foundations. Behind the ring, stood the Ironworks and the Simpson home for twenty five years, empty and abandoned.

Image: KY Collection

Malaga 2007. The bullring is visible bottom left; the site of the Simpson home is occupied by apartments.

Image: KY Collection

On the 18th December 1865 Ann Simpson, age 43, gave birth to another baby girl. This daughter, named Helen, was to be the last of the Simpson's children. James Simpson, perhaps with more concerns on his mind never got round to registering her arrival at the consulate so her date of birth was found in later records in Scotland. Helen had a very long life ahead of her. She would live through the reigns of six British monarchs; Victoria, Edward V11, George V, Edward VIII, George VI, and Elizabeth II. She would live through the Boer War, the Great War and WWII, and would see the demise of the British Empire, an event unimaginable at the time of her birth. She would live with the benefits of wonderful inventions; the motor car, radio, the aeroplane, electric light and electric appliances, the cinema and in 1953 she would watch the coronation of Queen Elizabeth II on television. In her last decade she would enjoy the benefits of Britain's welfare state. Sadly it seems very likely she never heard of the 'man with the donkey', her nephew, who had become a posthumous hero in Australia during the Great War.

In 1848 the Father of the Railways, George Stephenson went to Spain to weigh up the prospects for investment in railways.

On his return Stephenson reported succinctly;

> "I have been a whole month in the country but have not seen in the whole of that time enough people of the right sort to fill a train."

In one sentence he had summarised the situation neatly – a vast sparsely populated country, twice the size of Britain, with few sizeable cities, long distances apart, and in between, a scattered population of peasantry with little need for railways.

Nevertheless railway mania took a grip. Prior to 1855 only 456km of track had been laid. By the end of 1864 this had risen to 1,553km. Nine tenths of the money available for investment in Spain went into the railways. By the time the last length of rail was bolted onto the Malaga to Cordoba line in 1866, the Railway Companies were realising with dismay the simple truth of Stephenson's report. Revenues were not enough to pay running costs, far less pay dividends, interest or capital repayments. The railway boom had run into the buffers – just at the same time as the agrarian boom ended.

Railway at Malaga 1866. In1862, Queen Isabella inaugurated the Malaga – Cordova railway. Four years later, Malaga's industrial revolution, hit by severe recession was derailed. The Angel Ironworks went out of business. An embittered James Simpson took his entire family back to Glasgow in Scotland.

Image: www.costadelsol.medplaya.com

Recession hit Spain's iron industry and Malaga in the South with measurably higher raw material and transport costs than its rivals in the north at Bilbao and Barcelona, was most vulnerable. In Malaga itself the Angel Ironworks was at a disadvantage compared with its much larger competitor, Heredia's Constancia Works. Times must have been difficult for the management at the Angel with a shortfall on orders, with prices and margins squeezed, with the need to cut costs to the bone and the inevitable cash flow problems.

As Lord Palmerston had stated *"Wealth is within the reach of all,"* and in 25 years of employment in Spain, James Simpson must have accumulated substantial savings which had been remitted to Glasgow for investment on his behalf by his professional advisers. On the 21st day of February 1868 James signed a Trust Deposition Settlement (will) drawn up for him by Coupland, Cowan, Clapperton Sons and Barclay, Writers, Glasgow. James may have made these arrangements by correspondence, or he may have taken time off as business was slack, to make the trip to Glasgow in order to sort out his affairs. In this will James nominated four executors:

"Ann Hosgood or Simpson, his wife: David Simpson, Tailor and Clothier in Manchester (an elder brother):   Thomas Yarrow, Superintendent Railway Eng, Rutland Place, Govan Road, Glasgow: and Robert Hart, Iron founder, Rutland Crescent, Glasgow."

In view of the intricacies of making a will and contacting executors it seems likely that James was back in Glasgow at this time. James was certainly in Malaga in 1869 but he would soon be on a boat returning to Scotland - earlier than expected. About the end of 1868 it seems the Angel Ironworks stopped trading. The effect on James Simpson was traumatic. After 26 years of service, the last few of them working under unremitting pressure to keep worn out machinery running day and night, James found himself redundant. His ambitions and dreams of success were dashed on the factory floor and thrown out with the slag from the furnaces. The blow was too much for him and he had a mental break down. The family would later state that he was abroad and his age was 52 when his first breakdown occurred. The reason they gave for James' spell of insanity was: 'disappointment in business'- a massive understatement. Later events infer the parting from his Spanish employers was clouded by acrimony and rancour.

After recovery James turned his back on Malaga forever and returned to Scotland with his entire family. Perhaps just before they sailed Ann visited the English cemetery and left a few flowers and a prayer at the grave of her infant twins Julia and William.

Primary Reference Sources.

National Archives, Scotland – Old Parish Records
OPR Marriage, Kirkcaldy
        1803 James Simpson and Christian White
        1811 Jean Simpson
        1813 David Simpson
        1817 James Simpson
Glasgow Sheriff Court Probates 1897 - James Simpson SC 36/48/160
FO 927 Registers of Malaga Consulate 1837 – 1891 - National Archives (Kew)

Secondary Reference Sources.

Dubary, Rev. Thomas MA '**A Residence in the Canaries, South of Spain and Algiers'**, published Rivington, London 1851906
Ford, Richard '**Gatherings from Spain'** Published by J.M. Dent and Sons, London
Grice-Hutchinson, Marjorie 'The English Cemetery at Malaga'. Published by Author 2001
Harrison, Joseph '**An Economic History of Modern Spain'** 1978
Hobhouse, Hermoine '**The Crystal Palace and the Great Exhibition'** published Continium, London 2002

Chapter 5

THE SIMPSON FAMILY IN GOVAN AND LEITH
1869 – 1879

The Simpsons were able to celebrate Hogmanay and greet New Year's Day 1870 in the traditional Scottish manner, by opening their front door at midnight, greeting neighbours, first footing friends and toasting the New Year. The census return for the following year shows the family's front door was at 93 Gloucester Street, in the parish of Govan on the south bank of the river Clyde. The population of Govan grew from 9,000 in 1864 to 60,000 in 1880 the result of a massive expansion in shipping, ship building, marine engineering, locomotive engineering, sugar refining and textile machinery, together with innumerable supporting activities. The Simpson family made up 12 of this population explosion.

With three sons in his family, two of them already training to be engineers, James Simpson chose a place where they could complete their engineering training and have excellent employment prospects. James also had contacts in Govan. Two of the trustees named in his will, Thomas Yarrow and Robert Hart, lived in Govan and he may have hoped for support in resurrecting his own career.

The Ordnance Survey Map of 1854 shows the north side of Gloucester Street lined with tenement buildings, overlooking on the other side of the street the Clyde Rivet Works, West Street Chemical Works, Dundee Street Iron Foundry, and just round the next corner, the Eglinton Engine Works and the Tradeston Paint Mills. Public transport was practically non-existent; therefore workers had to live within walking distance of their employment.

Glasgow's answer to housing a rapidly expanding population was the tenement building, usually built of warm red sandstone and usually built four storeys high. The Glasgow tenement is wrongfully thought of as slum property. The tenements were built to house people of all classes from the labourers to the upper middle classes like the Simpsons and their neighbours. Certainly many of the over-crowded jerry built tenements did become slums, but many of the tenements survive into the 21st century and provide first class accommodation for today's upwardly mobile Glaswegians.

The Eglinton Engine Works. With no public transport in the mid-Victorian era, tenements had to stand within walking distance of factories, ship yards, engineering works etc. The above Works stood about 100 yards from the Simpson home in Gloucester Street. James Simpson had to locate where work was available for his three sons. His seven daughters were another problem.

Image: KY Collection

Pollock Street, Govan, Glasgow. On return to Govan, James Simpson and family lived at 93 Gloucester Street (now lost beneath the M8 motorway) moving later to Pollock Street as circumstances changed. The tenements occupied by the middle classes were of good quality. Many still exist and are highly desirable properties to this day.

Image: Courtesy of the Mitchell Library, Glasgow

A typical tenement was accessed from the street by a 'close' (passageway) which led to a central staircase. On each floor was a landing with the main doors to two apartments and usually a shared privy. Thus a four storey tenement would house eight families living in two apartments on each floor, all of them sharing the one close and the one staircase. Close, staircase and apartments were lit by gas lamp at this period. The passageway also gave access to the rear of the building where a communal wash house, midden and drying green were located. Each family had their designated day for the wash house and drying green. If it rained that day the washing would be dried on a pulley suspended from the kitchen ceiling. Thanks to a far sighted decision by the City Council, Glasgow enjoyed an excellent supply of clean water piped all the way from Loch Katrine by this period.

At the time of the 1871 census No. 93 Gloucester Street was the address for six families. It appears that the building had three main floors plus dormer attics on the fourth floor, as four of the apartments had 5 rooms with one or more windows, and two had 8 rooms with windows, probably on the top floor and attic. James and Ann Simpson with eight of their children occupied one of the larger apartments. The other 8 roomed flat was occupied by Archibald Campbell, grain merchant, his wife and seven children; the other four 5 roomed flats were occupied by Thomas Robertson, brass founder, his wife and five children; James Anderson, draper, his wife, 8 children and a domestic servant; James Baynes, with wife, four children and a domestic servant; Agnes McDougall, widow, with two adult sons, a married daughter, wife of a merchant navy captain, a daughter, a granddaughter, and two domestic servants. Although sharing their close with fairly well off neighbours the Simpsons, particularly Ann and the older daughters, must have felt it something of a comedown after living in a spacious villa in Malaga.

In the natural course of events fledglings fly the nest and by April 1871 the census for the civil parish of Govan shows two of the young Simpsons had already left, probably to escape the discord inevitable in a large family living in the confined space at 93 Gloucester Street. The census shows the occupants as follows;

James Simpson	Head	53	Marr	Engineer(unemployed)	Kirkcaldy, Fifeshire
Ann	Wife	48	Marr		Neath, Glamorgan
Christian W	Daur	24	Unmar	Milliner	Spain
Jane J	Daur	23		Dressmaker	Spain
Sebastion	Son	20		Engine Fitter (at works)	Spain
Ann	Daur	18		Dressmaker	Spain
Sarah	Daur	16		Scholar	Spain
Martha	Daur	12		Scholar	Spain
Julia	Daur	10		Scholar	Spain
Helen	Daur	5		Scholar	Spain

Missing from Gloucester Street are Samuel and James junior. Samuel does not appear anywhere in the 1871 census. On 3rd August 1870 Samuel signed on as an apprentice on the Glasgow registered sailing ship, the LOCH LEVEN CASTLE and at the time of the census his ship was in the Indian Ocean, nearing the Cape of Good Hope on the return voyage from Singapore. Although registered in Glasgow, this ship used Liverpool as its home port. Samuel's career in the merchant navy would take him round Cape Horn to the ports of Chile and Peru. He would cross the Pacific to Melbourne and the Lacepede Islands off Australia's North West coast. James Simpson junior, age 22 was recorded in the census for Greenock, a port and ship building centre on the lower Clyde, working as an Engine Fitter. He too would succumb later to the lure of the sea and would become the prototypical Scottish ship's engineer.

Also missing from the Simpson household is any reference to servants, although other residents at 3 Gloucester Street did have servants; the Andersons and the Baynes each had a resident servant and widow McDougall had two domestic servants living in. This has implications for the Simpson daughters in particular, prim young ladies who had been pampered by servants from birth until departure from Spain. They now had to learn new skills and perform menial tasks alien to their tastes. They would have had to learn to cook on an iron range; to clean out grates and set coal fires; to carry the ashes and other domestic refuse down stairs to be dumped in the midden; to take the family's turn at washing down the stairs; to spend one day a week in the wash house doing the family's not Inconsiderable washing; and after hanging it out to dry would have had to carry it back up four flights of stairs to be subsequently ironed. Mother Ann would have had to find local shops and her daughters would have been despatched on shopping errands. Perhaps James may have been generous enough to pay a laundress to relieve the ladies of one of the more onerous tasks or perhaps not. The employment of servants seems to have been a bone of contention between James, the head of the house, and the distaff members of his family.

Young Sarah, age 16, is recorded as a scholar although education was not compulsory for girls of her age at this time. She later stated her occupation as 'cook' so it is likely she was attending one of two cookery schools in the Govan area. A trained cook in the family would be a considerable asset complementing the skills of the other girls, millinery and dressmaking.

In 1872 three more of the children flew the nest. Sebastian attained his majority in August and followed his other two brothers into the mercantile marine. The two teenagers, Ann 19 and Sarah 17 also left home, though in circumstances unexplained and perhaps without the blessing of their parents. After the 1871 census no records have been found for Ann junior. She disappears without trace: no marriage, no death, no further mention in a census return: no mention in any family will or on the family grave stone. Did she also, like her brothers go to sea, or did she emigrate? Mysteries like this do happen in family research, but there is always the hope that a lead will turn up in the future.

The following year 1873, turned out to be *an Annus Horribilis* for mother Ann and James Simpson. A notice appeared in the Glasgow Herald of June 21st 1873 under the heading 'Deaths';

> *"At Fernando Po on the 13th ult., Sebastian Simpson, 22, engineer, S.S. Liberia – Friends please accept this intimation."*

Four days before the entry in the Glasgow Herald, the LIBERIA had docked in her home port Liverpool following a six week voyage to the West Coast of Africa. She was a modern screw steamer, registered tonnage 927, built in Govan 1870 by John Elder & Co. and managed by Elder Dempster Lines, Liverpool. The Master and the Company were very prompt in notifying the Simpsons of the death of their son. The news of Sebastian's death must have caused great sorrow for which there could be no closure from a funeral or a visit a visit to the grave. Ann had to lean on her religious faith for comfort. James it seems sank into depression. The return of Sebastian's effects a month later from the shipping company, together with his arrears of pay, £6.5/8, must have been a tearful time for Ann.

Ten weeks after Sebastian departed this world another Simpson entered in his stead, though his arrival may not have been an occasion for celebration in 93 Gloucester Street. Indeed we cannot be sure if James and Ann Simpson ever knew they had a grandson.

On 13th August the acting matron of the Royal Maternity Hospital, Edinburgh, Miss T Young, registered a birth on behalf of one of her patients. The Register of Births for the Saint Giles district of Edinburgh gives the following information:

Name and Surname:	*Alfred Simpson, Illegitimate.*
When and where born:	*1873, July Thirty First, 3 hr 20 mins*
	Royal Maternity Hospital, Edinburgh.
Sex:	M
Name, Surname & Rank or Profession of Father	----------------
Date and Place of Marriage:	-----------------
Name and Maiden Surname of Mother	*Sarah Simpson, Cook*
Informant:	*Miss T Young, acting Matron*

Only two years earlier Sarah had been listed in the 1871 census for Govan, age 16, a scholar, living in a comfortable middle class family home with her parents and siblings. How had such a dramatic change in her situation come about? The Hospital Admission Register gives some explanation, but as is often the case in family research, many more questions arise. Sarah was asked a number of questions on the day of her admission, July 11th. Her answers are most revealing and in one case chilling.

First she gave her name as Sarah Smith but had second thoughts and *"or Simpson"* was squeezed in by the clerk. She gave her present address as '6 Market Street, Edinburgh' and her previous residence as Malaga – NO mention of Govan! She told the admissions clerk her father was James Simpson, alive, previous residence Malaga Spain – again no mention of Govan! Her mother, she stated, was Ann Hosgood, **DEAD!!** – also of Malaga, Spain.

To the question about ' Husband or Father' she replied, **"Alfred Martin, Engineer"** and gave his address as, **"The Ne Plus Ultra, ship at sea"**.

Surprisingly Sarah concealed her connection with Govan. Astonishingly she stated that her mother was dead – why? After much reflection one can only conclude that she had become totally estranged from her family. She must have had a row of biblical proportions with her mother *'to wish her dead'*. Had she been driven from the family home because of her fall from grace? Sarah it seems was disowned by her family. The family door had been slammed in her face and she was so deeply hurt that she had no desire to see it opened again. An iron curtain had fallen between her and her family. She was alone in the world, age 18, with a young son to bring up.

Or was she alone – what of Alfred Martin, engineer on board the NE PLUS ULTRA? Two vessels of this name have been found in newspaper reports of Shipping Movements, neither of them British registered ships. One was an American Clipper Ship, homeport New York. She was a cargo ship plying her trade across the north Atlantic between New York, Liverpool and London . The second was a steamship reported arriving in South Shields from Bilbao, June 1876. The latter appears the more likely to be Alfred Martin's ship as he was an engineer and coming from Bilbao she may have been a Spanish registered ship. Perhaps Alfred Martin gave Sarah much needed financial support during her pregnancy. When Sarah gave birth on July 31st her baby weighed in at 13lbs 12 ounces, the heaviest baby recorded in the register that week and Midwife McFarlane recorded that the birth was normal and both mother and baby were 'well'. Sarah was evidently in very good health.

So many questions remain unanswered; where and when did Alfred Martin and 17 year old Sarah come together during 1872? Did Alfred make provision for Sarah and his son? How did Sarah come to be in Edinburgh for her confinement? The address she gave, 6 Market Street, was close to Waverley Railway Station and the 1871 census showed it to be a boarding house. Was Sarah staying there as a temporary guest or working as a cook? After this we lose track of Sarah for six years until 1879 when she is working as a stewardess on passenger ships supporting herself and son Alfred on a weekly wage of ten shillings. The door to the family home had been slammed forever in Sarah's face. Moreover she had no wish to open it. Her parents would never know this grandson or any other grandchildren.

The succeeding year 1874, passed without any recorded incident in the Simpson family, but in 1875, February 21st, Ann's father Sebastian Bond Hosgood, Civil Engineer, died in Cardiff at the age of 75. He had a good innings, having been married three times and had a very successful career as an engineer. Ann received a financial bequest, amount unstated, from her father's will. The inevitable passing of a parent is sad for a family but more bearable than the sudden loss of a son with a promising life ahead of him.

Ann's anguish continued in 1876 when her husband of thirty years succumbed to the succession of misfortunes he had experienced. He lost his reason completely and very sadly turned against his family. He threatened violence against his wife and daughters; he threatened to set fire to the house; he threatened suicide. His illness began in February. Ann found herself living in a nightmare, trying to shield her children, trying to pacify her irrational husband, and no doubt trying to conceal the family's troubles from friends and neighbours. Her adult daughters, Christian and Jane James, provided much needed support. At first, no doubt, Ann prayed that James' aberration would pass as had his previous bout in Malaga. As the months passed, however, James showed no sign of recovery, and after much heart searching, and perhaps on the advice of her doctor and her minister, Ann resigned herself to having James committed to a mental hospital. Telegrams or letters were sent informing Samuel and James junior, of the family crisis and calling for their return. The family solicitor was instructed to institute committal proceedings which entailed submission of a petition to the Sheriff Court in Glasgow, supported by reports from two doctors who had independently interviewed James for admission.

Samuel had sailed in March the previous year on board the ROSLIN CASTLE, a 644 ton sailing ship registered in Glasgow and owned by Thomas Skinner & Co., Gordon Street, Glasgow. The ROSLIN CASTLE was bound for Valparaiso in Chile on a voyage of up to two years. However she returned to Hamburg in March '76 with a cargo of guano (phosphate) and there Samuel could be contacted through the shipping company's agents. Samuel took his discharge in Hamburg, arriving home on 15th. July. James junior was more difficult to contact as he was 2nd engineer on board a Spanish ship working out of Bilbao, but he had left a contact address in Kirkdale, Liverpool where a letter might be sent in the hope of reaching him in time.

On 17th August, two doctors visited 93 Gloucester Street, Doctor John White, M.D. who probably walked the quarter mile from his address in Pollok Street, Govan and Doctor John H. Meiklem who had to take a carriage from his practice address in Central Glasgow. The doctors completed Medical Certificates to accompany the court petition, both concurring that: *"James Simpson is a person of unsound mind and a proper Person to be detained under Care and Treatment."* Curiously when answering the doctors' questions James used an antiquated style of language reminiscent of the King James Bible. He told Doctor Meiklem that:

> "..... he has got illuminated by Heavens and was insane 9 years, longer than Nebuchadnezzar but is now sane."

Clearly he had been well versed in the stories of the Old Testament during his formative years.

The doctors' reports were appended to the Petition to the Sheriff, a pre-printed document couched in legal terminology, with spaces for the case details to be entered by hand. The petition was originally made out in the name *of Ann Simpson, wife* but her name was scored out and that *of James Simpson, Son* written above the amendment. James arrived home at the eleventh hour and as male next of kin was the proper person to sign the document and to date it on the 18th August. The petition asked a number of questions from which it was ascertained that James' first attack was seven years earlier when abroad; that he was fifty two at the time; that the duration of the present attack was five months; and that the supposed cause was "Disappointment in Business". On 19th August Sheriff James Galbraith, signed an order authorising the transmission of James Simpson to the Glasgow Royal Asylum for Lunatics at Gartnavel.

Govan Ambulance c1880. In 1876 with deteriorating mental health, James Simpson was removed from 93 Gloucester Street to the Glasgow Royal Asylum for Lunatics at Gartnavel. He probably travelled in the above vehicle. Note the class distinctions in dress, from the gent in top hat down to the urchin, bare headed and shoeless. The spectators at James Simpson's removal from Gloucester Street were probably nearer the top end of the social scale.

Image: Courtesy of Mitchell Library, Glasgow

The following day perhaps, a horse drawn ambulance pulled up at 93 Gloucester Street, attracting as usual a group of interested spectators. Their curiosity was rewarded by the sight of the unfortunate James Simpson in a strait jacket being bundled out of the close entrance and into the back of the ambulance. As the rumble of the carriage receded in the distance and the crowd dispersed, what were the emotions of the Simpson family watching from behind their curtains? Would a forgiving God restore James as he had Nebuchadnezzar?

Gartnaval Mental Asylum. A grim combination of hospital cum prison – a far cry from sunny Malaga. *Image courtesy of Ned Parnell W.A.*

Ann had the consolation of having her two seafaring sons at home at the same time. Samuel who had been at home since mid-July applied to take his 2nd Mate examination and unhappily for him was given the date of 17th August, the same day his father was examined by two independent doctors. In the circumstances it is not surprising that the 18 year old failed at the first attempt. He reapplied and at the second attempt on 7th September he satisfied the examiners, passing in navigation, seamanship, and commercial code signals. Samuel remained at home until he signed on a Glasgow sailing ship the LOCH LOMOND, on 3rd October 1876.

James Simpson, junior, also took the chance of his spell ashore to further his career and successfully took his 1st Engineer exam in Liverpool on 26th September. Prior to coming home he had worked on a Spanish ship the RITA registered in Bilbao and after receiving his 1st Engineer's certificate he returned to the Spanish mercantile service on a ship called the NANA. These Spanish vessels must have been trading between Spain and Liverpool.

At home in Govan Ann, as James's wife and a trustee of his estate had to take over the management of the family affairs. In order to operate his bank accounts and manage his investments she needed a Power of Attorney. This may already have been arranged by her solicitor during the five months prior to James' committal when he was already deranged. Since James was not a pauper the family had to make regular payments to Gartnavel Hospital for his care and treatment. In order to economise Ann and the girls decided they no longer needed an eight roomed apartment and moved to a smaller house. Their new address at 85 Pollok Street was only about a quarter of a mile away and was also a tenement property but of good quality. The houses lining both sides of the street, had Georgian style facades. The street was exceptionally broad with a planting of trees running through the middle. At one end of the street was an established Church, at the other end a United Free Church of Scotland, and on nearly every street corner stood a public house where the sea faring sons may have had a convivial evening before they parted company for the last time. More important perhaps for Ann, both of the doctors who had examined her husband lived in Pollok Street. Ann had concerns about the health of her eldest daughter, Christian, who was not robust, and it was a comfort for her to have a doctor close at hand.

When the need for a doctor did arise, however, the call was not in respect of Christian but for 17 year old Julia. On February 11th 1878 tragedy struck the Simpson family once more when daughter Julia suffered an untimely death caused by diphtheria, a disease deadly at the time but now virtually eradicated by modern medicine. The diphtheria had lasted 20 days, complicated by meningitis for the last 5 days. Ann's grief must have been profound. She was unable to register the death herself and her daughter, Jane James undertook that sad task on her behalf. Jane probably also engaged the undertaker and made the funeral arrangements. A double lair was purchased in the name of James Simpson in a private cemetery at Craigton, near Govan. The cemetery is largely level but at the southern end, it rises steeply. The wealthy people of the district were buried on the hill while the hoi-polloi were buried on the lower ground, and as befitted their relative stations in Glasgow's Victorian society. The monuments of the wealthy were large and ostentatious while those below were more modest, and many graves had no marker at all. Ironically just outside the southern boundary of the cemetery now stands modern tower blocks housing ordinary families who now overlook the pretentious monuments of the Victorians below. As the funeral procession moved off from Pollok Street, as was the custom, neighbours closed their front curtains, nearby shops lowered their blinds, the loafers at the street corners doffed their caps and stood in silence as a token of respect for the deceased. In Scotland it was customary for men only to follow the hearse on foot. Women folk stayed at home to arrange hospitality for the returning mourners. However no male member of the Simpson family would be present at Julia's interment to lower her coffin into the grave. Her father was still in Gartnavel; her brother James was Second Engineer on board a tramp steamer trading between Singapore, Hong Kong and Shanghai; and Samuel was marooned on a group of tiny islands off the North West coast of Australia called the Lacepedes. It is conjectural but very likely that Ann and her daughters made their way separately to the graveside by carriage, so that some close family were there to say farewell to young Julia. At home, neighbours and friends from church may have rallied round to prepare the funeral meal. After standing on an open hillside on a cold February day the mourners in spite of their overcoats and top hats, would be in need of a hot cup of tea or a wee dram to warm their bones. The Simpson family story leaves Ann and her daughters to mourn.

In 1879, Samuel returned to Liverpool on the SCYTHIA as 2nd Mate at the age of 23. Did he then look up his Hosgood relatives in Wales? Was it only then he learned of the death of his younger sister Julia? He had about a fortnight's leave and it is earnestly hoped he took the train back to Glasgow to see his Mum and sisters. After a separation of two and a half years Ann must have been over joyed to have her boy home again; not a boy any longer but a mature weather beaten young man with the confidence to handle a full rigged sail ship in an Atlantic gale. All too soon the moment came for Sam's departure. When Ann kissed him goodbye it would be for the last time.

Sam re-joined the SCYTHIA in Cardiff on 16th June. The last crew members came on board 17th June and the SCYTHIA sailed on the 18th. The ship and her crew vanished in the vastness of the oceans. No trace of ship or crew was ever found. No one will ever know the fate of the SCYTHIA and her crew until Judgement Day when the seas shall give up their dead.

After eleven months with no sightings or reports of the SCYTHIA, the authorities accepted the ship was lost with all hands – 16 officers and crew, plus 4 apprentices. The deaths were recorded in the Marine Register, the date assumed to be the day after the ship sailed. The cause of death on Samuel's certificate reads, "Supposed Drowned". It would take a long time for the sad news to reach Pollok Street and may have been transmitted to Ann via the Mission to Seamen, a charity which maintained hostels in all the major ports around the world. The Simpsons did form a strong link with the charity and the final residue of the Simpson family wealth was bequeathed many years later to the Glasgow branch of the Seamen's Mission. However the news reached Ann, it came as another hammer blow to one whose spirit had already suffered more than it should.

This part of the Simpson family history runs up to April 1881, the date of the ten yearly census. The count for Govan shows the Simpsons still living in Pollok Street, but at a different address, number 118 which is a smaller apartment on the other side of the road.

> Anne, age 59 is shown as 'Head' and still 'Married'.
> Christian White, daughter, age 34, is still unmarried with no occupation.
> Jane James, daughter age 32, also unmarried is still a dressmaker.
> Martha, daughter age 22, is unmarried and a school teacher.
> Helen, daughter, age 18 is also unmarried and also a teacher.

In the preceding ten years since the last census, life had dealt Ann many cruel blows. She had lost her father; she had lost two sons, one dead in equatorial Africa, one lost at sea; she had lost two daughters who ran away from home; she had lost a 17 year old daughter to a deadly illness; and for the time being, her husband was locked in an asylum for the insane. Her two elder daughters were still spinsters, perhaps having lost their chances of marriage because of the turmoil in the family. On the brighter side, her two youngest daughters had embarked on professional careers as teachers. Her eldest son James had risen to the rank of First Engineer in the merchant navy, though his job had taken him to the Far East and she did not hear from him as much as she would like.

We leave the Simpsons in Govan for the time being and travel to Leith near Edinburgh to pick up the story of one of the daughters who ran away from home- Sarah.

Primary Reference Sources.
Hospital Records 1873 LHB3/16/1, and LHB3/14/2 Indoor Case Book
Edinburgh Royal Maternity, Lothian Health Service Authority
Register of Births 1873
Glasgow University Archives; NHSGGCBA Collections – Records of
Gartnavel.
Marine Register of Deaths; NASD 005796 May 1880.
Maritime History Archives Newfoundland; Sundry Crew Agreements.
Mitchell Library Glasgow; Records for Craigton Cemetery; Records of
Teachers' Services.
National Archives Kew; Consular Register, Kingdom of Granada
(Malaga) 1837 – 1891: FO 927
National Maritime Museum Greenwich; Mates' & Engineers' exam
applications and Certificates.
National Archives of Scotland; Wills.
Scotland's People; Old Parish Records pre 1855, Births and
Marriages: Births, Marriages, and Deaths 1855 onwards; Census
Returns 1871, 1881.

Secondary Sources.
Debary, Rev Thomas; **Notes of a Residence in the South of Spain,
etc.,** Travis & Rivington, London 1851.
Ford, Richard; **Gatherings from Spain**, Dent & Sons, London 1906.
Graham, Eric J; **Clyde Built**, Birlinn, 2006.
Grice-Hutchinson, Marjorie; **The English Cemetery at Malaga**,
published privately, 2001
Harrison, Joseph; **An Economic History of Modern Spain**,
Manchester University Press 1978.
Hobhouse, Hermione; **History of the Royal Commission for the
Exhibition of 1851,** Continium, London & New York, 2001.
National Library Australia; Website, Australian Newspapers,
Melbourne Argus Jan. 1877.
Oakley, C.A.; **The Second City**, Blackie & Sons, Glasgow 1967
Old Ordnance Survey Map, 1895, Glasgow, Pollokshields.

Chapter 6

LEITH: 1880 TO 1886

When the new decade dawned Queen Victoria, proclaimed Empress of India in 1877, reigned over a quarter of the world's population. The astonishing growth of the Empire during her forty three year reign, combined with the equally astonishing growth of Britain's industrial might, had brought great prosperity to the nation. Expansion of course, was not always peaceful and unhindered. By far the "jewel in the crown" was India, a jewel which attracted other envious eyes. In 1880, a British and Indian army was fighting in Afghanistan to prevent the intrusion of Russian influence on India's border. Britain succeeded, but at a bloody cost.

In South Africa, the mineral wealth, diamonds and gold, were attracting the imperialists and entrepreneurs. Not all in South Africa concurred with Britain's view of the road to economic progress. In 1879, an attempt to provoke a war with the Zulu nation resulted in a bloody nose for the British Lion, before superior fire power prevailed against spears and shields. By 1880, the Boer settlers in Transvaal and the Orange Free State were also disaffected and defending their way of life against British troops. With modern weapons they proved more than able to hold their own.

In Britain as the New Year and the new decade was greeted these minor setbacks in distant continents could be ignored. In Scotland, Hogmanay had always been a special celebration, a time to write off the disappointments of the 'Auld Year' and welcome the New Year with optimism; and perhaps a 'wee dram' or two to fortify that optimism.

In Leith, Robert Kirkpatrick, living in Tollbooth Wynd with his wife Mary and three sons, had good reason to be optimistic. By dint of his own abilities, he had risen from ordinary seaman age 13 on a small sailing brig, to the rank of First Mate on a modern steamship owned by the London and Edinburgh Shipping Company. Moreover he was soon to take the examination for his Master's Certificate and was confident of success. There was also another reason for an extra spring in his step. He was an expectant father once again. However he was a nervous expectant father, for it was not his wife Mary who was carrying his child, but the pert 26 year old stewardess, Sarah

Simpson who had served with him on board the IONA the previous year. Contrary currents were about to throw Robert's life into turmoil.

Crew List SS IONA 1879. Robert Kirkpatrick, 1st Mate age 41, and Sarah Simpson, Stewardess, age 24, began their affair after serving together on the IONA. (Entries 2 and 17 respectively)

Image courtesy of the Maritime History

As the end of the old year approached Scotland was being battered by severe storms, the kind of weather that caused anxiety for the wives and mothers in seafaring communities like Leith. On the morning of 29th December the citizens of Edinburgh awoke to news of a disaster almost beyond belief. The night before, around 7.15 pm, the Tay rail bridge, hailed as a marvel of Victorian engineering and only opened the previous year, collapsed from the buffeting by force 10 or 11 gales. An entire train, a locomotive and six carriages, which had set off from Edinburgh on a Sunday evening for Dundee, had plunged 88 feet into the icy waters of the river Tay. As the search for survivors in the aftermath went on, the full magnitude and horror of the tragedy captured the imagination of the nation. Seventy passengers and five train crew perished in the worst structural engineering disaster in British history. Queen Victoria herself had crossed the bridge earlier that year in her Royal Train.

The same storms that destroyed the Tay Bridge also disrupted sailing schedules between London and Leith, so when the church bells in Leith rang in the New Year, the IONA and its Scottish crew were four hundred miles away at the company's Irongate Wharf near the Tower of London. The IONA did not tie up again in Leith until 5th January 1880 when the crew had the option to take 'discharge' or 'remain' for a further six months. Most including Robert Kirkpatrick, chose to remain. The IONA had to average a round trip a week between London and Leith, and even when she was in port, she demanded much of Robert's time. As First Mate it was his responsibility to oversee the embarkation and disembarkation of passengers, as well as the loading and unloading of cargo.

Tolbooth Wynd, Leith. Robert Kirkpatrick was living at 19 Tolbooth Wynd when he applied for his Master's examination on February 7th 1881.

Image. KY Collection

In between his official tasks he had to divide his time in Leith between wife Mary and his sons, and his pregnant paramour, Sarah. It is easy to imagine him sneaking through Leith's gas lit wynds, his collar turned up and his cap pulled down in the wee small hours of the night.

On July 2nd at 5 Pattison Street, Sarah gave birth to a baby boy at 8.40 in the evening. Three weeks later, 23rd July, Sarah registered her son's birth, giving him the name James, after her elder brother perhaps who may have been the only member of the family with whom she still had contact. The name of the father was not registered, suggesting that Robert had managed to keep his affair clandestine so far. Sarah gave her occupation as 'stewardess'! The remainder of 1880 passed in the same manner, with Robert navigating up and down the treacherous east coast between Leith and London, and stealing brief moments with Sarah and his new son between trips. Somehow he managed to keep his adulterous affair secret – for a time at least.

Towards the end of the year newspaper readers found the following items in the overseas news printed by the *'Graphic'* on November 20th. United States – *'There is calm in political circles after the stirring campaign of the last few months and the Democrats have accepted defeat with as much philosophy as our Transatlantic brethren are capable of'. In Australia we hear from Melbourne that the noted bushranger, Ned Kelly, has been executed.*

At the start of 1881, with two homes to support, an increase in earning power was becoming imperative for Robert. On February 7th, he submitted an application to the Board of Trade, to take the examination for his Master's ticket, paying £1 for the privilege. The application shows his address as '19 Tolbooth Wynd'; apparently he was still living with Mary. The following day, the 8th February, he took his exam and emerged jubilant as 'MASTER OF A HOME TRADE PASSENGER SHIP', having satisfied the examiners as to his competency in navigation and seamanship. This was a qualified certification meaning Robert could not command a ship beyond British waters, which would restrict his employment prospects later in his career, but for now that did

Officer's cap badge of the London and Edinburgh Shipping Company.
Image. KY Collection

not matter. He could work as a Master for his employer, the London and Edinburgh Shipping Company. Promotion however was not automatic, and he would have to wait for an opening.

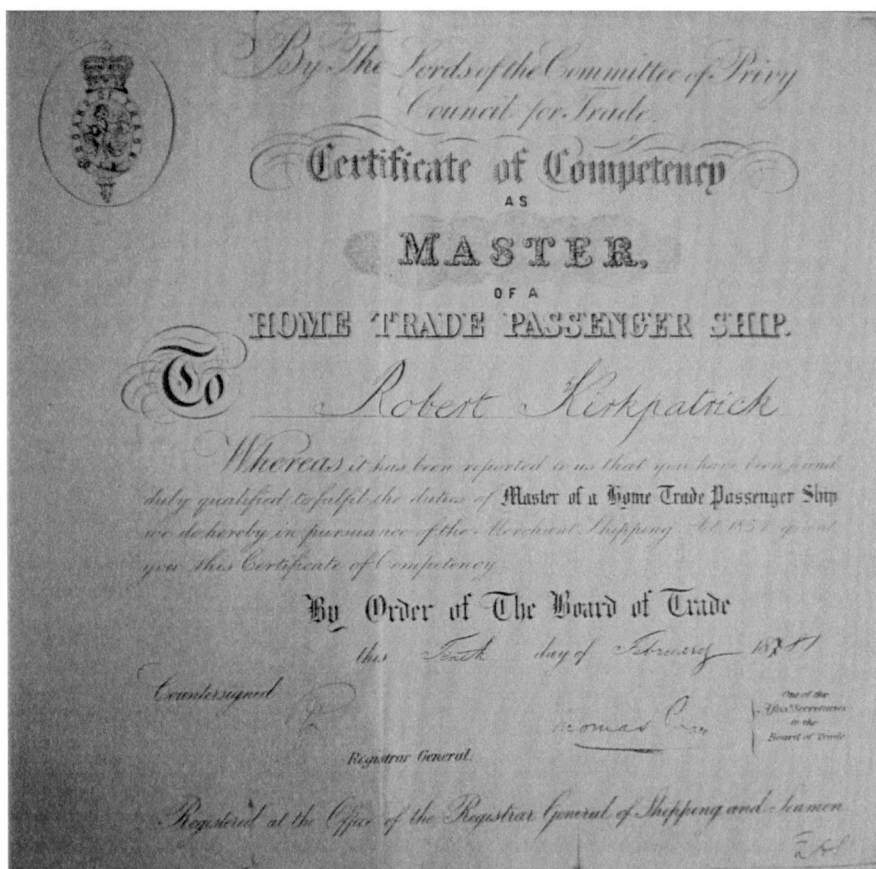

Robert Kirkpatrick at the age of 44 won his certificate of competence as Master, albeit limited to Home Trade Passenger Ships, no mean achievement for a seaman with no formal education beyond the age of 13.

Image: Courtesy of the National Maritime Museum

Two months later, the ten year census of April 1881 shows a dramatic change in the fortunes of the principals in this story. Sarah is still living at 5 Pattison Street in Leith with her two sons Alfred aged 8 and James 9 months. Never afraid of rolling up her sleeves, she was working as a Flax Dresser to support her children, probably in the Rope Works situated at the end of Pattison Street. Robert Kirkpatrick, still First Mate was on board the MARMION, anchored in the Firth of Forth. Mary, Robert's legal wife had quit Leith and is recorded as a boarder, along with her son William aged 7, in her brother's home at Whitekirk, near Berwick, 20 miles east of Leith. Her eldest son Robert, 19 years old, is working as a fitter in works at Kirkcaldy, Fife. Her second son Andrew, aged 16, somehow dodged the enumerators but turns up in the succeeding census working as a tailor in Kirkcaldy.

SS MARMION at Irongate Wharf, London. The London and Edinburgh Shipping Company vessel MARMION with its name visible on the lifebelts, taking passengers and cargo on board in London, a familiar sight for Robert Kilpatrick, 1st Mate 1878 and again 1880-81.

Image The Graphic 1874. KY Collection

Sometime between 8th February and the 5th April, the truth about Robert's double life had come to light. No doubt the gossips in Tolbooth Wynd had a field day with the scandal. Robert was forced to make a decision. He chose to abandon his wife of twenty years, Mary and his three sons and to live with the younger woman, Sarah, seventeen years his junior. Not surprisingly, Mary's descendants hold no forgiveness for Robert, and one elderly lady, with great dignity and restraint stated:

> *"His behaviour towards Mary was less than chivalrous, and he left her in a bit of a pickle."*

By the middle class, Presbyterian moral standards of Victorian Edinburgh, this is a massive understatement.

In spite of the difficulties in his private life, Robert Kirkpatrick achieved the promotion he had aspired to for so long when the London and Edinburgh Shipping Company appointed him to the Command of the IONA, one of their passenger/cargo ships on the London run. On the 5th May, Robert age 42 took his place as Master on the bridge of the IONA as she eased out of Leith harbour at high tide bound for London. It was rare for a seaman to rise through the ranks to the position of Master. The usual route to officer rank in the merchant service was via an apprenticeship whereby a lad was indentured to a ship's master on payment of a premium by the boy's father. The Shipping Master was obliged to feed cloth and educate the apprentice while at sea. A bright apprentice could pass his Board of Trade examinations in stages, 2nd Mate, 1st Mate and Master and he could be appointed to the captaincy of a ship in his mid-twenties. Robert Kirkpatrick's success was a praiseworthy achievement, but at 42 he was competing for a captaincy with men around his own age with 20 years' experience of sole command.

LONDON AND EDINBURGH SHIPPING CO.

LEITH AND LONDON THRICE WEEKLY.

S.S. MALVINA 190

SS MALVINA, London and Edinburgh Company advert. Robert Kirkpatrick's first two commands as Master were the IONA and the MALVINA, May to July 1881.

Image. Advertising Card. KY Collection

No doubt Sarah and her sons were on the dockside to wave a proud farewell to the IONA and her new master. The step from First Mate to Master was a huge one in terms of status. Masters were not waged employees, but earned a share of the profits from each trip, and many owned a share in the vessel. Robert commanded the IONA on her regular passenger runs to London until the 7th July when she was taken out of service for a rather special event. From July 15th to 29th, he commanded the MALVINA, another of the London and Edinburgh's passenger/cargo ships on the prestigious Leith-London run, after which he returned to the IONA.

The IONA had been taken out of service to prepare her for a part in celebrating a major event in the history of Leith docks. Since the beginning of the 19th Century, Leith had expanded and improved the docks almost continuously to keep abreast of the ever increasing volume of trade and the ever increasing size of the ships. The "Old Dock" begun in 1800 was completed in 1806, to be followed by the Queen's Dock completed in 1817. Both of these had a dry dock 136 x 36 ft. In 1825, an Act of Parliament was obtained to enable the construction of the West Pier and the extension of the East Pier, and in 1844, a further Act of Parliament modernised a mish-mash of management practices and piecemeal financial arrangements, by vesting the Harbour & Works in a newly incorporated body, the Leith Harbour Commission. This had been the situation when Robert Kirkpatrick first went to sea at the age of 13, in the schooner, GLANCE, registered tonnage 164 tons.

When Robert returned from Australia in 1860, he found Leith's harbour further enhanced by the Victoria Dock, and almost immediately thereafter, work commenced on the next extension, the Albert Dock, in use by 1870. A map of Leith, dated 1870 already shows the outline of a further proposed extension. Ten years later a Bartholmew's map of 1880 shows an unnamed "New Wet Dock, 16⅔ Acres," but by July 1881, completion was imminent and plans were well in hand for an elaborate opening ceremony. The new dock by then did have a name, "The Edinburgh Dock" and appropriately the opening was to be performed by none other than His Royal Highness, the Duke of Edinburgh, Queen Victoria's younger son.

The ceremony for opening the new dock was planned by the Dock Commissioners, chaired by James Currie owner of the Leith Hull Hamburg Line. Mr. Currie had a problem however with the arrangements. He had not been able to obtain approval from H.R.H. for his programme of events. The sailor prince as he was known, had been incommunicado for six weeks. He held the rank of Rear Admiral in command of Her Majesty's Reserve Fleet which had been on annual exercises in the North Sea and the Baltic. During this period, the Duke and his fleet of Ironclads, anchored first at Heligoland to visit the Danish Royal family; then at Kiel to visit German Royal cousins, and finally at Kronstadt, the fortress guarding the approach to St Petersburg, to pay further royal respects to the Tsar. The Duke of Edinburgh in his flagship HMS Hercules, did not arrive in the Firth of Forth until Monday 25th July, the day before the opening ceremony. That evening Mr. Currie and his entourage boarded HMS Hercules to present a loyal address to the Duke, and to obtain his approval for the next day's events. After the plans had been duly approved The Duke, Mr. Currie and their followers transferred to another ship, the GARTH CASTLE, where they were entertained to dinner by Sir Donald Currie, a brother of Mr James Currie, and owner of the Castle

Line which ran the mail ships to South Africa (he was the donor of the Currie Cup, a trophy still contested today in South African rugby).

OPENING THE NEW "EDINBURGH" DOCK AT LEITH: THE STEAMER BERLIN, WITH THE DUKE OF EDINBURGH ON BOARD, CUTTING THE BLUE RIBBON.
SEE PAGE 122.

Opening of the Edinburgh Dock, Leith, 26th July 1881 by HRH Duke of Edinburgh. Sarah Simpson was probably in the stand, while Robert was in the parade of ships.

Image. KY Collection

Edinburgh's daily newspaper, the Scotsman, gave an outline of the programme, from which the following précis has been extracted.

> *"The Dock Commissioners in the S.S BERLIN will proceed to the fleet about 12 o'clock to take on board His Royal Highness. The vessel will be followed by the London and Edinburgh screw steamer IONA, and Messrs Gibson and Company's steamer OSBORNE, with the Edinburgh and Leith Town Councils and other dignitaries. After receiving H.R.H. and the officers of his suite, the BERLIN will steam for the harbour and into the Edinburgh Dock, breaking the ribbon on her passage through the entrance. At this moment a Royal Salute will be fired by a battery of artillery sited to the east of the new dock. After disembarking H.R.H., Commissioners and guests will proceed to the banqueting shed for lunch, expected to last no more than an hour and a half. The lunch over, H.R.H will proceed via Leith Walk, to the Council Chambers in Edinburgh."*

The Dock Commissioners had planned the programme to the last detail, but they could not plan the weather. Tuesday the 26th dawned dull and grey, but windless. The Forth was as smooth as a mill pond, and a myriad of small

81

boats ventured out to view the impressive Ironclads and perhaps catch a glimpse of the royal Duke. When the SS BERLIN set out at mid-day to collect her Royal Guest, the sky was darkening to windward, and the Fife coast was obscured by mist. As the Duke transferred to the BERLIN, the band of the Leith Volunteers struck up "God save the Queen" and at around the same time the weather broke. The enthusiasm of the crowds was unimpaired however, and every craft cheered the royal progress. At the harbour, immense crowds swarmed over the piers, the roof tops, the decks and the rigging of every ship. At the entrance to the new dock stands, accommodating 1800 spectators had been erected – surely Robert Kirkpatrick as a senior officer with the London and Edinburgh Company would have been able to obtain tickets for Sarah and the boys. The Leith Volunteers lined the south side of the New Dock and the 42nd (Black Watch) lined the north side. Leith and Edinburgh would have looked most picturesque from the sea, said the Scotsman's reporter if it had not been for the pall of fog and smoke which shrouded the city.

When the flotilla entered the harbour the IONA and other steamers pulled up to allow the BERLIN to break through the ribbon into the new Edinburgh Dock. As she did so amidst enthusiastic cheers and flag waving, the band of the Volunteers played "Rule Britannia" most vigorously. When the BERLIN pulled up at her berth and the Duke alighted, the artillery battery sited to the east of the dock fired a royal salute. The guests then proceeded to lunch, expected to last two hours until around 3 o'clock. The Scotsman does not say if the crowds in the stands and on the piers waited two more hours in the rain for another glimpse of the royal prince. It does report large crowds gathering along the route from Leith to Edinburgh in the afternoon to view the royal procession heading to Edinburgh's Council Chambers for more loyal addresses, more toasts, and a sumptuous dinner. Being both a Royal Duke and a Rear Admiral must have been arduous at times.

It has not been ascertained if Robert Kirkpatrick was present in Leith to witness the opening of the Edinburgh Dock; he was more likely at sea with the MALVINA. Three days after the big event of 29th July, he quit the MALVINA in Leith and took command of the IONA once more. The London & Edinburgh Company took up residence in the new dock which became home port for Robert and his ships.

LEITH AND LONDON.

The London & Edinburgh Shipping Company's

FIRST-CLASS STEAMSHIPS

IONA, MALVINA, MARMION, MORNA,

(Iona and Malvina lighted by Electricity,)

Or other of the Company's vessels, are intended to Sail (till further notice) from

VICTORIA DOCK, LEITH, every Wednesday, Friday, & Saturday,

AND FROM

HERMITAGE STEAM WHARF, WAPPING, E.,

Every Tuesday, Wednesday, and Saturday,

AS UNDERNOTED :—

From LEITH.		From LONDON.	
AUGUST 1886.	SEPTEMBER 1886.	AUGUST 1886.	SEPTEMBER 1886.
Wednesday, 4th .. 3 P.M.	Wednesday, 1st .. 2 P.M.	Tuesday, 3rd .. 2 P.M.	Wednesday, 1st .. 1 P.M.
Friday, 6th .. 5 ,,	Friday, 3rd .. 4 ,,	Wednesday, 4th .. 3 ,,	Saturday, 4th .. 4 ,,
Saturday, 7th .. 6 ,,	Saturday, 4th .. 5 ,,	Saturday, 7th .. 5 ,,	Tuesday, 7th .. 8 A.M.
Wednesday, 11th .. 10 ,,	Wednesday, 8th .. 9 ,,	Tuesday, 10th .. 10 A.M.	Wednesday, 8th .. 10 ,,
Friday, 13th .. 1 ,,	Friday, 10th .. 10 ,,	Wednesday, 11th .. 11 ,,	Saturday, 11th .. 11 ,,
Saturday, 14th .. 2 ,,	Saturday, 11th .. 10 ,,	Saturday, 14th .. noon	Tuesday, 14th .. noon
Wednesday, 18th .. 3 ,,	Wednesday, 15th .. 2 ,,	Tuesday, 17th .. 2 P.M.	Wednesday, 15th .. 1 P.M.
Friday, 20th .. 4 ,,	Friday, 17th .. 3 ,,	Wednesday, 18th .. 2 ,,	Saturday, 18th .. 2 ,,
Saturday, 21st .. 4 ,,	Saturday, 18th .. 3 ,,	Saturday, 21st .. 4 ,,	Tuesday, 21st .. 4 ,,
Wednesday, 25th .. 9 ,,	Wednesday, 22nd .. 7 ,,	Tuesday, 24th .. 8 A.M.	Wednesday, 22nd .. 5 ,,
Friday, 27th .. 10 ,,	Friday, 24th .. 9 ,,	Wednesday, 25th .. 6 P.M.	Saturday, 25th .. 10 A.M.
Saturday, 28th .. 10 ,,	Saturday, 25th .. 10 ,,	Saturday, 28th .. 11 A.M.	Tuesday, 28th .. noon
	Wednesday, 29th .. 1 ,,	Tuesday, 31st .. 1 P.M.	Wednesday, 29th .. noon

FARES—First Cabin, including Steward's Fee, 22s. ; Second Cabin, 16s. ; State Rooms for Families, 10s. each Berth additional.   Deck (Soldiers and Sailors only), 10s.

RETURN TICKETS, available for Three Months (including Steward's Fee both ways)—
First Cabin, 34s. ; Second Cabin, 24s. 6d.

☞ *Provisions, &c., may be had from the Steward on moderate terms.*

Apply, in LONDON, to LONDON & EDINBURGH SHIPPING COMPANY, HERMITAGE STEAM WHARF, Wapping ; SEAWARD BROTHERS, 7 Eastcheap, E.C. ; ABERDEEN STEAM NAVIGATION CO., 102 Queen Victoria Street, E.C. ; R. THOMSON or M'DOUGALL & BONTHRON, 72 Mark Lane, E.C. ; G. W. WHEATLEY & Co., 23 Regent St. ; LAVINGTON BROTHERS, 69 Old Bailey ; EDINBURGH—Cowan & Co., 4 Princes St. ; GLASGOW—Cowan & Co., 23 St Vincent Place ; GREENOCK— D. MACDOUGALL, 1 Cross Shore Street ; and here to

8 & 9 COMMERCIAL STREET, LEITH.

THOMAS AITKEN.

Telegraphic Addresses { Leith . . "Aitken." London . "Edina." | Commercial Street Office Telephone No. ..403. Dock Office Telephone No. ....422.   [P.T.O.

Advertising leaflet for the London and Edinburgh Shipping Company 1886.

Image KY Collection

While the council workers were removing the bunting around Leith, plans were already advanced for staging a second major celebration in Edinburgh. New railway sidings were being laid and others extended. Officials of the Caledonian and North British Railways were working through piles of returns from the farthest corners of Scotland; from Galloway to Caithness, from the Western Isles to Berwick. Their aim was to bring 40,000 guests to the Queen's Park at Holyrood Palace on 25th August; and to have them assembled in a particular formation by 2pm in the afternoon in order to meet

Her Majesty Queen Victoria. The occasion was not the customary annual garden party, but a very special 21st anniversary.

In 1860, in face of a perceived threat of invasion from France, the government of the day, with the regular army scattered round the globe defending the Empire, appealed for volunteers to defend the homeland. The response was overwhelming. A wave of patriotism swept the country. Men flocked to the colours in thousands, infantry, yeomanry and artillery. They were true volunteers in every respect; giving their time freely, paying for their uniforms, accoutrements, and arms themselves. The emergency passed, but the enthusiasm of the volunteers continued unabated. A grateful Queen and government, realising the kingdom had a standing army at no cost to the Privy Purse were content to let the situation continue indefinitely. After 21 years, the volunteer movement was as vigorous as ever. When the railway officials collated the returns, they faced a huge logistical problem. They and the military solved the problem, with very minor hitches. New sidings were laid at Haymarket and others were extended. On the morning of the big event the volunteers arrived as follows:

Station of Arrival	No. of trains	Time	Numbers
Haymarket	27	5.35am – 10.30am	14,992
Leith Walk	10	7.35am – 10.50am	3,399
Duddingston	5	9.55am – 10.49am	2,368
Granton Pier	4	8.35am – 9.10am	2,753
Murrayfield	10	7.30am – 9.35am	6,542
Morrison Street	8	5.42am – 8.40am	4,540
Total	**64**		**34,594**

To this number must be added those who required no trains, the various units of the Edinburgh and Lothian Volunteers, plus a number of regular army units quartered in and around Edinburgh, bringing the total on parade that day to around 40,000 men.

Leith, on this second Royal Occasion of the summer season was not centre stage, but still played a supporting role. Around 7,000 men formed up in Leith and Granton and marched off up Leith Walk behind their pipe bands.

The morning was fine and the spectacle drew the citizens of Leith in large numbers. The throngs lined the streets decked in their finery and no doubt amongst the cheering crowds was Sarah Simpson, with her two sons Alfred and James. It is to be hoped however that Sarah took the boys home rather than follow the parade to Queen's Park adjacent to Holyrood Palace.

Between 12 o'clock and 2.00pm, the units formed up in the park. Assembly went with a precision which would have flattered the regular army. The sight of 40,000 soldiers, dressed in tartans, red, green and grey tunics was a magnificent sight, the biggest military assembly in Scotland since the Battle of Bannockburn 500 years earlier. (How times have changed! In 2010, Scotland could contribute only one regiment of 5 battalions to the regular British Army). The patriotism and the enthusiasm for soldiering of the Victorians have gone forever. That spirit still prevailed when the call to arms came in 1914, but the grim reality of the two world wars in the 20th century, has consigned those jingoistic emotions to the annals of history.

In a scene eerily reminiscent of the opening of the Edinburgh Dock the weather gods proved inexorably perverse. At midday the barometer was falling, and the wind was gathering strength from the east. At 2 o'clock, the start time of the ceremonies, the rain began to pour heavily and continued so throughout the rest of the day.

The Review was performed by Queen Victoria, in an open carriage; passing along the brigades as they stood, rank upon rank. The Scotsman reported *"The Volunteers behaved like tried soldiers, showing docility, training and endurance that could scarcely be equalled".* The Review was followed by the March Past which was *"more than creditable".* The men went at *"a swinging pace",* in spite of the mud and water which was ankle deep. The Scotsman concluded, *"No-one, either Sovereign or subject, but must feel pride in the evidence it afforded of the pith and endurance of Scottish Volunteers."*

The "Wet Review" may have been over, but the ordeal for the volunteers was not. While the good citizens of Edinburgh and Leith went home to dry their wet clothes in front of coal fires, 40,000 men went back to cold, empty trains to wring out their sodden tunics. They had no change of clothing. One ship returning to Fife on the other side of the Forth sank, but all 300 volunteers were landed safely. A few men died of pneumonia it is reported, but the Volunteers were justifiably proud of their achievement and formed a "Wet Review" Association, which was still meeting 50 years later. Scotland with a tenth of the population of England had turned out 40,000 Volunteers compared with England's 52,000, at an earlier event at Windsor. (*Please pardon a little Scottish pride even 130 years later in the 21st century*).

THE GRAPHIC

AN ILLUSTRATED WEEKLY NEWSPAPER

No. 614 Vol. XXIV. | SATURDAY, SEPTEMBER 3, 1881 | PRICE SIXPENCE

THE "LONDON SCOTTISH" DETRAINING AT LEITH WALK STATION

THE ROYAL REVIEW OF SCOTTISH VOLUNTEERS AT EDINBURGH

Wet Review. On the 2nd September 1881, Queen Victoria reviewed 40,000 Scottish volunteer soldiers in Holyrood Park, Edinburgh. 6,000 of these arrived in Leith and Granton and marched via Leith Walk into Edinburgh, watched by the good citizens of Leith. In the afternoon, the rain fell incessantly. Sarah and her two little sons were no doubt spectators.

Image. The Graphic, 3rd September 1881, KY Collection

As Leith dried out after the Wet Review, Robert Kirkpatrick continued as Master of the IONA on her regular sailings between Edinburgh and London. On 22nd September, Robert quit the IONA to take command of the OTTER, a cargo ship belonging to the Leith, London and Edinburgh Shipping Company and operating between Berwick and London. He was about to experience the wrath of nature at her worst. On the night of Thursday 13th and Friday 14th October, a storm of extraordinary violence hit Scotland, causing great destruction and loss of life. Communications between Scotland and England were completely severed as telegraph cables were wrecked, roads and railways were blocked by fallen trees and by floods. The women in the sea faring communities around the coast again spent an anxious night praying for the safety of their men folk.

It was Monday October 17th before the magnitude of the disaster began to dawn. The Edinburgh Evening News of that date reported:

> *"The disastrous results of the storm last week have now been properly realised and it is seen that so far as the Berwickshire fishing fleet is concerned, they are the most appalling that have ever befallen the fishing population of that quarter within living memory. Of the boats belonging to Eyemouth alone, several were wrecked within the sight of the harbour and altogether 64 lives are known to have been lost, while 11 boats with 74 persons on board are still missing. There is but too much reason to fear that most of them will never be heard of."*

One can hardly imagine the agony of Eyemouth's people watching in horror as the fishing boats foundered trying to re-enter the harbour and their menfolk drowned before their eyes.

At Newhaven, the fishing port next door to Leith, 17 fishermen perished, leaving 44 children unprovided for. Four of Leith's pilot boats were lost and 14 crew men killed. As with the fishing fleet, most small boats were crewed by family members. The Edinburgh Evening News tells of:

> *"A Mr Merrilees from Newhaven, who has been as far along the coast as Dunbar in his carriage, picked up the mast, tiller, rigging, compass box, a cravat and stocking belonging to the pilot boat Stormy Petrel, which was lost on passage home from Dunbar."*

The STORMY PETREL was crewed by a father and two sons - David Stevenson, Hugh Stevenson and Philip Stevenson. Their loss left 12 children fatherless. In total the seaport communities on Scotland's east coast lost 189 lives. Only 30 bodies were recovered from the sea. Charitable funds were immediately set up in Leith, to alleviate the hardship of stricken families. Contributions came from towns, cities and villages throughout England and Scotland. The Tay Bridge disaster fund sent a donation of £100 and Queen Victoria herself made a contribution. In two weeks the charitable funds raised £54,000 enough to maintain 73 widows for the rest of their lives. Today we tend to remember the hard times of Victoria's reign, but many philanthropists, charities and generous people gave their time, energy and money to improving the lot of the under-privileged in the absence of state intervention.

Only 22 months after the Tay Bridge tragedy, Scotland had suffered a second and even greater disaster. There was much grief in the sea ports of the Forth. There was also much relief among the families whose men returned safely. The larger sailing ships and the steamers mostly survived the storm. It would be a few agonising days later before Sarah would know if Robert was safe. He had sailed from Berwick for London, on board the SS OTTER, on the 12th October. The London and Edinburgh's office at 8 Commercial Street, Leith, would have no news of the OTTER until the telegraph lines were restored. The news eventually arrived that the OTTER docked safely at Irongate Wharf on the 14th October.

The IONA, which Robert had quit, was an old ship, built in 1866 and scheduled to be replaced by the company. His new command, the OTTER was considerably smaller, but of a more recent construction, built in 1877. She was a regular trader between Berwick and London. During the second half of 1881, the OTTER made 26 return trips to London, calling at Leith only four times in that period, a schedule not amenable to family life in Leith. The average return journey was 2 days out, Berwick to London, one day turn round, two days return, one day turn round and so on. Only one break was recorded, when the OTTER arrived at Berwick on the 18th October, and did not sail again until 26th October, a break of about a week.

On January 7th 1882, Robert once more took command of the MALVINA, and returned to the more prestigious passenger service, Leith to London, making one complete round trip per week. At this point, Sarah was about 8 months pregnant, so each return to Leith for Robert was filled with increasing expectation.

On February 2nd, at 5 Largo Place, Leith, Sarah gave birth to a baby daughter. Once again registration of the birth was left to Sarah, who did not get round to carrying out the formalities until 25th March. Her new daughter was registered as 'Maggie Low Kirkpatrick Simpson', the first two Christian names being those of Robert's mother. Sarah must still have been working prior to the birth since she gave her occupation as 'Ship Stewardess'. Largo Place is one of the few Simpson-Kirkpatrick addresses, still identifiable in 2012. It is a quiet cul-de-sac, with tenements on one side of the street and a small park on the other. At the end of the street, a pleasant walkway skirts along the River Leith. In 1882 the walkway was a branch of the North British Railway, running into the docks via the small 'Citadel' station.

Just 9 days after baby Maggie entered the world, Sarah's eldest sister, Christian White Simpson departed this world. She died of tuberculosis, just age 35, in the family home at 116 Pollok Street, Govan. Deaths from TB are now practically eradicated thanks to the effective use of modern antibiotics, but it was incurable in Queen Victoria's day. Mother Ann continued to live in Pollok Street with three remaining daughters Jane James, Martha and Helen. Sarah probably knew nothing of her sister's death for a long time. Would she have gone if invited to the funeral?

On the 10th April 1882, Robert was discharged from the MALVINA by 'mutual consent'- a phrase that suggests a falling out. The crew agreement nevertheless records both his 'Ability' and 'General Conduct' as 'V.G.' (Very Good) Three days later he took command of the OTTER and reverted to the Berwick-London trade. He was to continue in this service until the 30th June 1883, his career apparently having reached a plateau.

When the crew agreement for the OTTER expired at the end of June, it showed that Robert Kirkpatrick 'remains' for the second part of the year as master. However the OTTER could only have made three trips at most from Berwick to London when Robert received orders to bring the ship back to Leith. The Glasgow Herald of the 19th July 1883 recorded:

> "Shipping News: 18th July; Leith – Arrived, OTTER(S) from Berwick – light".

The (S) signifying a steamer and the "light" that she carried no cargo.

Just three days later Robert was transferred to the IONA, a brand new London and Scottish passenger ship, a replacement for the earlier IONA, but he did not transfer as master. He was demoted not one but two ranks to

Second Mate. His career appeared to be in free fall. What had gone wrong for him? How had he offended his employers?

The explanation came to light eventually in the Customs and Excise Out-Port Records in Leith, which show that the OTTER, just three days after Robert brought her back to Leith, was 'sold to a foreigner (Greek) – Registry cancelled 21st July 1883.'

It appears Robert was a victim of a downturn in the trade cycle, and a change of policy by the London and Edinburgh Shipping Company. Two years earlier, the company also sold off the BADGER, a sister ship built at the same time as the OTTER and in the same shipyard, this vessel having been sold to a Spanish owner. The London and Edinburgh was opting out of coastal trading to concentrate on the more lucrative passenger traffic between the capital cities, and so had a surplus of masters and mates. Robert, facing unemployment through no fault of his own, had little choice but to accept an inferior position, and a much lower salary. In Victorian times there were no redundancy payments and no state benefits to fall back on.

Most people are happy most of the time, or at least not unhappy, and the early years of the decade seem to have been happy times for Sarah and Robert. Sarah after the difficult years of the seventies could enjoy the warmth of family life, with a partner, two sons, Alfred aged 10, James aged 2, and a lovely baby daughter, Maggie. At this time, women with families were expected to stay at home and not go out to work, a convention which was the same for all levels of society. (Robert's first wife Mary had raised three boys and kept house as Robert's career progressed from seaman to mate, without any need to go out to work.)

Necessity of course, forced Sarah to earn a living in order to support herself and her children, but when she could have settled into domesticity, she continued to seek employment. In official documents at this time, she stated her occupation variously as Cook, Stewardess, Flax Dresser, Ship Stewardess and Factory Worker, with Stewardess probably her favourite.

On board passenger ships of the day, First and Second Class passengers formed the majority. Sarah was very much at home in the First Class salon, where the clients were very much her type of people. She and her sisters had been well tutored in the manners and etiquette of the upper crust, and for the first sixteen years of her life she had been one of them. Working as a stewardess she had the opportunity to dress smartly and to relive her happier days in Malaga; she could converse with ease, probably in a polite Scottish accent modified by her mother's Welsh diction and perhaps even in Spanish if the opportunity arose. Moreover she could be anonymous – no one knew her history. In short she was in her element – and she enjoyed it.

First Class Ship Salon 1880. Sarah Simpson, stewardess with her middle class upbringing, would have mixed easily in such company. Note the stewardess standing deferential, mid distance, left.

Image KY Collection

The escape from the humdrum routine of housework, however, presented Sarah with difficulties. A stewardess might have to be absent from home for several days at a time, which meant boarding her family with a third party. The first resort for child care at this time was grandparents or other relatives, but Sarah was totally estranged from her family and both Robert's parents were deceased. However, Robert had a widowed sister Margaret Brown living at 20 Pitt Street with three children, who made her living letting rooms. Pitt Street is only 500 yards from Largo Place, the address of Sarah and Robert at the time their daughter Maggie was born and Widow Brown may well have provided the mutually beneficial child minding service that allowed Sarah to hobnob with her erstwhile peers.

Apart from the six months in 1879 when Sarah served on the same ship as Robert - the old IONA, it has not been possible to discover what other ships Sarah served on. At this time over 100 ships were registered in Leith, and others registered elsewhere were regular visitors to the port. Theoretically it is possible to check the crew agreements of all these ships but this would take more resources in time and money than currently available. Sarah attended the passengers on the IONA along with a head steward, 2 stewards, an assistant steward, and an assistant stewardess. Her wage was only 10/- (ten shillings) a week, not much from which to pay for full time child care, but if modern practice can be taken as a guide, her wage would be well supplemented by tips from pleased customers.

The pattern of Sarah's life seems to have been spells at sea alternating with spells of pregnancy and child rearing during which she took factory work. The contrast between her two types of employment could not be greater. Her workmates on the factory floor would have been rough and ready in both manners and speech, but knowing her predicament would accept her sympathetically. Paradoxically Sarah could mix at the top and bottom ends of Leith's society, in the sophisticated atmosphere of the ship's salon, and among the clamour and grime of the shop floor. It was the strait-laced ranks of the middle class which were closed to her.

The year 1883 ended with Robert still employed as Second Mate on the IONA, but on Feb 16th 1884, his fortunes changed for the better when he was promoted to first Mate, the promotion bringing a substantial increase in his wage of 13/- per week, around 40%. At the end of June, Robert signed a further 6 month contract, remaining on the IONA still as First Mate. By the end of June, Sarah knew she was expecting another baby and would have to resign herself once again to factory work followed by unpaid maternity leave as the year end approached. Her son Alfred started the new school year in July aged 11 on what would be his final year of compulsory education. Leith Burgh managed nine schools, including Bonnington Road with 800 places and North Fort Street with 1040 places. Both are in streets close to where young Alfred lived, Bonnington Road perhaps being the more likely. James Simpson was only 4 at this time, not yet school age, and still in need of care while his mum was at work

Early in the morning of 16th December 1884, the local midwife was called to 6 Allan Street where Sarah had started her labour. At 9am Sarah gave birth to her second baby daughter. Allan Street has disappeared in re-developments over the years. Christmas must have been an especially happy occasion for Robert and Sarah. At the beginning of January 1885, Robert's contract as First Mate on the IONA was renewed for a further 6 months, and between trips he and Sarah attended the North Leith Registry Office on January 23rd. This time both parents signed the register, Robert as 'Mariner's Chief Mate (Merchant Service)' and Sarah as 'Factory Worker'. The proud parents named their daughter Sarah Simpson Kirkpatrick, making her extra special to her mother.

The year passed uneventfully until the 25th June. That day young James was unwell, showing signs of fever and a rash. A worried Sarah had to send for a doctor who confirmed Sarah's worst fears. He diagnosed Scarlet Fever, a disease readily treated today with antibiotics, but in 1885 it was often fatal. For six days and nights, Sarah nursed her little boy but she could do nothing to save him. On the 1st July he died before her eyes. The following day Sarah registered the death with the North Leith Registrar and arranged for James' burial.

The fates were showing no mercy to the distraught Sarah. On the 3rd July, baby Sarah, just six months old was displaying similar symptoms. Again the doctor, by a strange irony named James Simpson F.R.C.P.S. (Ed) made the same diagnosis. Again poor Sarah, living in the worst nightmare imaginable, prayed and nursed her sick child in vain. After a brief illness of seven days, baby Sarah went to join her brother with the angels on the 10th July. Once more it was Sarah who registered the death. Alone she also arranged Sarah's burial. Alone she stood at the graveside. Both children were interred in Rosebank Cemetery, off Bonnington Road, Leith. James on the 3rd and Sarah on the 12th July. Sarah could not afford to buy a burial plot so the children were buried in 'common ground', grave spaces H88 and H88.5 respectively. The graves are unmarked and the exact location within this section cannot be indicated.

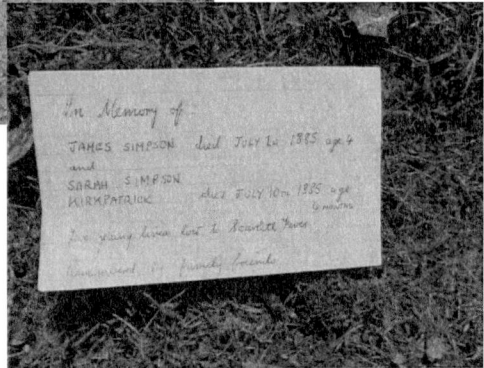

Rosebank Cemetery, Leith. In July 1885, Sarah Simpson lost two children to scarlet fever. While Robert was at sea, Sarah had to register the deaths and arrange the funerals. The children were buried in common ground with no markers.

Image KY Collection

Robert was away from home when the tragedy struck the family. Earlier in the year, April 24th, he left the IONA and went to work on board the OSSIAN, another London and Edinburgh Company vessel. The OSSIAN, a cargo ship only, was fairly new, built 1881, but a smaller ship than the IONA. She spent April and May on the west coast of Scotland, working around Glasgow, Greenock, Troon, and Ardrossan. By June, she was carrying coal between the Forth and France. On the 12th June, she arrived in Leith from Charente and on the 13th July she arrived in Dysart, one of the Forth's coal ports on the opposite shore to Leith, from Quimper. Given this latter date, Robert would have known nothing of the deaths of James and Sarah until he got home on the 14th July, two days after the burial of little Sarah. What a tearful reunion must have taken place at 6 Allan Street between Robert and Sarah.

The crew agreements for the OSSIAN for 1885 have not survived so it is not known for certain whether Robert sailed as Master or Mate. The fact that the OSSIAN was not in the 'home trade' when sailing to France makes it more likely that Robert was serving as Mate since his Master's certificate did not qualify him for the "foreign trade". Robert was allowed little respite to mourn his two children. He continued working on the OSSIAN until the 18th

94

October, when he rejoined the IONA once more as Mate, and returned to the Leith – Edinburgh - London run.

The year 1885 soon passed into history. At least two notable events had occurred in the year, one which made the headlines and gripped the public imagination and one which was scarcely noticed. General Gordon, a Victorian hero was killed at Khartoum by a besieging Muslim army, led by the Mahdi, a radical cleric. An expedition sent to rescue him by a dilatory, reluctant British government arrived just two days too late. The other event, which attracted little or no public interest, would within 80 years see the demise of the steam engine and the decline of the railways, a proposition impossible to imagine at that time. Two obscure German engineers, Gottlieb Daimler and Karl Benz, working separately, succeeded in inventing vehicles propelled by petrol engines, which needed no rails and could run on the roads. The first cars had been invented. Moreover the internal combustion engine opened the way to powered flight within 25 years.

At the beginning of January, Robert signed on once more as Mate on board the IONA. This, however, would be his last service with the London and Edinburgh Shipping Company. On the 12th March 1886, he took his discharge from the IONA. The next time his name appeared on a crew agreement was October 28th 1886, on a ship sailing out of South Shields. The Leith days for Robert and Sarah were over.

Note: Before following the Kirkpatricks to South Shields it may be opportune to make a record of Missing Persons.

a) **Ann Simpson** junior: Sarah's elder sister born Malaga September 1852. She was listed in the 1871 Govan census, age 18 a dressmaker, living with the family at 93 Gloucester Street. Thereafter no trace of her has been found in Scotland; no marriage, no death nor census return. Like Sarah she is not mentioned in any family wills nor on the family gravestone. The two sisters were closest in age and as rebellious teenagers may have quit the family home at the same time.

b) **Alfred Martin**: engineer on board the NE PLUS ULTRA, stated by Sarah to be the father of her first baby when she booked into Edinburgh Royal Maternity Hospital in July 1873. The register of certificated engineers held at the National Archives, Kew (ref. BT 139-141) has no record of an Alfred Martin at this period. His ship the NE PLUS ULTRA, was not registered in Britain according to Lloyd's

Register of Shipping. Two ships of this name were found in newspaper Shipping Reports. One was a clipper ship registered in New York, trading between London, Liverpool and New York and is unlikely to have had an engineer on board. The second was a modest steamer which delivered a cargo of iron ore to South Shields in June 1876, having sailed from Bilbao. Customs records are unclear as to whether she was French or Spanish. The circumstances which brought Sarah Simpson and Alfred Martin together remain a mystery.   A possible link may be Sarah's elder brother James, also a marine engineer, who spoke fluent Spanish and served for a time on Spanish boats.

 c) **Alfred Simpson**: Sarah's first child, born 31st July 1873 in Edinburgh Royal Maternity Hospital. Alfred was with his mother in Leith when the 1881 census was taken. After that he does not turn up in any of Scotland's official records. He was not counted in the census returns for South Shields either and does not seem to have accompanied his mother on the move. By 1886 when the family left Leith he was thirteen years old and had probably gone to sea as most lads did in a seaport town.

One lives in hope that that someday a breakthrough will occur and shed a little more light on Sarah's early years in Leith, 1873 to 1879.

Primary Reference Sources.

British Library – British Newspapers 1800 to 1900 (website) Shipping reports various dates.

Edinburgh City Council: Burial records for Rosebank Cemetery,

Lloyd's Shipping Registers.

Maritime History Archives, Newfoundland; Sundry Crew Agreements.

National Archives Scotland; Customs & Excise Out-Port Records, archives for London & Edinburgh Shipping Co.

National Maritime Museum Greenwich (NMM); Masters' and Mates' Certificates; Ship photo collection.

Scotland's People; Birth and death certificates; census 1881.

Secondary Sources.

Edinburgh Central Library; Scotsman Newspapers, Edinburgh Evening News (microfilms)

Fraser, Donald; ***Scottish Disasters****, Mercat Press, Edinburgh 1996.*

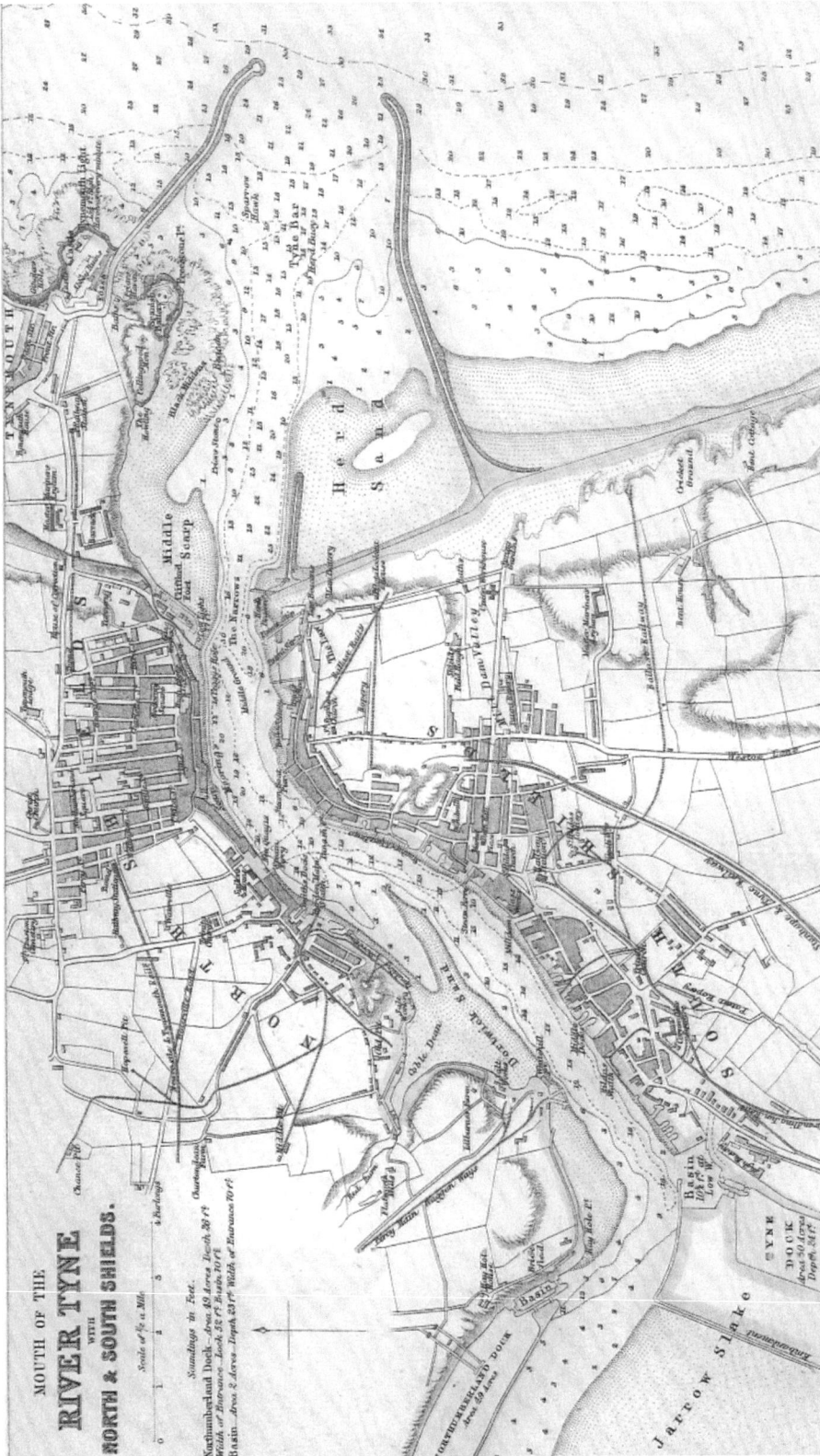

Image K Y Collection

Map of South Shields c 1870. Robert Kirkpatrick was discharged in South Shields from a ship named HEADQUARTERS in 1871. The town was then confined to the riverside. The seaward edge was used to dump ballast and waste from industry. There were no public parks. . The piers started in 1854, were not completed until the end of the century.

Chapter 7

ROBERT AND SARAH MOVE TO SOUTH SHIELDS: 1886

The story was handed down in the Kirkpatrick family that Robert took a ship to South Shields to be sold and liked the town so much that he decided to move the family there; so reported Sir Irving Benson after meeting Annie Simpson Kirkpatrick, Jack's younger sister. This is a very tenuous reason indeed for quitting a reasonably well paid job, uprooting one's family and moving home to a town a hundred miles away, with no guarantee of employment. A sceptic might suspect undisclosed motives lay behind the move.

South Shields in 1886 was not the attractive seaside resort of the later Edwardian postcards; nor was it new to Robert Kirkpatrick. In 1871 as mate on board a steamer named HEADQUARTERS he visited the Tyne on a return trip from Kronstadt near St. Petersburg in order to discharge a cargo of grain. The crew were also discharged at South Shields, a money saving dodge by the company. The last leg of the journey back to the home port of Leith was made on a Home Trade agreement which meant the crew had to provide their 'own provisions', a small saving to the owners. At that time the town of South Shields straggled along the southern bank of the river Tyne running for about two miles in a north easterly direction from the Tyne Dock basin to the narrows where the river emerges into the North Sea. The houses, two or three stories high, were closely built in narrow streets and alleys along the river side, many of them back to back. They were badly lit, almost destitute of the necessary conveniences; drainage was defective and water supplies to the poor were inadequate. A retired reporter of the Shields Gazette, Robert Fernandes, writing in 1949 about his memories of the town in his childhood days during the 1870s said:

> "My recollections are of poverty rampant among the people, of execrable sanitary conditions, of evil smelling paraffin lamps and tallow candles in the home; of primitive roads, rugged and broken, and churned into quagmires when it rained, swept by fiendish dust clouds when it was dry. The main roads, streets and back lanes were the only playgrounds for the children."

How did the town change between Robert's first visit in 1871 and his second in 1886 when he decided it would be a good place to raise a family?

HARD TIMES AND SOCIAL CHANGE

The town councillors in South Shields were highly conscious of the need 'to elevate the condition of the people' but the power to do so was not in their hands initially. By 1870 both the Liberals and Tories acknowledged the need to rectify the social problems caused by rapid, unregulated industrialisation. Between 1870 and 1874 a Liberal government lead by William Ewart Gladstone pushed through a raft of legislation aimed at improving the lot of Victoria's less privileged subjects; in 1870 The Education Act, one of the most far reaching, was placed on the Statute Book, giving local authorities power to appoint Education Boards, to build schools and to oversee the provision of education. More legislation followed; Cardwell's Army Reforms; the Bank Holiday Act, creating four public holidays a year; a Land Act to improve the rights of tenant farmers in Ireland; a Married Women's Property Act, allowing married women to keep £200 of their own money; A Trade Union Act, giving unions legal status (but not the right to strike); a Licensing Act, aimed at curbing the demon drink, by the licensing of premises for the sale of alcohol and by restricting opening hours. For many however the new laws did not go far enough, but ironically it was the last piece of legislation which occasioned Gladstone's downfall at the next election in 1874. Drinking was a national pastime and the new licensing laws alienated drinkers across the nation. Gladstone said of his election defeat, "I was borne down in a torrent of beer and gin".

Disraeli came to power on the pledge to 'elevate the condition of the people' and his term of office came to be known as 'the birth of Tory democracy'. The new government immediately relaxed the licensing laws in 1874 and the toast of "Cheers!" rang out in every pub across the land, in honour of the new Prime Minister. A programme of reform was set in motion with the Public Health Act of 1875, one of the most important reforms of Victoria's reign. Local authorities were empowered to set up Health Boards and appoint Medical Officers for public health. In 1876 an act promoted by a liberal, Samuel Plimsoll, to stop ships from being over loaded by unscrupulous owners, found its way onto the statute book, in spite of fierce opposition from the ship owners lobby. The Artisans Dwelling Act gave local authorities the powers to purchase and clear the worst slums; two Factory

Acts became law, limiting the working week to 56 hours and prohibiting children under 14 from working a full week; the Conspiracy and Property Act legalised peaceful picketing by strikers; and in 1880 Queen Victoria gave assent to another of the period's most important pieces of legislation, the Elementary Education Act which made education compulsory for children between the ages of 5 and 10 years. The timeliness of this reform became evident the following year, 1881, when the ten yearly census revealed the magnitude of the population explosion – 25% of the populace was under 10 years of age.

The consequences of this decade of legislation would soon be felt in South Shields and in Leith and would shape the lives not only of the Kirkpatrick family but the grandparents of people still alive in the present time. Leisure pursuits were playing an ever increasing part in working class lives outside the walls of the pub. Trains made days out at the seaside a possibility on Bank Holidays. In 1873 cricket's county championship was formed and five years later the first Australian national cricket team arrived on the shores of the mother country for a tour. They had travelled by steamer through the Suez Canal opened in 1869, making travelling time between Britain and her empire dramatically shorter. Music halls and theatres were springing up in every town and city. In London Richard D'Oyly Carte built the first ever theatre lit by electric light, to stage the comic operas of Gilbert and Sullivan, which rapidly became a success across the English speaking world, and the Mikado, the Pirates of Penzance etc. still have an affectionate following in the 21st century. On the soccer field the dominance of the Old Boys teams from the public schools, ended in 1883 when Blackburn Olympic, a team of weavers, factory hands and a dental assistant, defeated Old Etonians in the final of the F.A. cup. In 1882 the following obituary appeared in the London Times:

In Affectionate Remembrance of
ENGLISH CRICKET
which died at the Oval on
29th August, 1882
Deeply lamented by a large circle of sorrowing friends and acquaintances

R. I. P.
N.B. The body will be cremated and the ashes taken to Australia.

Thus the modern world began!

IMPROVEMENTS IN SOUTH SHIELDS

South Shields' councillors governed their parish from an antiquated, cramped and inadequate little building in the centre of the market square. Built in 1789 the old Town Hall, nick-named the 'Pepper Pot' by the Shield's Gazette still adorns the town centre market square. The council members were not however old fashioned and soon grasped the opportunity provided by the new legislation to improve conditions for the townsfolk.

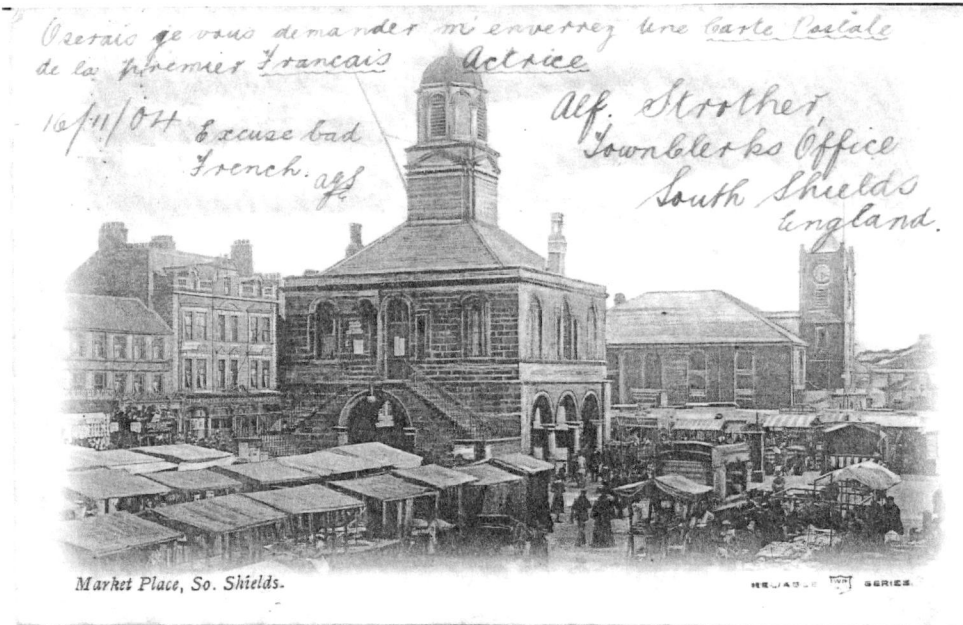

Market Place, So. Shields.

Old Town Hall, Market Place, built 1789 still stands in situ. Civic government moved to a new Town Hall in 1910. Alf Strother in the Town Clerk's Office had a French pen-pal in 1904, Madamoiselle E Wyrsch, at Plessis, Belleville, Oise.

Image KY Collection

By 1872, the council set up a sanitary department under the Borough Engineer to carry out scavenging in the town, but the real advance came in 1874 when after long and acrimonious debates, the Town council appointed a full time Medical Officer, Dr John Spear from Wigan. Iron ore, timber and cereals were not the only imports into the Tyne from European ports. Unwelcome imports in the form of cholera and smallpox epidemics also arrived. Dr Spear campaigned for the inspection of vessels entering the Tyne. In 1882, a Tyne Port Sanitary Authority was established with inspection and medical officers, and an old ferry steamer was converted into a well-equipped floating, quarantine ship. Pressed by successive medical officers, the council set up a small isolation hospital at the Deans.

Prior to the great Education Act of 1870, the Borough had an assortment of schools run by churches, charities and some philanthropic employers, but attendance at school was not compulsory. A few years earlier one of H.M. Inspectors concluded the children of the Borough were "beset by much ignorance and moral evils through want of school accommodation." South Shields was one of the earliest towns in the country to elect a School Board on January 27th 1871. The new Board discovered that they had a school population around 10,000, but places for only half that number. A building programme was launched. In 1883 the Board took over the Barnes School where Jack Kirkpatrick would begin his elementary education fourteen years later, and in 1901 the Mortimer Road School was opened, where Jack's schooling terminated when he was 13 years old.

The Town Council faced other problems with a continuous growth of population. Additional accommodation for the dead became a serious problem, only resolved in 1886 when the Burial Board purchased 31¼ acres of land between Westoe and Harton from the Ecclesiastical Commission. This new cemetery became the final resting place of Robert and Sarah Kirkpatrick.

Accommodation for the living was a much more intractable problem. Various schemes to clear the old slums along the waterfront fell through for lack of support. Meanwhile new streets and rows of terrace housing were springing up in the Tyne Dock ward of the town, such as South Eldon Street, Frederick Street and Bertram Street where the Kirkpatrick's lived at one time or another, and all within a few hundred yards of each other. The problem of slum clearance in Britain's major towns and cities would not be resolved until after World War 2. The Council did make progress with a number of amenities of a less daunting nature, e.g. a children's play area of four acres on the North Law; 1873 witnessed the opening of a Public Library and on the 1st August 1883, a horse drawn tramway opened, running between Tyne Dock and Ocean Road.

When Robert Kirkpatrick arrived in South Shields in 1886, Britain was in the throes of a prolonged depression, not the ideal time to move to a new region in search of a new job. The depression had started at the end of 1874 and lasted for 20 years. The depression hit agriculture first. The price of wheat plummeted, thanks to the opening up of vast tracks of fertile land in America's mid-west, combined with a dramatic fall in shipping rates, consequent on the ever increasing capacity of ships and the enhanced efficiency of compound marine engines. On top of this competition, Britain's wheat farmers suffered from a succession of bad summers and bad harvests. The same bad summers brought outbreaks of foot and mouth disease in cattle and foot rot amongst sheep. Tenant farmers, unable to pay the rents demanded by landlords, quit the land in droves not only in Ireland, but in large tracts of England. Many migrated to the towns in search of work; many more emigrated to North America and the antipodes in search of a new life. An estimated million workers were forced off the land.

In 1880, a Queensland farmer, Thomas McIlwraith chartered a steamship, the STRATHLEVEN, fitted her out with refrigeration equipment made in Glasgow, and despatched a cargo of frozen meat via the Suez Canal to London. When the holds were opened in Albert Dock, the meat was found to be in perfect condition. This venture opened a whole new world of international trade. Within two years frozen lamb and dairy products from New Zealand, frozen lamb and beef from Australia, and frozen meat from Argentina were filling the shelves of Britain's butchers and grocers. The arrival of cheap commodities was great news for the housewives like Sarah Simpson, but spelt disaster for British farmers who found it was not worthwhile to switch from cereal to meat production. The weekly cost of filling the family food basket fell by about a third, between 1877 and 1889.

In the international market for manufactured goods, Britain, the front runner in the industrial revolution during the first half of Victoria's reign, found herself overtaken by competitors, particularly in Germany and America. The latter with vast resources of immigrant manpower, both physical and intellectual, was rapidly becoming the world's leading economic power.

Paradoxically the Tyne, in spite of the depression was still shipping black diamonds (coal) in tonnages increasing year by year. Between 1871 and 1886, coal shipments rose from six to nine million tons, and would eventually reach 20 million by the outbreak of the Great War in 1914. This success was very much attributed to the Tyne Improvement Commission, set up in 1850, which turned the river from a shallow hazardous waterway, barely navigable for three hours each tide for shallow draught sailing ships, into a thoroughfare accessible for 12 miles inland by the largest steamers of the day. South Shields, near the entrance to the river blossomed, gaining tremendously as a seaport possessing first class facilities for bunkering, shipbuilding, ship repair, marine engineering and the shipment of coal. Tyne Dock became the largest coal handling port in the world. The work of the Commission was crowned by the building of the spectacular piers at the mouth of the river. The South Shields pier, extending for 5,155 feet, was begun in 1854 and completed in 1895.

South Shields pier under construction and still not complete in 1886. It was another nine years before the lighthouse at the end of the pier would light the way home for Robert Kirkpatrick. The north pier damaged several times by storms was not complete until 1904, Robert's last year at sea.
Image KY Collection

The north pier 2,950 feet long, took longer to complete being breached by storms in 1867 and in 1904. After a redesign to eliminate a curve in the structure, and to deepen the foundations, the pier was completed in 1907. The piers proved very popular, not only with mariners, but with strollers, anglers, photographers and postcard vendors.

South Shields had changed much since Robert Kirkpatrick's first visit in 1871, but it was by no means an attractive town. Railways carrying coal from the pits to the staithes in Tyne Dock straddled the town, claiming priority over streets and houses. Indeed two pits were situated within the borough boundaries. The streets were still lit by gas, generated by a malodourous gas works. The shore and parkland were covered by mountains of ballast off- loaded from the sailing colliers over centuries, and still brought by rail from the docks for dumping. The beautiful marine parks, electric street lighting, electric trams, public slaughter houses, public baths and wash houses were some years in the future.

South Shields shoreline before the ballast hills were replaced by the Marine Parks
Image South Tyneside Images

So what of the story that Robert brought a ship to South Shields to be sold, liked the town and decided to move the family there? It seems an unlikely tale. It is necessary to dig deeper for the true reason why Sarah and Robert took the decision to move from Leith.

In the town of Leith, Sarah Simpson and Robert Kirkpatrick were pariahs. They had transgressed against the seventh commandment and their conduct had scandalised respectable Presbyterian Leith. Both were strong characters however and for six years they had brazened the censure of their neighbours. Divorce was not an option for the working classes in Queen Victoria's days. The future facing their children was another matter. Victorian society stigmatised sternly illegitimacy and the sins of the parents were visited on the children. Sarah had probably seen her eldest son Alfred hurt by the taunts of his contemporaries and their parents, and was resolved that little Maggie and any future family should be spared from such hurt. At the same time it appears Robert's career with the London & Edinburgh Shipping Company was in decline, so they took the decision to move.

King Street, South Shields before the advent of horse drawn trams 1883.

Image KY Collection

By January 1887, the Kirkpatrick family were living at 47 Bede Street, South Shields, a town still struggling to improve its image. Emigration to America or to Britain's colonies, an obvious choice, would have offered a much better chance of a new life. Robert, an experienced merchant navy officer possessed transferable skills. His master's certificate however, only qualified him to command a 'Passenger Ship in the Home Trade' so perhaps he still aspired to resurrect his career as a captain, something he could not accomplish overseas. If so, he would be disappointed. The coal trade on the Tyne was booming, sustained partly by an insatiable demand for coal from London's gasworks, breweries and other industries. However there was over capacity in shipping. In April 1884, the managing owners of steamers in Newcastle agreed to lay up 25% of their fleets. Robert Kirkpatrick was unable to find a regular contract of employment for six and a half months after quitting the London & Edinburgh Shipping Company and moving to South Shields.

Custom House Shipping Office. Seamen in search of work frequented the shipping office. Robert Kirkpatrick, Mate and Master, spent six and a half months looking for a ship. Eventually in October 1886, he swallowed his pride and signed on as a fireman.
Image. KY Collection Vintage South Shields 206

When not working, no doubt Robert frequented the Shipping Office at South Shield's Custom House, at Mill Dam, where Master's came to find crew men. A young man, Arthur McClelland signing on as an apprentice in 1904, described the scene:

> *"The Shipping Office is a large oblong room along which runs a counter. In front of the counter are three pens and in these pens, men gather together with the master outside near the desk. The clerk puts down name and address, etc., and after some bargaining the wage. He then calls out the rules. The men show their discharge books, and then sign, the captain giving advanced notes."*

After six and a half months with no regular employment since discharging from the IONA in Leith on 12th March 1886, Robert signed on a collier steamer named CONSUL at South Shields 28th September 1886. By this time Robert's financial situation must have been fairly desperate. He signed on as a **Fireman!** In all his 36 years at sea he had never ever worked as a fireman. The fact that he was prepared to face the humiliation of dropping from Master on the bridge to shovelling coal in the stokehold is some measure of just how broke he must have been. The CONSUL was in the coasting trade and Robert signed on for a wage of £1-8/- per week, compared with a wage of £2 for the Mate. Robert stuck to his task as fireman for three voyages, two round trips to London and one to Hamburg, before quitting the CONSUL on 16th October. His earnings must have been enough to tide the family over as it was a further twelve days before he found another ship.

On 28th October 1886, Robert Kirkpatrick's fortunes took a turn for the better. Captain Matthew Gibb, master of the steam collier JULIA WIENER, had a problem. He had signed on his crew on 16th October, but with his ship loaded and ready to sail, his 1st Mate, Thomas Ropner from Cramlington, and his 2nd Mate, William Coates from Shields had 'not appeared'. Captain Gibb hurried to the Shipping Office in search of replacements. Robert Kirkpatrick happened to be there, produced his Mate's Certificate, Board of Trade No. 32186, and agreed with Captain Gibb to sign on as 1st Mate, giving the following information:

> "Age: 47
> Town where born: Leith
> Previous ship: COUNSEL" (should have been CONSUL)

His new ship was in the Foreign Trade and a wage of £7 per month with food provided, was agreed. Robert hurried home to Bede Street to give Sarah the good news together with an ADVANCE NOTE allowing her to draw money against his wages while he was at sea. Sarah at this date was around six months pregnant. Robert's wage was about £3 a month less than his wage on the IONA, but the country was still in recession, and he at last had the benefit of a regular job. After a brief farewell, Robert with sea chest on his shoulder and a spring in his step was off to join the JULIA WIENER. With pride restored and a fresh sea breeze on his face he took his place on the bridge as she sailed out of the Tyne.

The JULIA WIENER, although registered in the Port of London, was a 'Geordie' (Tynesider) from stem to stern. She was built in the Walker yard of C. Mitchell & Company, which later merged with Armstrongs, and her engines were manufactured by the North East Marine Engineering Company. Completed in 1876, she was a typical tramp steamer of the period: funnel amid ships, raised quarter deck, raised forecastle, length 220 feet, width 29.3 feet, depth 17.6 feet, and with a registered tonnage of 975 gross, 627 net. The JULIA WIENER became a second home for Robert

Kirkpatrick for the next two years. The close knit all male community on board ship comprised the captain, first and second mates, first and second engineers, ten able seamen, three firemen, a donkeyman engineer, a steward and a cook, making 21 men in total. When at sea, a steady speed of 13-14 knots needed a constant supply of steam. The three firemen must have worked like Trojans round the clock to earn their £3.10s a month, plus provisions. The JULIA WIENER carried no boys, no apprentices and no medical orderly. The Board of Trade 'By Authority' required every vessel to carry 'The Ship's Captain's Medical Guide' which informed the Captain how to deal with everything from 'Fireman's cramp' to fractures, fevers and venereal disease. 67 'medical diseases' and 12 'accidents' including 'hanging and drowning' were covered in the 14th edition of the 'Captain's Guide'.

The JULIA WIENER, with new First Mate, sailed from the Tyne, with a cargo of coal for the Baltic ports calling at Stettin on the 3 - 6th November and Riga on the 11 – 12th November. At Riga, the British Consul asked Captain Gibb to take on board a distressed British Seaman, Andrew Anderson, for conveyance to England. After visiting two Russian ports, the JULIA WIENER returned to the U.K. arriving at Cardiff on the 30th November. From there the ship proceeded to Algeria with a cargo of Welsh steam coal and discharged at Philippeville on 12 -18th December. Thereafter a cargo of grain, including barley, was loaded for delivery to Leith.

The JULIA WIENER terminated her voyage at Leith on the 12th January 1887 and the cargo of barley was delivered to Messrs Cochrane, Patterson & Co, while at the same time the Crew Agreement was terminated. The customers for the barley however, found their goods had been damaged in transit and claimed damages from the owners of the JULIA WIENER, John Johanssen and others, of £52. 4s. as reported by the Glasgow Herald of 26th February 1887. The plaintiffs claimed the owners of the vessel were at fault as the JULIA WIERNER was unseaworthy. The owners refuted the allegations, claiming that their ship had been 'under strain' from severe storms on the return journey. The parties eventually agreed on a settlement out of court of £30.

These last few paragraphs give a glimpse of the life of a humble tramp steamer and her crew over a two month period. What was the strain like on the crew of the JULIA WIENER as she battled through the winter storms in the notorious Bay of Biscay? The three firemen especially had a hard time, struggling to keep their balance as they shovelled coal frantically into a hot fire box.

While back in Leith Robert Kirkpatrick may have called upon his widowed sister, Margaret Brown, or perhaps after his furtive exodus from the town, he preferred to remain anonymous and to stay in the Seaman's Mission for a couple of nights. Robert and the crew were signed on again on the 15th January 1887, under a short Home Trade agreement to take the JULIA WIENER back to the Tyne where she tied up on the 17th January 1887. After two months and three weeks away from Sarah and little Maggie, Robert's heart and step must have been joyful as he hurried home towards 47 Bede Street. Would Sarah have given birth by now, he wondered? He soon found out. Another little girl was waiting for him, when he opened the door, born just two days earlier on the 15th January.

After five days the JULIA WIENER returned to the London coal trade, returning from the capital to Sunderland on the 17th February, but she made these runs without Robert Kirkpatrick who stayed at home with Sarah and their two young daughters. For Robert, this break from the rigours of the sea must have been a precious time. He and Sarah visited the Register Office in South Shields on the 23rd February to report the birth. Their new daughter was named Sarah Kirkpatrick, a replacement for the baby Sarah who died in Leith perhaps? It was a common practice at this time to re-use family names. Both parents are recorded as 'Informants'. Whilst maintaining the pretence of being married for the world at large, Sarah made no attempt to deceive officialdom, and correctly gave her name as Simpson. The short spell of domestic bliss could not last however. There was no holiday pay, the pennies were running out and Robert had to sign on for work once more.

After returning to Sunderland, the JULIA WIENER was laid up for a month, perhaps due to slackness of trade or perhaps she went into dock for repairs and refit. The owners had claimed previously in the Scottish Courts, that the ship suffered severe strain on the voyage from Algiers to Leith. Perhaps she needed some attention before returning to the foreign trade. Robert may have been unemployed for longer than he expected as the JULIA WIENER did not sign on a new crew until the 19th March. Once more Robert kissed Sarah and his girls goodbye and left not knowing when he would return. When he boarded the JULIA WIENER, Robert found to his surprise, that his old skipper Matthew Gibb, had been superceded two days earlier by Henry Wight of Herrington Road, Sunderland. His surprise was compounded when he discovered his new skipper was only 26 years of age and 22 years his

111

junior. What thoughts passed through his mind? Did he realise his chance of serving again as master were scuppered? The JULIA WIENER sailed on the 22nd March for London and from there to Penarth for Welsh coal; then onwards to the Baltic ports before returning via northern France, to South Shields. Robert spent the rest of the year sailing between the Tyne, the Baltic, Northern France and occasionally London.

A NEW LOOK FOR VICTORIAN SOUTH SHIELDS

In 1884, the Ecclesiastical Commissioners made a free gift of 31 acres to the Town Council of South Shields to enable preservation of open spaces on the seaward side of the town. The Council used the opportunity to create the South Marine Park. In July 1886, the Council engaged John Peebles, another Scotsman, as gardener to implement their plans for a park, and he also brought his family to live in South Shields.

Peebles tackled his new project with great energy. He was able to provide paid work for 200 of the town's unemployed and immediately set about laying out the paths. He had the lake dug out by September and it was filled by November. When it froze the following winter, the enterprising Peebles sold 8,942 tickets for skating and humbly petitioned the Council to install a few gas lamps around the lake so that the winter sports could continue after sunset. Peebles collected £111.15/6 for public funds. The creation of the parks was the most far-reaching decision ever made by the Council. The mines, the staithes, the collier ships, and the marine engineering have long since disappeared, but the parks along the seafront would still look very familiar to Jack Kirkpatrick and still make South Shields one of North East England's star attractions in the 21st century. On a sunny weekend it is near impossible to find a parking place on the seafront. Peebles' name is almost forgotten though his work endures in spectacular fashion.

Across the nation, Queen Victoria's golden jubilee on 21st June 1887 was celebrated with enthusiasm and affection. During her reign the population of Britain had doubled and her empire embraced a quarter of the world's people. Her sons, daughters and grandchildren occupied the thrones of most European nations and Britain had changed from a nation of peasants and farmers to one of urban dwellers. Britannia still ruled the waves but with steam driven ironclads in place of the sail clad 'wooden walls of England!' Victoria's name became synonymous with a complete age.

South Shields was not backward in celebrating. The Mayor and the Council finalised their plans in the Old Town Hall on Friday 27th May and decided that all children from elementary schools under 14 years of age, would be entertained at a cost of 3 pence per head. A permanent memorial to William Wouldhave, a townsman and inventor of the self-righting lifeboat would be erected in Ocean Road, the cost being funded by public subscription.

Wouldhave Memorial, South Shields   Valentines Series

Wouldhave Memorial, unveiled 1890 to the memory of the inventor of the self-righting lifeboat, Henry Wouldhave. The shrubs and trees of South Marine Park in the foreground are very new. When the Kirkpatricks arrived in March 1886, work had not started on the park. The Head Gardener, John Peebles, started landscaping the spoil heaps in July that year.

Image KY Collection

On June 20th, the evening before the jubilee, the Civil Service kicked off the celebrations with a Jubilee Dinner at the Criterion Hotel. Many toasts were drunk – the Queen, the Army, Navy and Volunteers, Civil Service, Colonial Office, HM Customs, Inland Revenue, Board of Trade and Port Office – a jolly time was had by all.

The weather on the morning of 21st June was described as 'charming' and the celebrants of the Civil Service were scarcely in bed when the bells of St Hilda's and Holy Trinity Churches began to chime at 6am. At 6.30am, the Postmaster and Staff of the South Shield's Post Office paraded outside their office and sang the National Anthem with the greatest and heartfelt enthusiasm, being listened to by a member of the public. Afterwards, they forwarded a telegram to the Queen embodying their warmest congratulations, and praying her Majesty may be long spared to reign over her loyal and beloved people.

King Street 1887 There was much to celebrate. Shields celebrated Queen Victoria's Golden Jubilee in great style. The Kirkpatricks celebrated the birth of a second daughter, Sarah on January 15th. Image South Tyneside Images STH 0000499

By chance the JULIA WIENER had docked at Shields the day before and Robert was home to complete the family's celebration. Little Maggie, now aged 5 and a pupil at Barnes Road School, was looking forward to the big party everyone had been talking about for days. Dressed in her Sunday best, Maggie probably went to school proudly holding her Dad's hand. After assembly, through the courtesy of the Town Council, the infants received a bag with a bun, an orange and sweets before dismissal. The older children marched from Tyne Dock to the Market Place for a rendezvous at 10am with other school children from around the borough. Seven thousand children assembled in the square.

Conspicuous were the Wellesley boys in naval uniform and carrying Martini carbines, who were naval cadets from H.M.S. Wellesley, an old wooden ship used to house and train destitute boys. Accompanied by the Dennison Family Brass Band, the children sang 'God Save the Queen', 'Rule Britannia', 'Now we Pray for our Country' and 'Hurrah, Hurrah for England', before returning to their respective schools to receive their buns, oranges

114

and bags of sweet just as the infants had done earlier. The Wellesley boys marched to the Marine Park where they gave a demonstration of precision arms drill.

The barefoot Wellesley boys on board their training ship carrying their Martini Carbines with their band on the poop deck behind. Hopefully they were issued with boots for the parade through the town.

Image KY Collection

One event which the Kirkpatrick family did not witness but worthy of note, occurred around 7am on the other side of town, when 200 - 300 men of the Swimming Association marched down Ocean Road, four abreast, carrying their swimming attire under their arms. Hundreds of onlookers watched as they headed for the beach. The men took a dip in the sea led by Father Neptune (alias Jim Pollard). In the water, the mermen joined together and sang the National anthem, then Rule Britannia and Auld Lang Syne. Anyone familiar with the temperature of the North Sea hereabouts will appreciate the fortitude of these brave souls and why there were no encores.

Horse Drawn Trams. These were operating from August 1st 1883. This single decker, nicknamed the 'Toast Rack' ran from the Tyne Dock area to the Market Place, King Street and Shore Road to the pier and sands.

Image KY Collection

For the Kirkpatricks, the festivities were only beginning. The people from the Tyne Dock area headed for the town either on foot or on the horse drawn trams which managed to run in spite of the throngs of people. The Shield's Gazette thought the bunting in King Street was meagre, but had high praise for the Railway Station's flags and bannerettes across the length of the platforms and the entrance, giving the place a holiday appearance. A most conspicuous flag on top of the Gas Company's new gasometer also merited a mention.

At 12 noon, the 3rd Durham Artillery Volunteers fired a Royal Salute of 50 guns from the battery at Trow Rocks and the beach was crowded from morning until late, though a heavy ground swell prevented the pleasure boats from working off the shore. The marine parks, though far from finished, were busy all day as spectators occupied every chair around the lake, watching model steam ships while in North Park enthusiasts celebrated the opening of a new bowling green.

A programme of music was laid on in North Marine Parade for the afternoon and evening:

Musical programme in the bandstand from 2 – 10pm

2 – 3	5th Durham Rifle Volunteers
3 – 4	Dennison Family Brass Band
4 – 5	Wellesley Band
7.00 – 8.30	Dennison Family Brass Band
8.30 – 10	Durham Rifle Volunteers & Wellesley Band

The Kirkpatricks with two young children could not wait for the evening festivities, a fireworks display when darkness fell followed by a beacon fire on top of the ballast hill at North Marine Park. It was 31 feet high and 14 feet wide at its base. Another bonfire was lit on the ballast hill behind Thames Street.

With the children safely tucked in bed, Robert and Sarah may have watched the pyrotechnics from afar. When they shut the door and settled down before their own fireplace, they probably felt content and happy with their move to South Shields – even if the first six months had been difficult.

The respite afforded by Victoria's Jubilee celebrations was brief. Three days later on the 24th June, Robert Kirkpatrick and the JULIA WIENER sailed once more, loaded with coal for London. In July, the ship returned to the Baltic followed by a visit to Northern France, before coming back to the Tyne; a pattern of trading which continued to the end of the year.

In South Shields, Sarah settled down to her domestic routine. Indeed this was probably the most settled period of her life since running away from home fourteen years earlier. She could walk her daughter to school in the mornings and have a friendly conversation with other young mothers; she could visit the neighbourhood shops and not be snubbed by fellow customers. Once a week, on Friday, she called at the Shipping Agent's Offices to draw an advance on Robert's pay, in order to fund her weekly household expenses. While at the office she would learn of Robert's whereabouts, thanks to the wonders of the modern telegraph system, the cables of which formed a network over the ocean's beds. The first cables connected London to France in 1850 and by 1876, a worldwide network reached every corner of Victoria's Empire, with the furthest extensions reaching Australia in 1872 and New Zealand in 1876.

Robert Kirkpatrick's wage, £7 a month in the Foreign Trade, with provisions included, or £2 a week in the Home Trade, but no provisions, provided a reasonable standard of living for his family. Sarah never returned to her earlier profession of 'stewardess', nor did she need to take factory work, like 'flax dresser' as in Leith. For the first time in her adult life, Sarah was enjoying a period of stability and of course she had her two little daughters, Maggie and Sarah on whom she could lavish all her love and care. At the back of her mind perhaps, like the wife of every other merchant seafarer, she would worry about her husband's safety. Being a seaman was one of the most hazardous occupations in the 19th century and the Shields Gazette reported accidents, mishaps and shipping losses in almost every daily issue. As for the past, Sarah appears to have committed that to oblivion, and no mention of her or Robert's antecedents would ever be disclosed to anyone, especially not her children.

In October, an event occurred in Glasgow that might have blown Sarah's cover if the news had travelled as far as South Shields. The mother, whom Sarah had vehemently declared to be dead 15 years earlier when she registered in Edinburgh Royal Maternity Hospital in July 1873, finally complied with her wish. Sarah's eldest surviving sister, Jane James Simpson reported their mother's death to the Registrar. Any chance of a reconciliation on this side of the grave had gone. The death certificate reads:

> *"Ann Simpson, wife of James Simpson, Mechanical Engineer, died October 22nd At 116 Pollock Street, Govan, aged 64; cause of death, apoplexy 5 days; deceased's parents, Sebastian Hosgood, Iron Works Manager and Jane Hosgood, m.s. James."*

Ann Simpson, nee Hosgood, aged 63 years, the mother with whom Sarah Simpson had a love/hate relationship. This Carte de Visite can be dated to 1886/87. Macnab, the photographer, opened a studio in Uddingston in 1886, and Ann Simpson died October 1887. The sitter is well dressed wearing jewellery and an expensively tailored coat, in keeping with her upper middleclass background.

Image courtesy of Paul Heiser, Queensland. The original is believed to be in the possession of the Parkin Family, Colchester. It was very likely passed to Sarah Simpson by her brother James who visited South Shields August 1889, before joining a new ship, the RION.

It fell to Jane James Simpson to arrange the funeral and in doing so she had a suitably imposing headstone erected at the family grave in Craigton Cemetery in the name of her unfortunate father who was still immured in Gartnavel Asylum. The stone erected records all the previous family deaths including the two sons who died at sea, Samuel and Sebastian. Jane James now took over the management of her father's affairs. Legally this role should have been fulfilled by James Simpson junior, the eldest son, but as a marine engineer, he was away at sea serving in the Far East. There is some indication later that Sarah may have been in touch with her brother James, but no evidence that Sarah ever had any communication with her three surviving sisters, Jane James, Martha and Helen. The iron curtain dividing the family stayed shut.

The JULIA WIENER, a tough little tramp steamer, spent most of the second half of 1887 shipping coal to London, but did carry four shipments to Hamburg. One cargo of 'black diamonds' was loaded in Newport, South Wales, one in Grangemouth, Scotland, and one in Sunderland, North East England, a rival port to Newcastle. Most loads were shipped from the staithes of South Shields, and in the course of six months, Robert Kirkpatrick managed to get home nine times, the final one of the 31st December. The crew agreement for the JULIA WIENER shows that on that date Robert 'Remains', i.e. was not discharged.

The crew agreement for the first half of the new year, 1888 shows a very high turnover of personnel, almost 100%, an indication perhaps that young Master Wight (now 27) commanded an unhappy ship. Maybe his man management skills did not match his skills in navigation and seamanship. In fact during the six months of the agreement, he had no fewer than three Chief Mates. The first to take his discharge was Robert Kirkpatrick who quit the JULIA WIENER as early as 31st January at Cardiff in South Wales. This ended Robert's connection with the JULIA WIENER, her owners, and her young captain. Later in the year, 5th June the JULIA WIENER was laid up, presumably because of slackness in trade.

A NEW SHIP AND STEADY EMPLOYMENT

On 5th March, Robert Kirkpatrick joined a new ship, the SOUTHMOOR, another of the sturdy collier steamers built at Redhead's yard on the Tyne in 1877. On that day, her Master Mr. E George left, the First Mate Abraham Harrison stepped up to Master leaving a vacancy which Robert was only too happy to fill especially as the weekly wage was £2 13/- a week, an increase of 13/- a week (32%) on his pay compared with that on the JULIA WIENER. The agreement contracted the crew to sail between any ports in the UK and any ports between the Elbe in Germany and Brest in Northern France. For the next 10 years, Robert would stow his gear in the Mate's cabin on the SOUTHMOOR. With the extra income, life for Sarah and Robert was even more settled, but not all plain sailing. On 22nd August, SOUTHMOOR returned to South Shields, loaded and sailed again on the same day. If Robert managed to snatch a few hours with Sarah who was six months pregnant once more, they would be the last for over three months.

On 25th August, a Lloyd's telegram reported:

> "The Steamer SOUTHMOOR of London, coal laden, and the WINSTON of West Hartlepool, bound down, collided in Limehouse Reach on the River Thames, early yesterday. The SOUTHMOOR sank. The WINSTON had her bows damaged."

The news which mentioned nothing of casualties, reached South Shields that day, causing heart stopping anxiety for Sarah and others. Eventually the waiting next of kin were relieved to learn that the crew had suffered no injuries. Although SOUTHMOOR sank in Limehouse Reach, the owners and insurers agreed she could be salvaged. The majority of the crew were discharged, but the Captain and his officers, including Robert Kirkpatrick, with two able seamen, a fireman, a donkeyman and the steward remained. After the cargo of precious coal was recovered, salvage work progressed, and a carpenter, three able seamen and a fireman were recruited on the 5th November. The SOUTHMOOR eventually returned to sea on the 7th December and Robert was re-united with his family on the 9th December at 45 Bede Street.

Robert no doubt received letters from Sarah while he was in London and already knew he had another daughter born on the 22nd November. Together Robert and Sarah registered the birth of Martha on 31st December 1888. On 3rd January 1889, the SOUTHMOOR cleared the bar at the mouth of the Tyne and the conveyor-like process of feeding London's insatiable appetite for coal rolled on into another year.

Earlier in the year, Queen Victoria lost a son-in-law when Frederick III of Prussia died prematurely, probably of throat cancer. Frederick who had experienced the waste and horror of the Franco-Prussian war, detested militarism; thoughtful and liberal minded he opposed Bismarck's attacks on constitutional rights and the press. Frederick was succeeded by his son Wilhelm II who was everything his father was not, a militarist, and imperialist, an autocrat and an Anglophobe who spoke of his grandmother, Queen Victoria, as an 'old hag'. Events were in train which would plunge the most civilised nations in the world into an unimaginably barbarous war – a war in which many sons yet to be born would be slaughtered.

The SOUTHMOOR's crew agreement for the first six months of the year shows that Robert Kirkpatrick re-enlisted as 2nd Mate with Ben Davison serving as 1st Mate. The agreement for the second half of the year shows they changed roles with Robert as 1st Mate and Ben as 2nd Mate. Was this a mutual agreement between colleagues to job share? For each man it meant six months earning £2.13/- per week and six months £1.18/- per week. The SOUTHMOOR logged 46 voyages in the first six months and 53 in the second, mostly between the Tyne and London but occasionally loading up at Newport or Cardiff and delivering to ports in north west Europe. Robert had little time at home and the onus of raising the family fell squarely on Sarah's shoulders, a situation common to all families whose breadwinner was a seafarer.

It is very likely that the Kirkpatrick children, Maggie aged 7, Sarah aged 2, and Martha who was 10 months, met an uncle in August 1889. In Palmer's yard, next door to South Shields, a comparatively new type of steamer was launched, a bulk oil carrier, gross tonnage 2196, and engines of a nominal 200 horse power. Hitherto oil was transported in metal cases. Registered in the port of Newcastle, the RION completed her trials and was ready to make her maiden voyage on 5th August when her crew signed on. Signing on as 2nd Engineer was James Simpson, aged 40, born in Malaga, Sarah Simpson's elder brother! James had been ashore since May 18th having been discharged from his previous ship ABYDOS, in Swansea following a voyage to Venezuela. Surely James must have visited his sister – perhaps even stayed with her. One small but significant clue lies in the Crew Agreement for the RION. James' wage was £11 per month out of which he made an allotment of half, £5.10/-, but to whom? James was a bachelor, his sisters in Glasgow were well off, he had made no allotments on board his previous ships, and he had no next of kin closer than Sarah. Moreover Sarah named her next son James and by April 1891, according to the census, she was sufficiently well off to employ a servant in her household. The odds are in favour of Sarah being the beneficiary of her brother's allotment. When Sarah and James met, she would learn of her mother's death. However,

Sarah maintained the blackout of her past history and only Maggie was old enough to have remembered a visit from an Uncle.

The RION and 2nd Engineer James Simpson made two trips to Batum, at the eastern end of the Black Sea to bring back cargoes of oil, not yet needed as fuel, but needed in ever greater quantities as a lubricant for the bearings of the industrial revolution. James Simpson took his discharge from the RION at London on the 11th November 1889, but there is no evidence of what he did next. He may have joined another ship or may have taken a job ashore.

When the new decade started, the SOUTHMOOR with Robert Kirkpatrick as 1st Mate continued to steam up and down England's treacherous east coast delivering coal from the Tyne to the Thames. At the start of the New Year, Sarah was already over six months pregnant and to her great delight was at last blessed with another son on the 7th March. The registration of his birth had to wait until 24th April when Robert and Sarah were able to visit the Registrar's Office together. Sarah very correctly registered as mother in her birth name, comfortable perhaps that the Registers were totally confidential. To give the child the surname Kirkpatrick, Robert had to be present at the Registrar's office as he and Sarah were unmarried in the eyes of the law. The register shows that their new son James, was born at 10 Lee Street, Westoe. This was the second time that Sarah had used the name James, perhaps in honour of her father, but more likely as namesake for her elder brother who had visited South Shields seven months earlier, and whose generosity may have been helping to support the family.

South Shields whose population had grown from around 20,000 at the beginning Victoria's reign, to 75,000 in 1890, was elevated to the status of a County Borough. The town, its Member of Parliament and its Council were on the liberal side of the political spectrum. The labour movement was still in its infancy and was two years away from sending an Independent Labour Candidate to Parliament. The Liberals therefore with popular support had done much to improve the conditions for the working classes of Shields and the jewel in the crown was to be the new Marine Park. The 25th June, the day set for the official opening of the new park remains an auspicious date in the history of South Shields. The Town Council declared that date a public holiday and organised a ceremony and celebrations reminiscent of the festivities three years earlier for the Queen's Jubilee. On the same day the new Lifeboat Memorial would be unveiled.

South Marine Park. The marine parks were officially opened on 25th June 1890. The Shields familiar to Jack Kirkpatrick was rapidly evolving.

Image KY Collection

The following extracts have been taken from the Newcastle Courant, published 27th June 1890:

"In the morning there were one or two sharp showers of rain, but a fresh westerly breeze drove away the clouds and tempered the atmosphere. In honour of the events, the bells of St Hilda's Church were rung at frequent intervals."

The centre of South Shields had *"probably never seen such a profusion of bunting and floral adornments… Venetian masts, festoons of evergreens, flowering plants and shrubs, together with pictures of lifeboat work, models of lifeboats, mottoes etc."*

The Town Hall *"was beautifully festooned with evergreens and adorned with pretty trophies of flags, surmounting shields and scarlet and gold cloth,"* while the L.N.E.R. (railway) bridge over King Street *"was decorated in the form of a triumphal arch, with flags and evergreens, and on either side of it in prominent letters were the words 'Welcome to South Shields."*

The parade began assembling in the market place at 2 o'clock.

"The Market Place, King Street and all the route was absolutely black with onlookers. Prompt at half past two, the procession headed by

124

*the band of the Wellesley Training Ship, followed by a band of the
South Shields Pilots and the Volunteer Life Brigade."*

Immediately behind came the carriages with the dignitaries. In the first, the Right Honourable Sir John R Mowbray, Bart., M.P., Chairman of the Ecclesiastical Commissioners who had donated 31½ acres for the park, and who was to perform the opening ceremony. With him were the Mayor, Alderman Shotton, Mr J. C. Stevenson, the local M.P., followed by numerous others including the Lifeboat Memorial Committee. On foot came the trades guilds, friendly societies and nearly every lodge in the town supported by another five bands, the West Docks, 3rd Durham Artillery Volunteers, South Shields Borough, Green's Home, and the St Bede's Chemical Company Band from Jarrow. Noticeably absent from the parade were the school children.

From a platform on the terrace in the park, the Town Clerk read an address on behalf of the Council thanking Sir John Mowbray and the Ecclesiastical Commissioners for their generosity. The Council, he reported had spent upwards of £22,000 on the creation of the park including an additional 14 acres, in an area which was formerly a barren waste and, he went on,

> *"The ambition of the Town Council is to alleviate and refine the lives
> and pleasures of the people of the present and succeeding
> generations so long as the Marine Park shall endure."*

The ambition of those long dead Town Councillors has been well and truly realised. One hundred and twenty two years later the lives and pleasures of the town's people and many, many visitors are still being 'refined'. They would be gratified to learn that in the 21st century, the final stage of the North East's famous annual half marathon ends on the Bents field near the park every year and that pictures of the occasion are broadcast to the world on something called television.

Sir John Mowbray thanked the Mayor, Aldermen and Councillors for the 'beautiful address', complimented them and the ratepayers on the intelligence, the spirit and the taste which made it all possible. Amid loud cheers, he declared the park open.

The proceedings then quit the park for the site on Ocean Road where the Lifeboat Memorial, inaugurated in celebration of Queen Victoria's Jubilee, and funded by public subscription was to be unveiled. The self-righting lifeboat was invented in South Shields in 1789 at the instigation of the town's

Coal Trade Committee. Distressed by the numbers of wrecks which occurred in the mouth of the Tyne within sight of spectators on the shore, the committee offered an award of Two Guineas (£2. 2/-) for the design of a lifeboat to be, if possible, unsinkable. Two entries came top, one submitted by William Wouldhave, parish clerk for St Hilda's, and other by Henry Greathead, a local boatbuilder. South Shields had the first true self-righting lifeboat built with a combination of ideas from both men. Both are commemorated on the monument unveiled in 1890 in a prominent position in Ocean Road.

Following the day's ceremonies, the Mayor hosted a banquet in the Public Library for his distinguished guests. Sadly the man who had actually created the marine park, John Peebles, head gardener, was not on the platform in the park, was not acknowledged in any of the speeches, nor was he invited to the banquet.

By the end of the year 1890, the features of South Shield that would be part of John Simpson Kirkpatrick's boyhood, and which would help to fashion the man, were now in place; the close knit community in the terraced houses around Tyne Dock, the horse drawn trams, the schools, the Marine Park, the pleasure beach with its donkey rides, the south pier (not quite complete) sheltering the Herd Sands, the river and the buzz of a major port crowded with ships and seamen from around the world. The arrival of John Simpson Kirkpatrick on the South Shields scene was only 19 months away.

On the world scene the Imperial Powers were still carving out their empires. That year, the British Government made a colonial swap with Germany, trading the islands of Heligoland off the German/Danish coast, seized by the British during the Napoleonic wars, for the Island of Zanzibar. The Kaiser apparently was delighted, but Queen Victoria was outraged, exclaiming "next we'd be giving up Gibraltar." That year, the Kaiser also removed from office his Chancellor, Otto von Bismarck, the elder statesman who had united Germany and maintained peace in Europe by balance-of-power diplomacy – an ominous portent.

During the whole of 1891, Robert Kirkpatrick remained as 1st Mate on the SOUTHMOOR, making 54 deliveries of coal to London. As fast as the ship could be loaded or unloaded, she put to sea again. Most of her cargoes were picked up that year at the staithes of Sunderland in the River Wear, some eight miles to the south of Shields.

Tyne Dock, South Shields. Robert Kirkpatrick averaged around 50 trips a year, many beginning and ending in Tyne Dock. Note coal waggon on staithes dropping coal via a spout (or chute) into the ship's hold. Empty collier ships await their turn for loading at the tiers.

Image KY Collection

Trimmers c 1900. It was the task of the trimmers to spread the coal evenly in the ship's hold. Robert as Mate, was responsible for loading the ship on an even keel, up to the Plimsoll Line and no more. *Image South Tyneside Images 0009722*

As 1st Mate, it was Robert's duty to supervise the loading of the ship, a process which involved manoeuvring the ship beneath the spouts or chutes on the staithes. The machinery on shore was operated by 'Teemers' and the coal in the holds was levelled out by the 'Trimmers', surely one of the dustiest jobs in the world. Apart from the Mate, the only other crewman necessary for loading was the donkeyman who operated the fore and aft winches to move the ship beneath the spouts, ensuring the holds were filled evenly. To ensure stability at sea the Mate had to keep the ship on an even keel, fore and aft, and abeam. Loading was complete when the water was level with the Plimsoll Line on each side. The 'Freeboard' amidships, the distance between the deck line and the Plimsoll Line was only 2ft 2inches in summer and 2ft 5inches in winter. Robert Kirkpatrick's time on shore was therefore much curtailed by his duties as First Mate, even more so by having to travel between Shields and Sunderland.

On the 8th February, the SOUTHMOOR sailed from the Thames in ballast. Thick fog on the night of the 8th/9th February made the trip hazardous. The SOUTHMOOR made it safely out to sea, but collisions were numerous. Two ships were sunk, one limped back into Millwall Dock, three more had to be run ashore to prevent sinking, one of these being the MALVINA, one of Robert's former ships. What were his feelings when he returned passing the grounded MALVINA at Gravesend four days later? Did he remark to anyone "I was Master of that ship back in July 1881".

On the night of Sunday, April 5th 1891, the date appointed for the decennial census, the SOUTHMOOR was anchored at Rotherhithe on the south bank of the Thames. In accordance with special arrangements for shipping, the Captain of the SOUTHMOOR, Abraham Harrison, completed a return of the crew and signed it in his own hand as witness. Robert Kirkpatrick, married, aged 52, 1st Mate, born Midlothian, Leith, is second on the list.

Strangely the census for the night of 5th April for Westoe, Tyne Dock Ward, shows the Kirkpatrick family living at 10 South Eldon Street, South Shields as follows:

Robert Kirkpatrick	Head	50	Seaman A.B.	Leith
Maggie	Daughter	9	Scholar	Leith
Sarah	Daughter	4		South Shields
Martha	Daughter	2		South Shields
James	Son	1		South Shields
Ellie Crosier	Single	15	General Servant/Domestic	South Shields

Firstly, Robert could not have been in South Shields as he was on-board the SOUTHMOOR in the Thames and he would not have given his rank as

Seaman A.B. (able seaman). Secondly, where was Sarah? The census registers for the whole of the United Kingdom have been searched with no result. Thirdly, who did fill in the census return? The servant Ettie Crosier would not have had the detailed knowledge of the family's ages and places of birth. Maggie, the oldest daughter, aged 9, was too young. Two or three days before the census date, the enumerator distributed census forms to each household in his district. These were to be completed, listing everyone in the household on the night of Sunday 5th April. The completed forms were collected the following day. Did Sarah have a dilemma with her form? If she gave her name as 'Kirkpatrick' she would be telling an untruth. If she gave it as 'Simpson' she would be revealing the secret that she was not married. Did she side step the question by leaving herself off the list and naming Robert as 'Head'? This is speculation but is the most likely answer, backed up by the fact that ten years later, Sarah's name is similarly missing from the UK census register.

The anomalies aside, the census shows the Kirkpatricks were certainly not at the bottom of the social pile. Their immediate neighbours were mainly skilled or semi-skilled tradesmen, another seaman A.B., a boilersmith, a dressmaker, a blacksmith, a joiner, a steam engine fitter and a moulder. The Kirkpatrick household was the only one out of five households on the census page employing a servant. Perhaps Sarah, still hankering after her youthful days in Malaga, when she was surrounded by servants, was indulging herself, with some financial support from elder brother James. The services of Ettie Crosier, domestic servant, aged 15, would have cost Sarah 5/- (five shillings) a week at most, possibly less given the amount of hardship in South Shields. Ettie's (Henrietta's) family were not untypical. Her mother Margaret, age 36, had been widowed about nine years earlier and left to bring up six children. At the time of the 1891 census her eldest son Joseph age 19 was a platelayer; her daughter Mary 17, was at home; daughter Margaret 16, was a domestic servant with the Lauder family in Napier Street; Ettie was with the Kirkpatricks at 10 South Eldon Street; her son John 11, was a scholar. Widow Crosier to make ends meet, had also taken in two lodgers, John Ripley age 63, a quarryman and his son Allan age 19, a labourer. The Crosiers and their lodgers managed to fit into a three roomed terrace house. The above addresses are all in the Tyne Dock Ward of the town. This typifies a close knit working community willingly offering mutual support to friends, family and neighbours. The day would come when Sarah Simpson would have to take similar measures as widow Crosier did in order to get by.

For women without partners, life could be really tough. Woman loading props onto open railway wagon at Tyne Dock Timber Yards.
Image South Tyneside Images

The SOUTHMOOR continued to pound her way up and down the North Sea coast without a break until the 4th October. The ship and crew then enjoyed a furlo' of ten days before they headed out to sea once more. For an all too brief interval Robert enjoyed family life with his four young children and with Sarah. The sequel to this brief furlough would emerge nine months later.

In South Shields in 1891, an Electricity Order became law. The effect was not immediate but the door was opened for electric street lighting, electric trams and eventually electricity in homes. Further afield voices were raised in Australia demanding trade protection and unification. Germany, ahead of the rest of Europe introduced a State Pension Scheme, and Tsarist Russia inaugurated the Trans-Siberian Railway.

Primary Reference Sources.

Maritime History Archives, Newfoundland – Sundry Crew Agreements
UK Census 1891 South Shields and Rotherhithe
Scotland's People Deaths
Burial Records for Craigton Cemetery, Mitchell Library, Glasgow

Secondary Sources

Glasgow Herald - February 26 1887   Julia Wiener
Glasgow Herald - May   24 1887   Court Case
'**Looking Back at Britain 1870's**' Jeremy Harwood, published by Reader's Digest
'**Looking Back at Britain 1880's**' Brian Moynihan, published by Reader's Digest
South Shields Gazette Centenary 1849 – 1949. Published by South Shields Gazette
South Shields Gazette Diamond Jubilee Souvenir 1849 – 1909. Published by South Shields Gazette
South Shields Centenary 1850 – 1950 . Published by South Shields Gazette
The Banks of the Tyne, edited by Geo. B Hodgson 1899. Published by South Shields Gazette
South Shields – A Gossiping Guide, Aaron Watson 1892. Published by South Shields Gazette
The History of South Shields, Geo. B Hodgson, published Reid and Co. Newcastle
South Marine Park, David Bell, Jargram Publications 2007
South Shields 100 years of Public Transport, Tyne and Wear Public Transport Exec.
From Tyne to Tsar, Arthur McLelland, University of Sunderland Press, 2007
South Shields Gazette 28th May, 21st June, 22nd June 1887

Chapter 8

ENTER JOHN SIMPSON KIRKPATRICK

When the bells of St Hilda's Church greeted the New Year 1892, the Kirkpatricks could look forward with some optimism. Robert was in virtually permanent employment as First Mate on the SOUTHMOOR, his home from home. His ship spent most of the year shuttling between Sunderland and London, with occasional diversions to Hull, Cardiff, Grangemouth and northern France. She only returned to the Tyne on one occasion. At the start of the year, Sarah suspected she was pregnant once more. At 10 South Eldon Street, a three roomed house, Sarah ruled the roost over her growing family, Maggie aged 10, Sarah aged 5, Martha aged 3: her pride and joy – only son James aged 2 and her servant girl Ettie. On the 6th July, Ettie Crosier was sent to fetch the midwife who presided over the birth of another son for Mrs Kirkpatrick. It was almost a month later, 3rd August before Robert and Sarah found the opportunity to attend the Register Office together in order to register the birth of their boy. They gave his name as 'John'. To his family and friends in South Shields he was known as 'Jack'. Later in life he would be known to the mercantile service as Kirkpatrick; to the Australian Army as Simpson; to his mates as 'Simmo'; and to posterity as 'the man with the donkey'. In the genes inherited from his parents, nature had already played her part in shaping Jack's destiny. From here on nurture would take over the task, along with the environment in which he spent his childhood.

Shield's South Marine Park laid out and still supervised by Mr Peebles, was maturing in spite of initial doubts about the exposed situation and the poor quality of the soil. Whiteleas Smallpox Hospital was opened this year to the gratification of the Borough Council, though thankfully its services would not be needed by the Kirkpatrick Family. At national level, the first ever Labour M.P., Keir Hardie, a former miner from the Scottish coalfields, was elected to Parliament, representing the London constituency of West Ham. He caused a furore in the House of Commons when he entered Parliament, wearing a tweed suit and a cloth cap. He was evicted on the orders of the Speaker of the House, but refused to back down, being permitted to take a seat sometime later on his own terms. The following year the Independent Labour Party was formed in the UK.

Nothing untoward troubled the Kirkpatrick family in South Shields in 1893. Robert continued to serve on the SOUTHMOOR as First Mate, though under a new Master, Fred Koster from Sunderland, the ship fetching and carrying coals to the same ports as before. Sarah on summer Sundays, could take her enhanced family to the Marine Parks which were flourishing literally under the management of John Peebles. On sunny days, elegant ladies and nannies pushing prams, strolled through the sheltered walks; crowds on the terraces enjoyed the views and the sea air as they listened and relaxed while the bands played popular music; boys of all ages sailed their boats on the lake; and the sands across the road were thronged with pleasure seekers. The donkeys which would play a crucial part in young Jack Kirkpatrick's career were already giving rides on the beach. Photography, a rapidly growing hobby, was attracting a new breed of enthusiasts who found a plethora of subject matter in the combination of sand, sea, river, shipping, piers, parks and people. Boats were picking up passengers from the beach for a short sail; fairground amusements, ice cream and refreshments were on offer. These early photographers have left a rich visual record of South Shields in the era of the Kirkpatrick family.

Mr George and the Donkeys c 1900-1901. Jack worked on the sands with Mr George's donkeys in the summertime. Is he in this photograph? Inscribed on the reverse is "Mrs J George, 1 Florence Street, The Deans, High Shields", only a couple of streets away from Jack's home in Bertram Street.

Image KY Collection

In 1871, Newcastle had demolished its 18th century stone bridge of many arches which blocked the passage of ships other than the traditional twenty ton keel boats. Its place was taken by the Armstrong swing bridge, still in use 140 years later. This new bridge combined with dredging and other improvements implemented by the Tyne Commission made the river navigable up to twelve miles from its mouth. On the north bank of the river, Lord Armstrong's complex of factories developed rapidly; ship building, hydraulic engineering, bridge building and armaments. Armstrong's breech loading rifled guns, invented after the Crimean War, became a 'must have' for every nation with military and naval aspirations. Armstrong with complete impartiality sold his guns to both sides in the American Civil War 1861 to 1865. On the south bank opposite the Armstrong industries, the North Eastern Railways (N.E.R.) built substantial new staithes in 1893 at Dunston. These shortened the distance from Durham's inland pits to the point of loading and greatly increased the capacity of the Tyne for shipping coal. For Robert Kirkpatrick and the SOUTHMOOR, this was a mixed blessing. Turn round times for ships were improved, but for Robert it was less convenient, sometimes having to sail twelve miles beyond Tyne Dock and home. The extensive wooden structure of the staithes still stands 120 years later, its machinery painted and apparently in working order, waiting for ships that will never return, its purpose forgotten. The last vestige of the Armstrong industrial empire on the opposite bank, a workshop building tanks, is scheduled for closure, as Britain decimates its armed forces and takes another step back from its role as a world power.

On the far side of the world, New Zealand became the first of Queen Victoria's self-governing dominions to introduce votes for women in 1893. For Sarah the years were passing quickly. By mid-1894, she knew she was pregnant once more, and nearing 40 years of age, she realised this might be her last time. On 10th November, she gave birth to a healthy daughter, later christened Annie. Less than a month later as she was recovering, her worst nightmare returned. Her four year old son James took ill. With sinking heart she recognised the symptoms of scarlett fever, the killer disease which had robbed her of the first James and first Sarah in Leith in July 1885. She was now fighting two desperate battles, the first to save James and the second to prevent the rest of her children from catching the fatal fever. She won the second battle but lost the first. On 10th December 1894, James died. The effect on the family was profound. Young Jack, just two years old, did not only lose a brother, he became the sole male heir to the Kirkpatrick name. To his parents, he suddenly became doubly precious. His mother Sarah would cosset and spoil him making the bond between mother and son exceptionally strong, directing for better or worse the major decisions and actions in his short life. The Christmas celebrations that year were tinged with sadness.

During 1894 – 1895, the North Marine Park was extended by another 14 acres. John Peebles gained a promotion being appointed Head Gardener for both parks at a salary of £1.15/- per week, considerably less than Robert Kirkpatrick's £2.10/- a week as First Mate on a collier ship. However, John Peebles was given possession of the handsome lodge in North Marine Park, 'free of rent, coal, gas and water', a valuable perk for a man with a wife and four young children.

Robert Kirkpatrick, to earn his £2.10/- a week was averaging over one return trip a week between the Tyne and the south of England, or the near continent. When returning to the Tyne, it was the practice to have a watch 'aboard' and a watch 'ashore'. The watch ashore comprised the men from Shields and surrounding areas so that they could have time with their families. When the ship arrived in the Thames, the watches changed roles. The men 'ashore', quit the ship when she moored at the tiers, rows of buoys, awaiting her turn for loading at the staithes. The crew took no part in the loading. This operation was carried out by 'teemers' and 'trimmers'. The former operated the machinery on the staithes, positioning coal wagons above the spouts (chutes), then opening the trap doors beneath, letting gravity send the coal cascading into the open holds of the ship below. A typical collier could have four holds which needed to be filled evenly, with water being pumped out of the ballast tanks as needed to keep the ship on an even keel particularly important at low tide. One end or other resting on the river bed would have been a serious embarrassment for the Mate. By the 1890's, using gravity spouts, a collier could take on board 1,000 tons of coal in four or five hours. The round trip to London took four days normally, but undue waiting time at the tiers and storms at sea could disrupt schedules.

The Tyne Improvement Commission started building the north and south piers at the river entrance in 1854. It was not until 1895 that Robert Kirkpatrick was able to bring the SOUTHMOOR passed the completed south pier. The north pier beset with problems and damaged by storms would not be completed during Robert's working life.

A milestone in the family's life was reached on February 2nd 1894 when eldest daughter Maggie reached the age of 12, school leaving age and would have left at the end of the school year in July. She may have taken Ettie Crosier's place in the home, helping her Mum look after the younger children and learning domestic skills like washing and ironing her Dad's shirts. Alternatively she may have found employment to add a few shillings to the household income.

The course followed by the SOUTHMOOR, plying between the Tyne and the Thames, 307 nautical miles, passed Whitby, Flamborough Head, Spurn Head, Yarmouth, Lowestoft, Orfordness and the treacherous sands off the Lincolnshire, Norfolk and Essex coasts, was much the same route Robert had traversed for nine years in the steamers of the London and Edinburgh Shipping Company, except for the stretch between the Tyne and the Forth. Robert often saw the flag and funnels of his old company in the course of his travels. Bad news in maritime circles travelled fast even in Victorian times. On the morning of Tuesday 17th September 1895, British newspapers, from the Aberdeen Journal in the north east to the Bristol Mercury in the south west, carried the sensational story of a shipping disaster in the Thames estuary. Even the New York Times of the same date was able to publish the story with the headline – *'FATAL FIRE ON THE IONA'*, thanks to the transatlantic telegraph cable.

The IONA had left Leith at 7o'clock in the evening of Sunday 15th September. At 1.20a.m., the following morning, George Thompson, the Captain who was on the bridge, perceived smoke issuing from the skylights of the second class dining room. He immediately ordered the engines into full reverse to stop the ship and went to investigate. He found fire had caught hold in the forward section of the ship, burning most fiercely on the port side where the women's cabins were located. It took the ship's engineers three hours to extinguish the fire, before they could enter the cabins. There they found six *"bodies so charred and burned to be scarcely recognisable"*. One woman was found face down holding the hand of a child.

The story was particularly chilling for Robert Kirkpatrick. The IONA was his last ship before leaving the London and Edinburgh Shipping Company. The story was equally poignant for Sarah. The dead woman found holding the hand of the child was a young stewardess, 20 year old, Edith Leadenham who was seen rushing into a blazing cabin to rescue a child. She was not seen alive again. *"There but for the Grace of God go I"*, thought Robert and Sarah.

With the fire extinguished, the IONA completed the voyage to her berth at Irongate Wharf, near the Tower of London, where passengers and cargo were discharged and the Master of the ship reported to the Coroner's Office. The following month an enquiry was heard in the Coroner's Court and the New York Times reported the verdict of the Coroner in its issue of October 4th 1895. The Coroner found the officers of the steamer were culpable for their failure to rescue the women and children passengers when the fire broke out. The Captain was also found guilty of negligence in failing to ring the alarm bell when the flames were discovered.

Captain George Thompson's career was 'ruined' and his Master's Certificate was probably revoked. The London and Edinburgh Shipping Company did recover from the bad publicity, and continued trading through two world wars in the 20th century, only succumbing to competition from the rapid expansion of air traffic after WWII.

The year 1895, saw a number of inventions, cinematography, wireless telegraphy, safety razors, the discovery of X-rays, and one which, perhaps unexpectedly, would benefit South Shields, the advent of picture postcards. Use of these spread rapidly. In their time, they were the equivalent of today's emails and text messages. Postal deliveries in towns were so frequent that it was possible to advise a friend by a card posted in the morning, of arrival by a specific train later the same day. South Shields with parks, piers, sea, river and ships was very picturesque, and a boon to card manufacturers as a result of which, images of South Shields' best aspects were reaching every corner of the globe, many sent by seamen visiting the Tyne. Many of the images used came from earlier photographs, so it is possible today by collecting postcards, to see South Shields of the late Victorian and Edwardian era, the South Shields familiar to the Kirkpatrick family.

When Robert Kirkpatrick signed on the SOUTHMOOR's crew agreement for 1896, he erred with his year of birth, stating it to be 1842, thus knocking four years off his age, making him 54 instead of 58. Was he becoming sensitive about his age? This vagueness was corrected when he signed on for the second half of the year. The SOUTHMOOR loaded mostly at Sunderland that year, with only occasional calls at Hartlepool, Hebburn, Shields and Tyne Dock. The South Shields Borough Council continued its programme of improvement, widening streets and starting to replace gas lamps with electric lighting. On the seaward face of the borough, more ballast hills were levelled and South Marine Park was extended via Bents Park southwards to

Trow Rocks. Further afield, the modern Olympic Games were inaugurated in Greece, thanks to the drive and initiative of Baron de Coubertin.

Steam crane at work removing ballast hills to make way for the new parks.   *Image South Tyneside Images*

THE PIER SOUTH SHIELDS.

The Pier, South Shields. Completed in 1895 but not opened to the public until a dispute between the Town Council and the Tyne Commissioners was settled in the Courts in 1897. It has become the most photographed scene in South Shields, a boon for postcard manufacturers for over a century.

Image KY Collection

QUEEN VICTORIA - 60 YEARS ON THE THRONE

As 1897 dawned, the nation was beginning to look forward to the celebration of Queen Victoria's Diamond Jubilee. It would also be an eventful years for the Kirkpatricks, though maybe not for the best of reasons. Robert resumed work on the SOUTHMOOR, signing a new agreement on January 1st. On March 22nd however, he was discharged. The vessel continued trading and Robert was replaced by William Phillips. Robert had served nine years on the SOUTHMOOR and there was no obvious reason for his discharge. Robert did not find another ship until October and was apparently out of work for 6½ months, the most likely explanation being a health related problem. If this was the case, Sarah must have had a difficult time financially but she was resourceful. In the past she showed she would take on any task from stewardess to flax dresser to feed and clothe her family. In Shields in times of hardship she reputedly took in laundry. At this time Maggie, aged 15 was old enough to roll up her sleeves and play a part in the laundry business. For Robert, there was the consolation that he had time to get to know his younger children. Sarah had no family near at hand who could help. Her sisters in Glasgow were well off, but totally estranged. Maybe her elder brother James was still able to help? Maybe she also had some savings to fall back on and there was always credit at the Co-op.

The Coat of Arms of the Borough of South Shields carried the words on a ribbon below a shield 'COURAGE, HUMANITY, COMMERCE', in plain English – no pretentious Latin. COURAGE is exemplified on the central shield by a manned lifeboat with the words above it 'ALWAYS READY'. HUMANITY and COMMERCE are represented by the shield's supporters, the former by a young woman carrying the staff of Aesculapius (the God of Medicine) and the latter by a mariner carrying a sextant. The Town Council's plans for the celebration of Queen Victoria's Diamond Jubilee on the 22nd June 1897 reflected, perhaps unconsciously, the intrinsic characteristics of which the town prided itself.

The festivities were to follow the pattern set ten years earlier for the Golden Jubilee. Music would abound; the main streets, market place and Town Hall would be 'illuminated and ornamented' lavishly. The children of the town were to play a prominent part in the celebrations and special arrangements were to be made for the poor. At Harton Workhouse, the inmates would be entertained to dinner similar to that held on Christmas Day. From two o'clock until 8 o'clock, the adults and children would be able to enjoy celebrations outdoors, but with no intoxicating liquor. The men would receive an ounce of tobacco, and the women and children would get 1 shilling each, total cost reckoned to be £115. Arrangements were also made to entertain 2,000 of the poorest children in the town.

The Mayor, Alderman Readhead, launched an appeal for donations to fund the Jubilee celebrations, but money was slow in coming in at first. On the 14th June, the Shields Gazette published a list of the benefactors and the amounts donated, ranging from one to thirty guineas. This had the desired result as the list showed not only the names of donors, but prompted those whose names were missing to dig into their pockets. By June 19th, the Shields Gazette could compliment the local inhabitants on their 'liberality and enthusiasm'. £600 had been raised for feeding the poor, street ornamentation, music in the parks, fireworks and bonfires. Any money left over would be given to the Infirmary Extension Fund.

Rejoicing began on the eve of the Jubilee, when crowds come out in the fine weather to see the decorations and illuminations. The Mayor had received a grant from the Corporation specifically for the 'illumination and ornamentation' of the Town Hall. Devices in electricity and gas were lit around the building in a full dress rehearsal. Thousands turned out and even after midnight it was still very busy. *"Shields had surpassed itself"*, reported the Gazette. Among the spectators, no doubt, were the Kirkpatricks, enjoying a rare occasion when the entire family could turn out together.

King Street 1897. Decked out to celebrate Queen Victoria's Diamond Jubilee.
Jack aged 5 was old enough to enjoy the festivities.
Image South Tyneside Images 0000508

It is almost certain Sarah Simpson was unaware that an attendant from Gartnavel Royal Lunatic Asylum in Glasgow had registered the death of her father earlier that day.

Typical Victorian funeral. James Simpson's last journey from Gartnavel Asylum to Craigton Cemetery in June 1897 was made in similar fashion. Traffic and bareheaded spectators alike stopped in respect for the deceased.
Image Courtesy of Sheffield City Libraries

The last entry in James Simpson's case notes reads:

"June 19th, He gradually got worse and died today.
Death on June 19th 1897.
Cause of death: Senile decay and old age. No P.M. (post mortem)"

James, 'Engineer and Millwright' aged 80, was at last released from 20 years of mental torment, as Victoria's Jubilee celebrations proceeded regardless.

The 22nd itself, was a day of fine weather. The bathing fraternity in the Borough celebrated the occasion in their own peculiar way. At 7a.m. they marched down Ocean Road headed by Father Neptune. Many thousands lined the route despite the early hour. They sang the National Anthem prior to their dip in the North Sea and then marched to the park for a commemorative photograph.

Later in the morning, 12,000 children from 38 Sunday Schools in the Borough formed a procession, following the Mayor, Alderman R. Readhead in his carriage. They marched through the town, stopping outside the

Mayor's home in Westoe, where they sang the National Anthem accompanied by the Garibaldi Band and three Salvation Army Bands. They then moved to the fields opposite Ogle Terrace where Jubilee hymns approved by Queen Victoria were sung. The demonstration dispersed at 12.30p.m.

In the town, local publicans closed at 1p.m to allow managers and staff to join their families in the festivities. This was also beneficial for public order, it was thought. On the river, proposals for a water pageant were dropped, but the lifeboat crews launched three boats, rowing them to Tyne Dock, then to the harbour entrance, before returning to their stations. In North Marine Park, three bands, The Borough, the 3rd Durhams, and the West Dock provided a programme of music from forenoon until 11pm. On the terrace of South Park there was continuous music from noon until 11pm, while in the Market Place, bands performed from morning to night in two hour sessions, pausing periodically for the ringing of joyous peals from the bells of St Hilda's Tower.

Festivities for the poor began at 12 noon, when 2,000 of the poorest children in the town assembled in the Market Square. Headed by a band, they marched, many barefooted, through the town to Mitchelson's field where they had tea and an excellent programme of children's sports and amusements. At 4pm, 600 of the aged poor, male and female, were treated to a knife and fork tea at St Thomas's Hall, followed by a programme of entertainment. These events were additional to the fare provided at Harton Workhouse, where the regulations, although relaxed slightly, prevented the inmates, adults and children alike, from leaving the establishment. The inmates enjoyed a dinner of roast beef and plum pudding followed by music and entertainment in the evening.

In spite of the temporary hardship caused by Robert Kirkpatrick's unemployment it is near certain that Sarah ensured her children paraded with the Sunday School Union and not with the procession for the 'poorest'.

As dusk approached, hundreds of children pleaded with their parents to be allowed to stay up to watch the fireworks and the bonfires atop the ballast hills. For many, like 5 years old Jack (John) Kirkpatrick, it would be an unforgettable experience and, as a permanent souvenir, all 12,000 children in the town were given a Diamond Jubilee Medal by courtesy of the borough. The Kirkpatrick children should have received four, one each for Sarah, Martha, Jack and Annie.

Reporting on the events of 22nd June, the Gazette stated proudly: *"South Shields had shown herself worthy of her motto 'ALWAYS READY".*

Barnes Road School on the junction of Barnes Road and South Eldon Street where Jack began his education in September of the Jubilee year.

Image South Tyneside Images 0004862

In September when the new school term started Jack was age to begin his education and he duly took his place in Barnes Road School only a few hundred yards from his home in South Eldon Street. There he embarked on the basics of 'reading, writing, arithmetic and recitation.'

Removal of household furniture. The Kirkpatricks moved frequently. Their final move was from South Frederick Street to 14 Bertram Street.

Image K Y Collection

South Eldon Street. A typical street in the Tyne Dock Ward of South Shields. On 6th July 1892, John Simpson Kirkpatrick was born at Number 10. At least five addresses for the Kirkpatricks have been found. Writers have speculated that they had trouble paying the rent – NOT so. All the addresses are in the same neighbourhood. The reason is more mundane. Children were growing in numbers and in age.

Image South Tyneside Images 0003139

NEW COMPANY, NEW SHIP, NEW CENTURY

The following month his father's luck took a turn for the better. While Robert was frequenting the Shipping Office daily in search of work, the master of a collier steamer, the ETHEL, came looking for a 2nd Mate. The Crew Agreement shows Robert signed on 6/10/97, previous ship SOUTHMOOR, weekly wage £1 -18/-. The Master of the ETHEL, J Cook, made an entry in the ship's log:

> *"Shields 6/10/97. At the time of sailing W Hector 2nd Mate failed to join. Engaged R Kirkpatrick in his place."*

The ETHEL was fairly new, registered in South Shields June 1895 at 1035 gross tons. She was in the coasting trade, loading in Shields, Sunderland and Blyth; and delivering to London, Cherbourg, Hamburg, Amsterdam and

144

Haven, routes and ports very familiar to Robert. However the ETHEL appears to have been an unlucky ship. Her log shows that on 7th November when leaving Blythe harbour on passage for Hamburg, she ran aground and was stuck fast for five hours, being refloated without assistance and with no apparent damage. Thirteen days later on 15th November, when returning from Cherbourg and off the Dudgeon Light, ETHEL suffered a break in her main steam pipe. Obliged to put back to Great Yarmouth in a strong north easterly gale, with a strong sea, the ship 'falling off beam' threw Able Seaman Robertson over the wheel, breaking his leg. The ETHEL was not to Robert's liking and when the half year crew agreement expired at the end of December he did not re-engage.

The newly completed south pier was the site of an unusual confrontation on 31st December '98. The builders of the pier, The Tyne Improvement Commission claimed the right to control access to the pier and to charge admission fees. The Town Council vigorously opposed this and claimed a public right of way on the pier for its citizens. To make their point the Tyne Commissioners erected barricades at the entrance to the pier. On 31st December the Mayor, Alderman Imrie, accompanied by a number of fellow councillors and a team of Council workmen, marched from the Town Hall to the pier and, in front of a bemused Tyne Commission police officer, had the barricades pulled down. The dispute went to Court and judgement went against the Town Council. However South Shields won in the end and the pier today is an excellent amenity for anglers, sight-seers and strollers.

On 3rd Jan. '98 Robert signed on as 2nd Mate on the BERRINGTON, a vessel owned by J. Fenwick & Son, a company with whom he would remain for the rest of his working life. His new job came with an increase of 6 pence a week. When Robert signed on he understated his age by 5 years, a white lie he would perpetuate to the end of his service. The company could easily have checked his age against his Mate's Certificate. If they did, it did not seem to concern them. The crew agreements give the impression that the relationship between Robert and Fenwick & Son was mutually satisfactory.

During the whole of 1898, the BERRINGTON plied the old familiar trade route from Tyne to Thames with an occasional detour to the near continent. Traffic in these two rivers was dense, and inevitably, as on modern city thoroughfares, shunts and bumps occurred. The BERRINGTON was not immune. On 22nd December 1898, the Master, S Merriman made an entry in his log:

*'at 6pm, while said Steamer was at anchor, Waiting Tide to enter
Regent's Canal for the Purpose of Discharging, the SS Tay of
London collided with our Starboard Bow doing considerable damage
to Deck Fretting and Bow plate.'*

The spelling, punctuation and the use of capital letters are those of Mr
Merriman, who was a Shields man living at 410 South Alice Street in the
town.

Robert Kirkpatrick held the rank of Second Mate throughout the year and his
weekly wage of £1 -10/- kept the family in comfortable circumstances.

As the calendar changed from '98 to '99, the end of the century was in sight,
and then end of Victoria's reign, she was now 80 years old, was also
approaching. Sadly for the much loved Queen, her final years were not to be
blessed with peace. War with the Boer Republic in South Africa broke out
once more. It began at 5 o'clock on the 17th October – just at tea-time, the
London Times noted. Before it ended, the Empire would have a new
monarch. The British professional army commanded by General Buller was,
of course, expected to put the recalcitrant Boer farmers promptly in their
place. The Boers mobilised their Commandos quickly and made pre-emptive
strikes, laying siege at Ladysmith, Kimberley and Mafeking, The British Army
marched to the relief of these towns, but in what came to be known as 'Black
Week', the Boers inflicted disastrous defeats on the world's greatest military
Power, at Sturmberg on the 10th December, at Magersfontein on the 11th and
at Colenso on the 15th, where 8,000 Boers in well-chosen positions, inflicted
a humiliating defeat on a British force of 27,000 regular soldiers. The news
was greeted in London with disbelief. "Our Generals," exclaimed Herbert
Asquith, "seem neither able to win victories, nor give convincing reasons for
their defeats." Around the world, Britain's rivals rejoiced at her discomfiture
and in Europe there was much sympathy for the Boers, especially among
the Germans who were only too happy to supply the Boers with Mauser rifles
and Krupp field pieces. The year and the century came to an end with Britain
calling up reservists and assembling the largest army to leave her shores up
to this point in history.

The Shield's Gazette, thanks to international telephone cables and news
agencies, published a daily column with the latest news of the war, though
the paper looks odd to modern eyes, as it contained no photographs. In spite
of the blow to Britannia's pride, the public were enthusiastic for the war.

Kipling wrote popular jingoistic poems, patriotic songs were sung in the music halls, and regiments marching to the stations and the docks could hardly pass through the cheering crowds. Enthusiasm in South Shields matched that of any town in the United Kingdom.

As Britain stumbled towards war with the Boer Republic, the BERRINGTON continued her relentless schedule between Tyne and Thames. From the 5th to the 19th April, Robert Kirkpatrick's career enjoyed a boost when he was temporarily promoted to First Mate. The day after his promotion, he found himself having to sign an entry in the log, recording another collision, this time in the Tyne.

> *'At 9.00am unmoored Ship from Buoys abreast of Bulack spouts for the purpose of entering into Tyne Dock.*
>
> *9.30am SS Walton coming down river against the flood tide. I gave three Blasts on our Whistle to indicate we wanted to come astern. Seeing he was determined to come on we lay stationary in water not be'in able to go ahead, our Bow be'in close to the SS Quickstep, the SS Walton came on striking the SS Berrington in the Stern with great force, forcing us ahead into the Quickstep, doing considerable damage, also damaging our Stern.*
> (signed)   S Merriman, Master
> (signed) Robert Kirkpatrick, Mate'

Such accidents were common and don't seem to have damaged the careers of the Master and the Mate. Later in the year, 27th September, Robert was promoted to full-time First Mate at £2-10/- per week.

Just before the British Force, in South Africa suffered its 'Black Week', the BERRINGTON blotted her copy book once more on the 5th December, when she collided with the Schooner Northern Star, emerging from Mill Dam, at South Shields. There is no mention of damage to the BERRINGTON.

The first year of the new century would prove to be crucial for British arms in South Africa, and eventful for South Shields and the Kirkpatrick family who would celebrate a wedding and lament a death. General Redvers Buller was out of his depth and knew it. He had the good sense to ask the government in London to relieve him of his command. On the 10th January, Victoria's most able general, Field Marshall Lord Roberts, (popularly known as 'Bob') accompanied by Kitchener, landed in South Africa, taking command of an ever growing army, the numbers rising eventually to 180,000 including 25,000 Australian, New Zealand and Canadian volunteers.

The Boer President, Paul Kruger, had hoped for quick victories, accompanied by an uprising of the Boer population in the Cape Provence, to bring Britain to the conference table on his terms. As British numbers in the field grew, his strategic aims were fading but not without a fight. An impetuous young British officer, working as a war correspondent reckoned that one Boer, armed and mounted, in the right country was worth five British regulars. The young correspondent was captured by the Boers, but made a highly publicised escape – his name was Winston Churchill.

One of Roberts' priorities was the relief of the besieged garrisons. Kimberley was relieved first on 15th February. Just before sunset on the 28th February, Major Gough of the 16th Lancers splashed across the Klip River at the head of his squadron to be greeted with indescribable enthusiasm by the emaciated defenders of Ladysmith. At Mafeking, the Boers tore up the railway lines and cut off the town on 13th October '99. Ably commanded by Colonel Robert Baden-Powell, the garrison was still holding out at the beginning of May the following year. Roberts, by now making his main thrust through the Transvaal and the Orange Free State, detached a flying column for Mafeking's Relief on the 4th May. Reuters News Agency had kept world informed almost daily of the events in Mafeking, capturing the imagination of people in every corner of the English speaking world. Well aware of the universal interest, Roberts included in the relieving force of 1149 men, troops from Australia, New Zealand, Canada, Natal , Cape Colony, as well as contingents from English, Scottish, Irish and Welsh regiments.

In Britain, public excitement was building daily in anticipation of the relief of the beleaguered garrison in Mafeking. The Reuter's news bulletins were read avidly; everyone knew the end of the siege was imminent. The Reuter's News Agency received a message from its correspondent in Pretoria at 9.17pm on the 18th May. He reported that the Transvaal Government had announced its abandonment of the siege.

Every town in Britain had been preparing to celebrate. In South Shields, the chief reporter of the Gazette, Robert Fernandes felt the town's people were

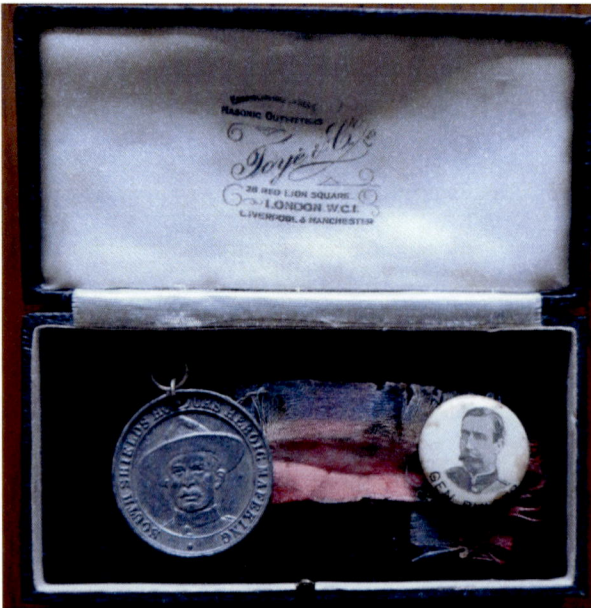

dragging their heels. Writing a column in the Gazette, under the nom-de-plume 'Odd Man Out', he twitted the town with lagging behind. Fernandes also gives us a glimpse of how passionately Britons felt about the war in South Africa when in 1949 he recalled:

Mafeking Medal 1901. The Relief of Mafeking on the 17th May 1901 occasioned almost hysterical celebrations throughout Britain and the Empire. Shields Town Council presented a commemorative medal to every child in the borough, 25,000 were commissioned. Both Jack aged 9 and his sister Annie aged 7 would have received one, but probably appreciated the extra day off school most. The medal bears the image of Baden Powell who organised the defence of Mafeking. Generals Roberts, Buller and White appear on the reverse.
Image KY Collection

"I shall never wipe out the memories of Colenso and Mafeking. Colenso was the third of a sequence of disasters to the British arms in South Africa. Only those who lived in the peaceful years of Queen Victoria's reign could realise the distressing blow that hit our prestige and struck terror to the hearts of the people."

The day following his twitter, Fernandes met the town's Mayor, Alderman Marshall, who gave the go-ahead for a Mafeking Relief Committee. A programme of celebrations was quickly organised including a cycle carnival, a torch light procession, bonfires, firework displays and a musical fête. The Mafeking Committee commissioned 25,000 medals bearing the impress of Baden-Powell, the hero of Mafeking, for presentation to the schoolchildren. So Jack and Annie, not only enjoyed a day off school, filled with fun and jollification, but received a souvenir of the occasion, a medal, complete with red, white and blue ribbon, manufactured by Toye and Company, the leading supplier in the United Kingdom of Orders, Medals, Decorations and Masonic Regalia. Celebrations in Shields went on all day and night.

In London, wild celebrations reached hysterical levels subsiding only after three days and were echoed around the empire. Bonfires were lit on the hills surrounding Wellington in New Zealand, public holidays were declared, salutes were fired in cities as far apart as Montreal, Canada and Melbourne, Australia, and church bells were rung in major cities in every dominion. A new word entered the English language, "*to maffick*".

Robert Kirkpatrick missed the 'mafficking' celebrations in Shields by a day. The BERRINGTON loaded up at Dunston Staithes on the River Tyne, and sailed for Rotterdam on the 17th May, not returning to the Tyne until the 21st, when the celebrations were petering out. At home Jack and Annie proudly showed their Dad the Mafeking medals in their presentation cases from Toye and Company. Jack's next medal would be awarded posthumously.

On the 1st September, the BERRINGTON and Robert Kirkpatrick returned to Dunston, higher up the Tyne from Shields. The following day, his eldest daughter was married in Sunderland in the Parish Church. The entry in the register shows that William Thompson Balneaves, aged 23, bachelor, photographer by profession, married Marguerite Lowe Simpson Kirkpatrick, aged 18, for whom no profession or occupation was recorded. Marguerite, 'Peggy' to her family, had dropped her baptismal name of 'Maggie'. She might have chosen 'Margaret', the English version of 'Maggie', but she has gone further opting for the rather posh sounding French version 'Marguerite'. The marriage entry shows the address for both bride and groom being 7 Ann Street, Sunderland. The witnesses were Alex S. Balneaves, and Joseph Robinson. Will Balneaves was a Scot, born in Aberdeen into a middle class family. His father was a cashier. His best man and witness, elder brother Alex, was a teacher.

Will and Peggy Balneaves. Peggy, organist at St Mary's Church, South Shields, wearing necklace presented by Ladies Guild in 1912 - a contrary image to that painted by Jack in his letters.

Image courtesy of Pat Coomber, Queensland, Australia

South Frederick Street. By October 1900, the Kirkpatricks had moved to 141 South Frederick Street in the same locality. Daughter Martha died there in 22nd October 1900. The photograph is slightly later than 1906.

Image South Tyneside Images 0001848

The following month, Sarah and Robert lost another child. At 141 South Frederick Street, on the 22nd October, Martha Simpson, aged 11 years, daughter of Sarah Simpson (the names are as shown on the Entry of Death certificate), died of 'hip joint disease and pulmonary phithisis'. It appears that Martha had not been of a robust constitution and contracted tuberculosis which would have caused her to suffer over a protracted length of time. Martha's father was in Rotterdam on the day she died, but returned to Dunston on the 24th with the BERRINGTON. He registered Martha's death on the 25th October. With Peggy and Martha gone within a couple of months, the household comprising Robert and Sarah, Sarah junior, Jack and Annie must have seemed unusually spacious and empty.

Meanwhile the Boer War dragged on into 1901, and when the bells tolled for the New Year, everyone in the land knew Queen Victoria was dying. The Royal family gathered from across Europe to say farewell and a proposed visit to Australia by the Duke of York was postponed. Kaiser Wilhelm II, in spite of the hostility current between Germany and Britain, arrived in London and conducted himself with great dignity to the surprise of the British press. On Sunday 20th January, the Queen's physicians, R Douglas Powell M.D. and James Reid M.D. issued bulletins from Osbourne House at 11am 4.30pm and midnight, the third one stating,

> *"The Queen's condition has late this evening become more serious, with increasing weakness and diminished powers of taking nourishment."*

These bulletins were published in the Shields Gazette on Monday 21st January. The issue of January 23rd carried the large headline. *"DEATH OF THE QUEEN".* Victoria had died the previous evening at half past six, *"in the presence of an august group of her children and grandchildren"*! The Gazette reported:

> *"The sad news caused profound regret among all classes of the community in South Shields.' Groups of people discussed everywhere the mournful intelligence, and in every possible way, manifestations were given of the real sorrow that was felt."*

At the Post Office and other public buildings the blinds were drawn and Union Jacks floated at half-mast.

"The solemnity of the occasion was intensified by the pealing of the bells from St Hilda's Church in muffled tones."

The Unionist and Liberal clubs closed their doors early, and at a concert, the audience stood, heads uncovered, as the orchestra played the 'Dead March' from Saul.

The front page of the Gazette for Friday 1st February was filled by announcements from local shops and businesses intimating they would be closed all day on Saturday 2nd February, the day of Queen Victoria's funeral. Captain Taylor, Commanding Officer of the 5th Volunteer Battalion, Durham Light Infantry, promulgated the army's orders for mourning: Officers to wear black crepe, 3½ inches wide on the left arm; the detachment attending the service in St Michael's Church, to be in Dress Review Order, with Helmets and side arms; Officers, N.C.O's and men to wear white gloves.

5th Volunteer Battalion DLI parade for Queen Victoria's funeral

Image South Tyneside Images

On Saturday the 2nd, six of the town's bands assembled in the market place, before the Town Hall steps. Each set off from a different assembly point, the Harmonic from Ogle Terrace, the Garibaldi from Chichester Road, the Town Silver from Ocean Road, the Mission from Bank Top, the Temperance from Princess Street, and the Borough from Trinity Church. Their marches, playing suitable hymnal music were timed to arrive at the market place at a quarter to 12 midday. There they played a selection of hymn tunes, concluding with the Dead March, before returning to their starting point. One wonders what the children of the town made of these ceremonies compared with those of the Diamond Jubilee four years earlier. For Jack and Annie, there were no medals this time, only memories.

For their father there may have been no memories of the occasion. The Shipping News in the Gazette of Monday 4th February shows the BERRINGTON returned from Rotterdam on Saturday 2nd, but did she dock in time to let the crew witness the mourning rituals? Neither the coal trade nor the war in South Africa could pause for the funeral of a monarch – not even the longest reigning Empress of the world's largest ever Empire.

Britain's pride and self-confidence had been badly shaken by the reverses inflicted on her armed services by the Boers. To this was added the burden of gloom caused by the death of the much loved Queen, and on top of this came the apprehension concerning her successor. Her 59 year old son, Edward VII, was the antithesis of his parents, a bon viveur, a libertine, a playboy, spoilt, self-indulgent and with no experience of Government. What kind of king would he be? The nation, in the upper echelons at least, felt fragile and vulnerable.

South Shields put away the mourning clothes, rolled up its sleeves and got back to work. London and the rest of the world still needed fuel and coal shipments from the Tyne were increasing every year. The BERRINGTON was playing her part assiduously, delivering 16 cargoes of coal to Rotterdam, four to London and one to Portsmouth (for the Royal Navy perhaps?). Between the 3rd January and the 8th June, Robert Kirkpatrick made all of these voyages as First Mate, though under three different Masters. In June, Samuel Merriman of 72 Dean Road, South Shields, handed over to Edwin Brooks of North Shields. He in turn was superseded by T. M. Cheyne of 43 Oxford Terrace, Westoe, South Shields – no promotion for Robert Kirkpatrick, not even on a temporary basis.

The BERRINGTON arrived at Dunston in the Tyne on Sunday 31st March in time for Robert Kirkpatrick to be included in the headcount of the 1901 census, scheduled for that night. The family at 141 South Frederick Street were recorded as follows:

Robert Kirkpatrick	Head	56	Chief Mate Seas	Leith, Scotland,
Sarah	Daur	14		South Shields
John	Son	8		South Shields
Annie	Daur	6		South Shields

As in the previous census of 1891, Sarah Simpson (aged 46) is missing. She does not show up anywhere in the U.K census. If she was not at home, when Robert was at sea, who looked after the children? Was she again dodging the census taker for her own mysterious reasons?

The census for the St Paul's Parish in Sunderland shows Marguerite (Peggy) and Will Balneaves at 7 Ann Street, the same address as when they were married in September the previous year. There have been no additions to their family. William was recorded as a photographer's assistant, Marguerite with no occupation.

The South Shield's census also shows another family in very similar circumstances to the Kirkpatricks. The creator of the South Marine Park, John Peebles, also a Scot, was living with his wife Alice, and family in north Marine Park Lodge. He also had three daughters and a son John aged 8 years. Sarah Simpson and Alice Peebles would experience similar heartbreaks in the next 14 years.

Robert Kirkpatrick continued to serve as First Mate on the BERRINGTON for the remainder of the year and into 1902, until the ship was laid up in the Tyne on the 27th March 1902, presumably due to a downturn in trade. Journeys had been split between London and Rotterdam, which curiously was deemed to 'In the Coasting Trade'. Robert was unemployed for almost four months until signing on as First Mate on the BERRINGTON once more on the 12th July, trading this time mostly with London, excepting two trips to Dunkirk. When signing on, Robert gave his previous ship as the BERRINGTON, inferring he had not worked since March. Sarah's resourcefulness to keep the family fed and clothed was tested once again. Sarah junior, was of working age and may have contributed a few shillings to the household budget.

In South Africa, the war had become messy with both sides adopting unorthodox and unscrupulous tactics. The Boers mounted a campaign of guerrilla warfare. The British as a counter measure declared martial law and cleared the Boer families from their farms, incarcerating women and children in prison camps in harsh conditions. President Kruger clung to the hope that the Germans might come to his aid. Towards this end he visited Berlin, but his hopes were dashed when the Kaiser refused to meet him. The Boer leaders arrived in Pretoria on 31st May to meet Lord Milner, the British High Commissioner and Lord Kitchener. There they signed the terms of surrender, accepting British Rule, with a promise of self-government later, and a £3 million grant to assist with reconstruction; the question of votes for natives not to be decided before self-government.

From July to the end of the year the BERRINGTON traded between Tyne and Thames once more. Perhaps economic confidence was recovering after the end of the war. On August 9th, Edward VII was crowned in Westminster Abbey. On a sunny day, crowds lined the streets, cheering a glittering procession of Europe's royalty and Britain's good and great. In South Shields however, the Peebles family were not celebrating. John Peebles was unwell and on the 19th June, he wrote to the council stating he had been advised by his doctor to take three or four weeks leave as a means of restoring his health. The council granted his request, but sadly the recommended cure was ineffective. John Peebles never returned to work and died on the 20th August. He was only 52, leaving a widow to raise three young daughters and a son.

Sometime before November 1902 the Balneaves, Peggy, Will and daughter Martha quit Sunderland and moved to South Shields, taking up residence with the Kirkpatricks at 141 South Frederick Street. The house must have been crowded but was about to become even more so. On 10th November Peggy gave birth to a son, who was christened John Robert, making his uncle Jack and his grandfather proud men. What prompted the Balneaves' move?

The BERRINGTON and Robert Kirkpatrick were back at sea, but the days of non-stop steaming, it seems were over. The log for the BERRINGTON for the first half of 1903, ended abruptly with the following entry on 21st February 1903.

> *"This is to certify that the Berrington arrived in Howden dock at 10am, of the 21st inst., to lay up, was securely made fast and cleared up over the decks, all ship's papers handing over into the marine superintendent's (Captain Geary's) hands, and ship left in charge of the 1st Officer as watchman.*

> Wm.
> Turnbull, Master
> Robert
> Kirkpatrick, Mate"

The BERRINGTON may have been laid up idle, but Robert still had employment. Indeed this period may have been a 'cushy number' for him – no crew, no coal, no high seas and every night at home. What a great opportunity for his 10 year old son to explore every corner of a Tyne Collier and to sit in the 1st Mate's cabin listening to exciting tales of his father's life at sea. One can imagine young Jack in the school playground with his mates, bragging about his father's adventures in distant oceans and in strange lands.

There are clues that Jack was conversant with his father's maritime career. When Sir Irving Benson visited South Shields 'in search of Simpson', he met one of Jack's schoolboy friends, W.J. Bowman, who could tell Benson that Jack's father was a Master Mariner who had been in Australia during the gold rush. This is confirmed by an unexplained gap in Robert Kirkpatrick's maritime service, between 10 June 1852 when he was discharged from the brig SWIFT in Leith, and December 17th 1856 when he signed on the BRITISH LION in Melbourne. Most of the crew of this ship appear to have deserted to go prospecting, a regular hazard for ships arriving in Melbourne. The Master of the BRITISH LION had to find 19 new crew men before he could sail for London with a consignment of gold. Jack also shows knowledge of his father's ships in a letter sent to his mother from Newcastle, New South Wales, dated 1 March 1912. He mentions meeting a Shield's man, Jack Waters who claimed "he was second engineer in the old SOUTHMOOR with my father". "He is a hell of a liar", stated Jack. When Robert Kirkpatrick quit the SOUTHMOOR, Jack was only five years old but was evidently familiar with his Dad's ship.

Robert's sojourn as watchman on the BERRINGTON lasted until June 6th 1903, when Fenwick & Son called him up for active eservice one more, this time as 2nd Mate on the TWIZELL, one of their modern vessels, built in Sunderland by S.P. Austin in 1901. Robert's wage was £2 2/- a week, but as the ship was 'in the Coasting Trade', he (and the rest of the crew) had to find their own provisions. In spite of being 'in the Coasting Trade', the TWIZELL was carrying coals regularly across the North Sea to Hamburg, a round trip of six or seven days. Happily for the Kirkpatrick family, the TWIZELL loaded every time in Tyne Dock, a 15 minute walk between ship and home.

On 19 November 1903, Robert bade farewell to the family and the TWIZELL made passage from the Tyne once more for Hamburg. For sailor's wives, it was an uneasy time of the year, a time when winter gales rattled the windows and left wives staring into the fire at night with thoughts of those in peril on the sea. The night of Friday 20 November was particularly wild in the North Sea and the following day rumours were circulating round the streets of Tyne Dock. One ship was overdue at Rendsberg, the SS ESLINGTON with a number of Shield's men on board, and another, the SS TWIZELL, bound for Hamburg was aground near Cuxhaven. With racing hearts, wives and mothers hurried to the shipping office in search of news.

North Sea Cuxhaven. On the night of 19th November 1903, Robert Kirkpatrick's life was in jeopardy when his ship the TWIZELL grounded and was wrecked off this coast. The entire crew were rescued by the lifeboat from Niewerk.

Image KY Collection

A Lloyd's telegram eventually arrived from Cuxhaven stating:

> "The British Steamer Twizell, Shields for Hamburg with coals, is
> ashore and will probably be a wreck. She lies in an exposed position
> off Rottenplate, near Schaararven Beacon. Blowing hard with a
> heavy sea. Crew saved in their own boats and lifeboat from Niewerk."

Sarah and the wives of the TWIZELL men could go home with relieved
minds. The relatives of the ESLINGTON men received some re-assurance
as a report came in that one of the ship's lifeboats had been washed ashore
empty, the belief being that that crew had been rescued from their boats by
another ship. On Monday 23 November, the Shield's Gazette published the
contents of the Lloyd's telegram and added the information 'that the sea is
completely sweeping over the steamer (*Twizell)* and she is likely to become
a total wreck?'

The crew was transferred from Cuxhaven to Hamburg where Captain Jobling
of the TWIZELL punctiliously completed the ship's log with the following
entry, before lodging the Articles with the British Consul.

> "Date of Occurrence: November 20/03
> Date of Entry: 23/11/03
>
> At 5.45pm weather thick with rain blowing a strong gale from the
> S.W.; while preparing to take a cast of the lead, broken water was
> reported ahead, the helm was put hard astarboard & before the
> vessel answered the helm, she struck the ground bumping very
> heavy the sea breaking all over the ship. Port lifeboat and jolly boat
> got ready to launch and kept the engines working full astern from
> 5.45pm, until 1.00 am on the 21st November. At this time we found
> the ship was making water in the engine room to fast to be kept down
> by the pumps, also the ballast tanks were all full. Finding it was
> impossible to save the ship, the boats were provisioned and all hands
> left with the same at 7.45am on the 21st. After running three miles, we
> were picked up by the Niewark lifeboat and taken to Cuxhaven,
> arriving there at 1.0pm.
>
>   J.R.Jobling, Master
>   J Inkster, Mate"

In Hamburg, His Britannic Majesty's Vice Consul signed the last page of the Twizell's logbook certifying that he sanctioned the discharge of the crew following shipwreck, and the loss of the vessel, and that the seamen had received their balances of wages, signing the release in his presence. It was standard practice in the Merchant Navy that seamen's wages ceased the day the ship was lost. The crew would stay in the Seaman's Mission until repatriated.

Most of the crew reached South Shields on 27 November, where they were met by the Shields Gazette reporter as well as friends and relatives. The account in the Gazette the following day, was somewhat more graphic than Captain Jobling's prosaic entry in the ship's log, and included an anecdote concerning the Captain himself.

> *"The Master, Captain Jobling had rather a narrow escape while going aft to the cabin (the crew had been sheltering in the foc'sle). He was caught by a heavy breaker and washed about the decks but he fortunately escaped practically unhurt."*

No doubt he returned to his cabin to secure the ship's articles and logbook which he later completed at the British Consulate in Hamburg. The crew lost 'the whole of their clothes and effects.

The kinsfolk of the ESLINGTON's crew were not so fortunate. The early hope that their men had been saved by another ship quickly faded as each day passed with no word. Neither crew nor ship were found. With pay stopped on the sinking of the TWIZELL, Robert Kirkpatrick had only a short respite from work.

Elsewhere in the world, new enterprises which would reshape the 20th century were getting off the ground, literally in one case. On 17 December, two brothers named Wright, managed to get a heavier-than-air machine off the beach at Kitty Hawk, North Carolina, and stay aloft in controlled flight for nearly a minute. The length of the flight was 850 feet. Elsewhere in the USA, on June 16th, Henry Ford set up a motor company, producing cars by a novel method on an assembly line.

At the beginning of January, Robert Kirkpatrick signed a new six month agreement on another Fenwick ship, the SUNNINGDALE. Robert signed on 6 January 1904, as Second Mate, replacing John C. Peacock who signed off that date after only two days on the ship. It appears Fenwick and Son were shuffling crew around to accommodate the survivors from the wrecked TWIZELL. The SUNNINGDALE would be Robert's last ship and 1904 would see his career reputedly ended by a crippling accident. Once again Robert erred in stating his age as 59, when he was in fact 66. The SUNNINGDALE, commanded by Captain Robert Scarfe, 279 Stanhope Road, Tyne Dock, South Shields was 'in the Coasting Trade, between the River Elbe and Brest inclusive.' In fact SUNNINGDALE, made only one trip to Hamburg on the Elbe in May. The rest of the six month period, she traded between the Tyne and London.

Only one accident is reported in the ship's log for the first half of the year. On 20 February 1904, C. Heslop, able seaman, working on the aft winch, while heaving in slack rope, 'somehow slipped and his arm got between the crank and the whipping shaft, breaking his arm and other serious injury'. He was immediately conveyed to the Ingham Infirmary, South Shields, where he was detained. His effects and balance of wages were forwarded to his home address in South Shields. The log entry was signed by the Master and First Mate. Robert Kirkpatrick, Second Mate, apparently was not involved.

The SUNNINGDALE continued trading to London in the second half of the year with Robert still as Second Mate, with the exception of one visit to Hamburg in August. There at the request of the British Consul, the Master took on board Cornelius Gellhoed. This Scandinavian seaman was landed at South Shields shipping office on 27 August together with a Consular report.

ROBERT KIRKPATRICK BEACHED

On 31 December, when the crew agreement expired, the SUNNINGDALE was docked in the Thames at Erith, and Robert signed a new agreement on the 1st January 1905. He suffered **NO** crippling accident in 1904! Another Kirkpatrick story turns out to be a myth.

So how did the story of the crippling accident in 1904 originate? It appears in Sir Irving Benson's "The Man with the Donkey". Benson writes, "Then a serious accident in 1904 left him permanently incapacitated until his death in 1909. There was no compensation in those days and it was difficult to maintain the family." This was part of the history given to Benson by Annie (Pearson), Jack's younger sister. Was Annie recounting a family story, dramatized and exaggerated over the years, a not uncommon occurrence in family histories or was it Benson's interpretation of the story?

Crew Agreement of the SUNNINGDALE 1905. This shows Robert Kirkpatrick signed on "1.1.05" (column 6) at Erith, London, as Mate. He left the ship "21.1" at "T Dock" and he signed himself for his pay £1.10.0. This refutes clearly another myth, that Robert's career was ended by a crippling accident in 1904. This falsehood seems to originate from Sir Irving Benson's meeting with Annie Kirkpatrick in South Shields in 1956. The tale has been further dramatized and embroidered by later writers, notably Tom Curran in "Across the Bar". Robert quit because of age and degenerating health. The SUNNINGDALE's Log Book confirms there were NO accidents.

Image courtesy of the National Maritime Museum, Greenwich

Tom Curran in his 1994 biography of Simpson "Across the Bar" not only plagiarises the myth, but embellishes it even further, inventing without foundation a conversation between young Jack and a friend Geordie.

> "*How bad is he"* asks Geordie.
> "*He's bad"* then after a pause, *"they brought him back off his boat. He's in the hospital. But me Ma won't say what's wrang with him."*

Curran has now added to the myth, having Robert Kirkpatrick brought back off his boat and putting him in hospital. This over dramatization, makes good reading, but is entirely reprehensible on the part of a biographer-cum-historian.

Robert Kirkpatrick actually signed on the SUNNINGDALE at Erith on 1 January 1905 once more as Second Mate at £2.2/- per week. He made five more journeys between London and the Tyne before taking his discharge at Tyne Dock on 21st January 1905. He was well enough to sign for the balance of his pay £1 10/-, and his character was recorded as 'V.G.' for Ability and 'V.G.' for Conduct. He signed his name in full, and his writing is clear and legible, if a mite spidery.

There was NO accident and therefore no question of compensation, as mentioned by Benson, perhaps to evoke the reader's sympathy.

When Robert signed on for the last time on 1 January, he gave his age as 60. He was in fact 67 on his previous birthday, 26 November 1904, and had been at sea for 54 years. He had been falsifying his age since he joined Fenwick and Son in January 1898, perhaps in an effort to prolong his working life. Robert unwittingly was paying the penalty for starting a second family with a woman who was seventeen years his junior. At a time in life when the families of most men have flown the nest, or are at least contributing to the household income, Robert was compelled to work flat out to maintain a young family. It very nearly cost him his life when the TWIZELL foundered off the German coast.

Robert would live for another four years and nine months after retiring. His death certificate in 1909 gives the cause of death as 'Dropsy and Heart Disease', nothing that suggests a serious accident. It seems more likely that the onset of heart disease forced his retirement. The British army in the 19th century used a stock phrase when discharging soldiers, namely 'Length of

Service and Worn Out', equally apt for an old sea salt like Robert perhaps. At sea since the age 13, he had survived tempests in southern seas, storms, fog, collisions, shipwreck, cold and wet and a lifetime of sleep deprivation. It would be nice to think that the deterioration of his health over his last four years was gradual and that he was well enough to enjoy his children and grandchildren for much of that time.

Benson was right on one point – it would be 'difficult to maintain the family.' For most families their lives changed gradually with the passing of the years and their expectations for better or worse changed accordingly. Occasionally a sudden occurrence can throw expectations into turmoil. The abrupt grounding of Robert Kirkpatrick's career was such an event. Robert himself knew he would not work again and wondered how much time he had left; Sarah knew she was likely to become a widow and to live as such for a good number of years; Peggy and young Sarah were adult, married and had their own lives to lead; Jack was deeply affected. At the age of 12, he took on the role of the breadwinner. For the rest of his short life, every pound he could spare from his earnings went to support his mother and younger sister Annie, aged 10.

Jack Kirkpatrick as a lad – exact date unknown, perhaps c 1903/4.
Image courtesy of the Australian War Memorial

Annie Kirkpatrick as a girl – exact date unknown, perhaps c 1907/8.
Image courtesy of the Australian War Memorial

Jack left Mortimer Road School in the summer of 1905, a fact established in *"Dust, donkeys and Delusions"* by Graham Wilson, who consulted the 'Tyne and Wear County Archives' (TW116-1/8). However Tom Curran who had contact with the family descendants states in his book *"Across the Bar"*: *"In 1904 Jack began work for Fred Patterson, the local milk merchant in South Frederick Street"*. This was stated in the context of Jack's father supposedly suffering a crippling accident in 1904. This conflicts with the Tyne and Wear County Archives which are factual.

The likely scenario is that Jack started work with Fred Patterson on a part-time basis doing early morning rounds, while still attending Mortimer Road School. He was thus in a good position to move up to full-time work with Patterson when he left school in July 1905.

According to family legend, Sarah took in washing while Jack pursued his career as a dairyman. At that time the houses in Shields did not have fridges and dairymen did not deliver milk in bottles. Housewives bought only as much milk as they needed daily. The supply chain from farm to consumer had to be fast and regular. Farmers delivered milk in 17 gallon churns for transport by rail. Milk trains travelled to cities and towns like South Shields during the night. Dairymen like Fred Patterson collected their churns from the station by horse and cart, leaving the previous day's churns to be returned by train to the farms. For delivery in the vicinity of the dairy, two wheeled hand carts were used. Jack's first training was pulling one of these bogies under the supervision of a regular man round the back lanes. A bogie comprised two small cartwheels, a frame to take a 17 gallon churn, and a small 5 gallon churn plus ladles for 1 pint and a 'half' pint.

Jack had to start at 5 am summer and winter, come rain, hail, snow and sunshine. After a probationary period, probably while still at school, Jack got his own bogie and his own round. He announced his presence in the street each morning with a hand bell, and ladled out the milk into customers' jugs. Jack had to have his wits about him. Business was on a cash basis, no tick (credit) and at the age of 13 or 14 he not only handled the cash, but had to deal with some hard cases. Any shortages had to be made up from his wages, a common practice in many occupations.

The time spent by the Balneaves at 141 South Frederick Street may have been short. By May 1905, they were living at 30 Atkinson Road in the Benwell district of Newcastle, where on the 8th May they had another son,

165

George Alexander Leonard, the choice of names this time favouring the father's family. The registrar made an understandable error in recording the baby's mother as 'Margaret'. Peggy was not having that. 'Margaret' was deleted and 'Marguerite' inserted above. William Balneaves was still a Photographer's Assistant and may have moved for a change of employer. Benwell is to the west of Newcastle and not as convenient as Sunderland was for a family visit. Grandmother Sarah would have to travel by train or tram from South Shields to Newcastle to see her newest grandson.

Early in 1905, the Mayor of South Shield, Alderman Lawson lifted the first cobbles in Stanhope Road to commence construction of a new electric tramway system. Fred Patterson's milk men were hampered in making their deliveries by road works for the next two years. On September 27th, Alderman Lawson inaugurated another reconstruction programme, this time laying the foundation stone for a new Town Hall.

In the Far East, a new Imperial Power was flexing its martial muscle. Japan, closed to Western trade and influences until 1853, was fast emerging as an imperial super power, and was expanding into Korea and Manchuria at the expense of Tsarist Russia. In January a 20,000 Russian force surrendered at Port Arthur. At Mukden in Manchuria, a Russia Army of 200,000 was annihilated during May. On the 28th of the month, the Russian Baltic Fleet, after sailing halfway round the world, was destroyed in the Strait of Tsushima, 35 out of 38 warships being sunk or disabled by the Japanese Imperial Fleet commanded by Admiral Togo. At home, the Tzar was faced with strikes, rebellion in the streets, mutiny and murder in his Army and Navy. The Romanoff dynasty was stumbling towards its end.

On the 30th March 1906, Jack had completed his early morning delivery before the Opening Ceremony for the new Electric Tram Service took place. Three miles of track from Fowler Street to Stanhope Road via Westoe had been laid and the inaugural run was made by a procession of three cars, the leading car being driven by Alderman W.C. Wylie. The horse drawn tram service, operating since 1887, terminated on 1st February. Disruption to traffic continued but progress was rapid. By March 1907, the layout of routes was complete and 35 cars were in service.

SOUVENIR

Opening of South Shields Electric Tramways,
March 30th, 1906.

Advent of Electric Trams 1906. The horse trams were replaced in 1906 by electric trams. This one is in Frederick Street. What did Jack think? Did he regret the passing of the horses? The upheaval in the street must have disrupted his milk round. *Postcard KY Collection.*

Jack proved to be an efficient delivery man and was promoted from bogie to float. Around the time the electric tram route was complete, he was given command of his own float, a two wheeled horse drawn vehicle, with his own delivery run. It says much for Jack's character that his employer was willing to trust a 14 year old to take a valuable pony and cart onto the streets every morning to run a mini business on his own. Not many 14 year olds would merit such trust.

Milk cart c 1905. Six months after his father retired, Jack left school and started work as a milk boy, aged 13. He may even have started a delivery before leaving school. Many boys made delivery rounds, delivering rolls, bread and newspapers before starting their school day. Jack's round initially with a hand cart, had regular stopping points beneath a lamp post, essential at 6am on dark winter mornings.
Image South Tyneside Images 0000721

Jack's four legged assistant was a dapple grey pony called Andrew, and a very experienced assistant he was. He knew every inch of the route, every lane, and every stopping point (often under a gas lamp to make work easier on dark mornings). He knew exactly when to move from one stopping point to the next and would do so without word of command. The delivery run would finish late morning, but Jack's work was not complete until he had fed and groomed Andrew, cleaned tack, mucked out the stable and scoured the milk churns ready for exchange at the station next morning. Driving through streets, weaving in and out among trams and other vehicles, Jack had a different view of the world. Anyone who rides a horse or drives a carriage is literally looking down on the world around them. Jack must have enjoyed this feeling, perhaps a little bit like his Dad on the bridge of his ship. He was in control.

Jack was proud of his little command, and he was working independent of close supervision. He loved his job and his best friend Andrew. In spite of the long hours he got great satisfaction from his work. It was vastly preferable to driving a pit pony several hundred feet below ground. However living alongside a great seaport, and imbued with his father's stories of the sea, ships and foreign lands, he could not avoid the lure of a life at sea. But that could wait until he was old enough. These teenage years were probably the happiest in his working life.

On Friday November 17th 1933, the Shield's Gazette published a letter from Mr John Shaw of Mowbray Road, who remembered John Kirkpatrick as a boy. The following is a transcription of Mr Shaw's letter:

> "He worked for the late Mr Fred Patterson, South Frederick Street, a milkman. I can vividly recall, as though it were yesterday, when boy Kirkpatrick used to come to the shop of the late Mr Andrew Anderson, shipping butcher, to get milk orders for ships.
>
> He asked me on one occasion to be allowed to go with me to the boat, and I said 'Yes'. I remember that it was blowing pretty hard on the river, and poor Kirkpatrick fell overboard while we were close to a ship called the 'Bride', belonging to Wilson, of Hull, and laden with grass.
>
> I tried to pull him out of danger, but he slipped back into the water. When ultimately I got him back into the boat, the first words he used

were "Look at my tabs"! He was holding a penny packet of woodbines. They were soaked with the river water. I said "Never mind your tabs, man; it's your life you've got to think about."

If I remember right, he lived at that time with his mother and two sisters in Bertram Street. I have often thought since that the life of John Kirkpatrick was spared then that he might save the lives of others.

He used to leave his milk can standing near the first stairs at Tyne Dock while he went with me, then a butcher lad, to the ships. I shall always remember him with kindly feelings."

The letter was prompted by the unveiling of a statuette in South Shields Central Library of John Simpson Kirkpatrick, as part of the Remembrance Day ceremonies. The statuette was presented to the Library and Museum by the Freemasons.

The anecdote, interesting in itself, reveals a significant trait of Jack's character. He was apparently fearless. Another indication of this trait occurs in a story related by Jack's sister Annie to Sir Irving Benson, when he visited South Shields in 'search of Simpson'. Benson reports being taken by Annie to the 'Gutt' or ramp where horse drawn carts could back down to the water for loading. Annie told him:

"Two children fell into the water there one Saturday and Jack promptly jumped in and   rescued them."

There is no indication of Jack's age in the story, but if accurate, it illustrates once again Jack's lack of fear. Fearlessness is not the same as bravery. Many acts of bravery are performed in spite of fear.

On 20th September 1906, crowds gathered on both banks of the river to witness one of the Tyne's historic events. The yard of Swan Hunter and Wigham Richardson at Wallsend launched a new Cunard liner, the MAURETANIA. The epitome of luxury and weighing almost 32,000 gross tons, she had quadruple screws driven by steam turbines, giving her a service speed of 25 knots. She would go on to hold the Blue Riband for the fastest Atlantic crossing for 20 years. Jack like every other Tynesider would have gone to see the MAURETANIA and hopefully his father was well enough to join him. A few months after Robert Kirkpatrick was born, a Leith built paddle steamer, the SIRIUS made the first ever east to west crossing of the Atlantic powered solely by steam. He must have marvelled at the incredible advance in ship design and technology during his lifetime.

Mauretania Leaving the Tyne 1907. The whole of Tyneside turned out to watch the Mauretania, a Cunarder and the largest, fastest liner of the day, leaving the River Tyne. What thoughts must have passed through the mind of the frail Robert Kirkpatrick watching with his son Jack?

Image KY Collection

3rd Durham Garrison Artillery (Volunteers) pre 1908. Jack, by now promoted to driving a milk float for Pattinson's Dairies may also have joined the Volunteers.

Image South Tyneside images 0005332

170

When Jack was about 16, he spotted a further opportunity to earn himself some extra money and to indulge his passion for equine quadrupeds at the same time. On the 1st April 1908, the Territorial and Reserve Forces Act of 1907 came into effect abolishing the centuries old Militia and the 19th century Volunteers. These units were incorporated into the structure of the British Army as the Territorial Force. In South Shields, the 3rd Durham Royal Garrison Artillery (Volunteers) re-enrolled as Royal Field Artillery, being designated as the 4th Durham (Howitzer) Battery of the 4th Northumbrian Brigade RFA, part of the Northumbrian Division (Territorial Forces). No. 4 Battery was based with its headquarters in South Shields. The unit swapped its Quick Firing (QF) 4.7 inch guns for 4.5 inch howitzers.

Jack Kirkpatrick did enlist in the territorials but the date of his enlistment is a moot point. Recruits to the territorials had to be 5 foot 3 inches tall or over and aged 17 years. In theory, Jack could not enlist until his 17th birthday on 6th July 1909. However a photograph of Jack at annual T.A. camp in June 1909 exists and the dates are confirmed by correspondence between Jack and his family.

Also, when Jack enlisted in the Australian Imperial Force in 1914, he stated under 'previous service' that he had served 12 months with the 4th Durhams. If correct, this means he must have enlisted in the summer of 1908 when he was only 16 years of age. He must have lied about his age on enlistment, as many young men would do later in the 1914-18 conflict. Another possibility is that he was already a member of the 3rd Artillery Volunteers when they were embodied in the Territorial Force, 1st April 1908 and redesignated as the 4th Durhams.

The photograph of Jack, alongside the wheel of a gun limber and a gun crew at annual camp in June 1909 shows he had no problem meeting the height requirement.

4th Northumberland (County of Durham) Howitzer Brigade 1908. In April 1908, Britain established the Territorial Army (TA) embodying volunteers and militia into the British Army. Jack's attestation form for the Australian Army shows he served 12 months with the TA in South Shields before joining the Merchant Navy. Photograph of Jack looking over gun wheel was taken at annual summer camp in 1909.

Image courtesy of the Australian War Memorial PO1446.002

On 7th May 1908, the Liberal Chancellor, Herbert Asquith announced the introduction of pensions in the UK; 5/- per week for men over 70 years of age, and 7/6 for married couples, if both over 70, something of a relief for Robert and Sarah.

The previous year, Annie had finished her schooling and became a wage earner. Jack and his pony Andrew continued their milk round for the rest of the year manoeuvring through the road works as streets were widened, cobbles lifted and tram rails laid.

On 1st January 1909, Robert Kirkpatrick, aged 71, should have queued up at the Post Office – if he was fit enough – to collect his first weekly pension of 5 shillings. It was no longer in his interest to understate his age as he had done in earlier crew agreements. Robert's health was failing and he would not celebrate his 72nd birthday.

On Sunday 20th June 1909, the 4th and 5th Durham (RFA) Howitzer Batteries, the first from South Shields, the latter from neighbouring Hebburn, together with the 4th Brigade Headquarters and the Brigade Ammunition Column embarked by train for their annual camp at Knott End Camp, Fleetwood, Lancashire. That evening Jack Kirkpatrick sent a humorous postcard (Benson Papers, AWM, Canberra) to the family. It was addressed to 'Mrs Kirkpatrick, 14 Bertram Street, South Shields, Durham. Oddly perhaps, he did not address it to Mr and Mrs Kirkpatrick. How ill was his father?

> *"Dear Mother, We arrived at Fleetwood at 6.30. We have just been having tea, two jam wedges and 1 pint of dirty water. I am now going down into the town, so time is precious as it is now 8 o'clock and we have to be back by 10. I remain yours truly, Jack."*

Inland postal services in Edwardian times were vastly more efficient than in the 21st century. Jack's postcard, sent after 8 o'clock on a Sunday evening, crossed from the west coast to the east overnight, was delivered next day and his sister Annie replied on the 21st. Annie's card was addressed to 'Gunner Kirkpatrick', 4th Howz. Batt., Knott End Camp, Fleetwood.

> *"Dear Jack, Mother received your P.C. this morning. There are 8 pigeons in your duckett now, of course, including the young ones. I hope you enjoy yourself on Wednesday. Sarah and I are going to the Knutson's house for the afternoon instead of going to the picnic."*

It sounds as though Jack had a small dovecote in the back yard for his pigeons. Note there is no mention of rabbits. Annie says she and her sister Sarah are going to the Knutsons, a Swedish Family, living at 80 Dean Road. The family had a daughter Jenny, the same age as Annie.

On July 25th, Frenchman Louis Bleriot became aviation's latest hero when he crossed the English Channel from Sangatte, near Calais in France, and landed in Dover, taking 43 minutes for the 31 mile flight. In doing so he won a £1,000 prize offered by the Daily Mail.
On the 15th September 1909, Sarah junior aged 22, married Samuel Young Christie, aged 21, a Ships Plater living at 57 Pearson Street. Sam was born in Hebburn, of Scottish parents. The wedding was solemnized at the Register Office, perhaps being a quiet affair in view of Sarah's father's poor health. The witnesses were J Campbell and E Kayes, not recognisable family names. No occupation, rank or profession was recorded for Sarah.

Just 25 days after her marriage, Sarah Christie returned to the Register Office. Robert Kirkpatrick, Master Mariner (Merchant Service) ended his earthly voyage, on the 10th October 1909. His daughter, Sarah Christie, present at the death, at 14 Bertram Street, was the person who informed the Registrar. The cause of death was 'Heart Disease and Dropsy'. The death certificate gives Robert's age as 65, however his date of birth was 26th November 1837 making him a month short of his 72nd birthday, when he died. He was buried in Harton Cemetery, South Shields, but a stone was not erected until he was joined by his partner Sarah in 1933.   He left Sarah Simpson with a son and three daughters, two of them married. In his final hours, did Robert spare a thought for Mary McLean and his other three sons?

Primary Reference Sources.

GRO Births and Deaths, South Shields
Maritime History Archives, Newfoundland – Sundry Crew Agreements
UK Census 1901 South Shields, Sunderland and Newcastle
Scotland's People Deaths
School Records, TW116 – 1/8 Tyne and Wear Archives

Secondary Sources

South Shields Gazette, June 1897,
South Shields Gazette 1887, 1901, 1903, 1933
'Dust, Donkeys and Delusions', *Graham Wilson 2012*
South Shields Centenary1850 – 1950. *Published by South Shields Gazette*
South Shields Gazette Centenary 1849 – 1949. *Published by South Shields Gazette*
South Shields Gazette Diamond Jubilee Souvenir 1849 – 1909. Published by South Shields Gazette
The History of South Shields, *Geo. B Hodgson, published Reid and Co. Newcastle*
South Shields 100 years of Public Transport, *Tyne and Wear Public Transport Exec.*

Chapter 9

JACK LEAVES HOME: 1909 – 1915

Robert Kirkpatrick was interred at Harton Cemetery on Tuesday 12th October 1909. The burial record held in South Shields Central Library reads;

> *"No 844. Robert Kirkpatrick, Mariner, died at 14 Bertram Street, South Shields, aged 65, buried 12th October 1909."*

His father's death gave Jack a jolt. Two days after the funeral, he quit his job as a milkman, abandoned home and embarked on a career at sea, signing on as 'Mess Room Steward' on a local tramp steamer, the HEIGHINGTON for a monthly wage of £2. 10/-. From this he allotted £1. 5/- presumably to his mother. When signing, he falsified his age claiming to be 19 instead of 17. Jack's departure was sudden. He was off within hours of learning of the post on the HEIGHINGTON as he reveals in a later letter. Jack's motivation for going to sea so abruptly is not explained. Mess Room Steward was the lowest paid berth on the ship, but perhaps better paid than a milkman. Perhaps he felt cramped with his brother-in-law in the house. The crew agreement for the HEIGHINGTON clearly schedules her voyage to be from the 'Tyne to Genoa'. Jack's first letter home however shows he expected to go via Madeira to Valparaiso in South America, and thence to Australia. Did he get it wrong in his haste to leave?

After 12 days at sea on the HEIGHINGTON, Jack wrote home to his mother from Madeira. His career as a merchant seaman did not have an auspicious start. Following a rough passage through the notoriously stormy Bay of Biscay, he was a homesick and seasick boy.

His first letter home is reproduced in full so that the readers may appreciate for themselves, Jack's style of writing. Jack's words and spelling have not been corrected. Moreover he had no respect for punctuation, so a few commas have been inserted to ease readability. Subsequent letters have been abridged to save time and space, leaving out the inconsequential pleasantries and cliches, but all quotations are identified in italics.

> *"This is written from S.S. Heighington – my dear brother sailed in this ship 14th October 1909. He was then only 17 years and 3 months. (Note added by sister Annie)*

Heighington, Madeira, 26th October 1909

Dear Mother,

Just a few lines to let you know that we arrived in Madera this morning after a twelve days passage which I can tell you that we have had a rare old putting up right from the time we left the Tyne, until we got through the Bay of Biscay. We were very nearly four days in the Bay instead of about 38 hours and not only that but the forecastle has been flooded all the time everything floating about and in the bunkers you are very nearly up to the knees in water. She is a proper wreck and nearly everybody is about full up with her already. We are just calling in at Madera for bunkers and we will leave tonight again for Valparaiso after that we expect to go to Sydney and if she does, everybody will be clearing out for she is a rotten packet altogether and the grub is not up to much either so that we are not getting much encouragement to stop in her. Now Mother I think I have given you all the news at present, so give my love to Annie and with best love to yourself.

I remain

Your ever loving and affectionate son

Jack

PS Tell Peggie I have not had time to write her from here and give my love to the kids. Now Mother, do not forget to write to Valparaiso c/o British Consul, so with love from Jack.

Clearly Jack still expected the HEIGHINGTON to continue to Australia via Valparaiso on Chile's Pacific coast. The P.S. shows he was still on very good terms with his elder sister Peggie Balneaves and her children when he left home. This friendliness would turn very sour over the years of his exile.

Jack's letters are archived at the Australian War Memorial, Canberra, having been preserved by the family, and passed to the Australian War Memorial by Jack's sister Annie, via the hands of Sir Irving Benson Australian biographers have used them to account for Jack's time in Australia. In this account the letters are used to explore the relationships in the family amongst whom Jack spent his formative years.

Jack's second letter, dated 26th October 1909, did not come from Valparaiso, Chile, as expected, but from Genoa in Italy. His morale was transformed and he was back to his usual cheery self. He has time on his hands and writes a four page letter, one of his longest. He says to his mother:

> "Now I do hope you are keeping your pecker up and not worrying yourself about me for you have no call at all, here I am having grand weather and little work and plenty of good grub and eating any Gods amount of it".

The letter goes on at length about how well he is eating, how easy the work is, and he thinks "it is money for nowt".

Jack with considerable brashness for a 17 year old, is forward in dishing out advice to his mother and his eldest sister Peggie. He counsels:

> "I am glad you and Peggie are getting on all right and hope it will last and if Peggie gives you any lip, give her a thick ear to be going on with till I get home, and mother don't let your temper get the better of you or I will tell Peggie to give you the same".

This confirms that Sarah Simpson had a fiery temper, a trait which seems to have run through the female side of the family, and may well explain why Sarah and her mother had an irreconcilable quarrel in 1872, causing Sarah to leave home forever and to declare her mother 'Dead' when she registered at Edinburgh Royal Maternity Hospital.

Jack goes on to mention all the family. He apologises to his youngest sister Annie for not saying farewell (she must have been out at work) saying:

> "I am sorry I did not bid her goodbye, but that was no fault of mine as I did not expect to go away so soon."

He thanks Will Balneaves, Peggie's husband, a photographer by profession for 'taking them photos'. Jack asks his mother to tell Sarah (his other married sister) "I hope Sam is working". Sam was a plater in a shipyard. The shipbuilding industry was experiencing a period of industrial unrest at national level, as workers fought for shorter hours and better conditions – strikes by workers were being countered with lock-outs by employers. Jack also asks his mother to give a message to Peggie's two young sons, his only nephews:

> "Tell Bob and George that I will not forget that parrot and monkey".

A promise he was never able to fulfil. He was also sorry to hear that Martha, Peggie's little daughter was poorly.

Finally he chides his mother gently:

> "Now mother, you forgot to put the cards and dominoes in my bag, but that is not surprising   seeing the state you were in. But now owld lass, you will not have to worry any more for I am as happy as a linty and I don't see why you should not be the same now".

The 'state' Sarah was in at her son's hasty departure would not have been eased by Jack's earlier depressing letter from Madeira, but this second letter must have been vastly reassuring. The use of the expression 'owld lass' by Jack, reveals a closeness between mother and son. Not many 17 year old lads would get away with addressing their mother in such an uncomplimentary but affectionate term.

In this one letter, Jack mentioned every one of his close family. He would never be so solicitous again. As time passed, his concern would only be for his mother and younger sister Annie.

The HEIGHINGTON loitered in the western Mediterranean for just over a month, from 27th October until 30th November, giving ample time for an exchange of mail between South Shields and the ship. As well as letters from his mother, Jack received letters from sisters Peggie and Sarah, a postcard from Annie and a letter from someone called 'Bob', not his young nephew this time, but someone who was advising Sarah about an insurance claim, perhaps a friend of her late husband or perhaps an almoner from the Tyne Dock Masonic Lodge. Jack's replies to his Mum give further glimpses of her state of mind:

> "Thanks for the photos, but mother you might have tried to look a bit pleasanter. You look as if you had lost a tanner (a six penny coin) and found a threepenny dodger",

and more seriously:

> "Peggie tells me she had you out for an afternoon at Sunderland. 'Well done………..' Peggie tells me she has never seen you in a bad temper since I went away. Now that's what I call a good change."

Jack commiserates with his younger sister Annie on losing her job as a 'Lady Clerk' and assures her that something better will turn up soon.

After visiting ports on the north African coast, Tunis, Bona, Phillipsville, Jijelli, and Algiers, the HEIGHINGTON set off for the U.K. carrying a cargo of barley and locust beans (a substitute for chocolate). The ship arrived in Leith, Scotland, via London, where Jack had time to write home telling his mother:

> "I will be home for my Duck at Xmas. I say do you remember when I pinched that duck, so mind you watch it well this time".

A tendency to petty larceny perhaps when hungry? He also told her how frosty and bitterly cold Leith was, but makes no comment that it was once his parent's home. Perhaps he did not know!

THE BUILDING NEWS. DEC. 15, 1882.

LEITH SAILORS' HOME
Perspective View

Charles S.S. Johnston, Architect

Leith Sailor's Home. Two months after leaving home, Jack's first voyage ended in Leith, the home of his parents before their move to South Shields, not in Australia as he hoped.

Image KY Collection

The HEIGHINGTON paid off on the 20th December. Jack collected the balance of his pay £2.19/6 and went home to the warmth of 14 Bertram Street, South Shields. Christmas 1909 would be the last he would celebrate with his mother, Annie and the rest of his close-knit family, though other Christmases would be notable for different reasons.

After six weeks, Jack's pay of £2.19/6 from his first voyage was running out. At the Shipping Office at Mill Dam, he found the Glasgow registered ship, the

YEDDO signing on crew for a trip to the West Coast of America, duration 'not exceeding 3 years'. For this voyage Jack signed on as a fireman at the wage of £4 per month, out of which he made an allotment of £2 to his mother. Of the 12 Firemen who signed on, 11 came from South Shields. Jack gave his age as 19, although still only 17. Only two of the crew were younger than him, two lads from the Training Ship Wellesley stationed at North Shields, Fred Thompson, Mess Room Steward and Chris Sebody, Assistant Cook, both aged 16. The YEDDO sailed from his beloved Shields on the 9th February 1910. The start of a voyage of course, is a time of optimism and every seaman fully expects to return home.

For three and a half months, Sarah watched for the postman, her anxiety increasing as every day passed, waiting for a letter from her beloved son. Eventually it arrived, written on the 16th April 1910 in Valparaiso, Chile, just over two months after Jack's farewell. She scanned it quickly:

> "received your letters all right……… good passage from Madeira to Valparaiso …………………   it is a long time to be in the stokehole without a spell (break) for we were fifty days from the Tyne to Valparaiso ……. we were all rare and thin when we got in ……… getting fed on all sorts of rubbish ………………… had no potatoes shortly after leaving Madeira ………… it was nothing but preserved spuds and peas and beans ………………….. been making up for it here……………. getting well fed and I am getting as fat as can be."

The YEDDO had been in port for 12 days before Jack wrote:

> "Now Mother, you will have had two half pays by the time you get this letter. I can't tell you where we are going to. If they get no orders by the time we are finished unloading, we will be going to Newcastle, New South Wales ………… If things are alright out there I am going to have a try at the pits. Give my love to Annie and with love to yourself".

Sarah could sleep with an easier mind for a while.

Jack has already signalled his intention to quit the YEDDO and seek work in Australia. The YEDDO sailed for Newcastle on the 22nd April 1910, and arrived there on the 30th May 1910, around the same time as Jack's letter from Chile reached South Shields. Stories of high wages in Australia and New Zealand attracted many men from the old country.

Valparaiso, on the Pacific coast of Chile. Jack arrived here from Madeira on the YEDDO on 16th April 1910. He wrote home confirming he was en route to Australia.

Image KY Collection

Newcastle Harbour N.S.W. After a 38 day passage from Chile, the YEDDO reached Newcastle, where Jack jumped ship 15th June 1910.

Image KY Collection

Sarah's next letter from Jack was written in Coledale, New South Wales on Sunday 31st July 1910. Earlier that month, Jack reached 18 years of age but he made no mention of birthday celebrations. This letter gives an account of Jack's adventures in Australia from the time he deserted the YEDDO, after arrival in Newcastle, NSW until his arrival in Coledale. This letter is reproduced in full. Jack's exploits may strike a chord with the Australians, but it does contain anomalies in need of explanation.

"31st July 1910

Dear Mother

I am writing to you a few lines and not before time you will be thinking, but never mind, better late than never. Now I told you that I was clearing out of the Yeddo in my letter which I wrote from Newcastle on the sixth of May. Well I stopped by her a fortnight in Newcastle until 13th. I did not want to leave her before the 12th of May because if I had, the skipper would have wired home and stopped the half pay which was due on the twelfth, so I knew you would draw it on the 12th, so on the 13th there 14 of us firemen and sailors cleared out. There was another man and me beat our way down to Sydney. We were knocking about Sydney for about a fortnight and we could not get a day's work nowhere. I was properly sick of it so I worked my passage right away up into the north of Queensland and I got a start cutting sugar cane on the plantations but it only lasted a week and I wasn't sorry either for the heat was terrible. It was 110 degrees in the shade and the money was small, so me and another chap bought a swag between us: the blankets, billycan and tent and beat our way through the bush for about 150 miles till we struck the first cattle station. We got a start for ten bob a week and our keep but at the end of the week, the boss sacked my mate because he couldn't manage the job, but he offered to keep me on and give me 1 pound but I wanted 30 bob a week. He would not give me it so I told him to keep his quid and get somebody else. I always fancied when I was in the old country that a job riding about on a horse all day would be alright but I had my belly full of riding in that one week. You get into the saddle at daylight and your galloping about till dark, change your horse twice a day. I soon found that a cowboy's life was no catch so we 'padded the oof' down to the coast again at Cairns. We struck the coast at Cairns and I left my mate there and I came down south. I worked my passage down form Cairns when one off the firemen took

182

sick and the chief engineer offered me the job until the man got better and you can just bet your life I jumped at the chance of getting a bob or two. Well, I was on her for about a fortnight. We came down to Brisbane; from Brisbane to Sydney; Sydney to Melbourne; Melbourne back to Sydney. Well, I got a couple of quid off the chief and ten bob off the second , so I made off for the mines at once, so by the time I have paid my train fare down to Coledale and bought some working clothes, I have not much left, but I am sending you a post office order for a quid. I have got to start at Coledale pit on Monday night and will have to work 3 weeks before I get pay, so it will be three weeks before I can send you any more money.

Now Mother, when you answer this letter address it to me c/o Post Office, Coledale, New South Wales, because it is only a little township and there is no postman. Now give my love to Annie and with love to yourself

I remain
Your loving and affectionate son
x x x x   Jack   x x x x x x

P.S. I enclose PO for 1 pound. Hows the dog going on?

Jack claims he did not want to clear out from the YEDDO before the 12th May to ensure the skipper could not stop the half pay allotment to be paid to his mother on that date. He goes on to say on the "…. 13th, there 14 of us firemen and sailors cleared out". His dates are quite wrong. The YEDDO'S log shows she did not arrive in Newcastle, N.S.W. until 30th May.

The section of the log book of the YEDDO, reproduced below, tells a different story from Jack's letter to home. On arrival from Valparaiso, the Master of the YEDDO deposited the ship's articles at the Shipping Master's Office on the 30th May 1910, and when the Articles were returned to the Master prior to sailing on 15th June 1910, only six men including Kirkpatrick were reported to the Shipping Master 'as deserters'.

CERTIFICATES

Or Indorsements made by Consuls or by Officers in British Possessions Abroad.

SHIPPING MASTER'S OFFICE.

NEWCASTLE 15—6—1910.

ARTICLES DEPOSITED 30—5—1910.

ARTICLES RETURNED 15. 6. 1910.

DESERTED.

I HEREBY CERTIFY that the under-mentioned seamen have been reported to me as deserters at this port; and proper entries in the Official Log Book have been produced to me viz:- J. E. Judson & Robinson G. Andrews, J. Fitzgibbon & Kirkpatrick, R. Cole.

I hereby certify that I have sanctioned the discharge of the under-mentioned seamen upon the grounds of mutual consent and that the balance of wages as expressed against their signatures has been paid them in my presence. viz R.J. Hansen, J. Bite.

I hereby certify that I have sanctioned the engagement of the within named and under mentioned Seamen upon the terms mentioned in the within written agreement and I have ascertained and am satisfied that the said seamen fully understand the said agreement and that they have signed the same in my presence.

Shipping Master

BRITISH CONSULATE GENERAL

VALPARAISO

Vessel arrived...4.1.1/.910................

Articles deposited ...53............

Articles returned..22. 4. 10......

AVERAGE RATE OF EXCHANGE IN TOWN 10/4 PENCE PER DOLLAR

Consul

I hereby certify that I have sanctioned the engagement of the undermentioned seamen upon the terms of the within written agreement which has been signed in my presence with a full understanding of the same

Jack was at sea throughout the whole of May and could not have sent a letter to his mother from Newcastle on the 6th May. How could he make such a mistake? There is no doubt the dates recorded in the YEDDO's log by the Shipping Master's Office are correct; which means that from the time he actually deserted in Newcastle on the 14th June, to the time he wrote to his mother from Coledale on 31st July, Jack had only 48 days in which to cram in the adventures he recounted in his letter to his mother. Using Jack's own timings a schedule of his movements can be reconstructed.

		No. of days
1.	"Another man and me beat our way down to Sydney"	0.5
2.	"We were knocking about Sydney for about a fortnight and we could not get a day's work."	14
3.	"I worked my passage right way up into the north of Queensland". (estimate sailing time for steamer averaging 240 miles a day)	6.5
4.	"...... cutting sugar cane on the plantations but it still only lasted a week".	6
5.	"...... beat our way through the bush for about 150 miles till we struck the first cattle station." (estimated 30 miles a day)	5
6.	"At the end of the week the boss sacked my mate ...... I told him to keep his quid and get somebody else."	6
7.	"....... 'We padded the oof' down to the coast, we struck the coast at Cairns". (Another trek of 150 miles presumably)	5
8.	Jack found a ship at Cairns. "I was on her for about a fortnight. We came down to Brisbane; from Brisbane to Sydney; Sydney to Melbourne; Melbourne back to Sydney."	14
9.	A day to "buy some working clothes", take the train to Coledale and then find digs.	1
	Total	59 Days

The actual time between desertion and writing his first letter from Coledale is only 48 days. If taken literally, Jack's timetable far exceeded the 48 days between desertion and arrival at Coledale. However some of his times and distances are vague and his travels might have been accomplished within 48 days. Time in Sydney may have been a few days less than a fortnight; he may have worked less than a week cane cutting; and his trek through the bush, 150 miles, may be exaggerated. His description of life as a 'cowboy' certainly has a ring of authenticity. Did he lose track of time after such a hectic introduction to life in Australia – mistaking May for June?

The men who deserted the YEDDO along with Jack were all from the Tyne area, six from South Shields and one from a pit village 7½ miles south west of Newcastle, England. The six men from South Shields comprised one Able Seaman J. Robinson, aged 29 and five Firemen: A. Leslie, aged 43, Thomas Dick, age 34, C Andrews, age 35, J Fitzgibbon age 32, and J.S. Kirkpatrick, age 19. The odd man out was J.C. Anderson, aged 19, 2nd Steward from Long Row, Lintz Colliery who may have been the mate with whom Jack set off in search of work. Their ages were compatible. The Master of the YEDDO, Sydney C. Robson managed to sign on five replacement firemen on the 15th June, the day the ship sailed, but they were signed on at £5 per month, £1 (a quid in Jack's jargon) or 25% more than Jack and the other firemen who jumped ship. If Jack had stuck with the YEDDO, he would not have returned to the U.K. until the 17th November 1911 when she docked in Liverpool, a voyage of one year and nine months.

We do not have Sarah's letters, but judging by Jack's assurances about swagmen being 'respectable', she must have been horrified at the thought of her well brought up son being a tramp. The reassurance that he was about to start in the pits was no great comfort but at least it was something she could understand.

Swagman. Jack and friend bought a swag and set out to become ranchers, but without the luxury of two wheeled transport.
Image courtesy of Bill Chapman, Wollongong, N.S.W.

Cutting Sugar Cane, Queensland. After failing to find work in Sydney, Jack and a mate tried cane cutting, but could not get into the rhythm of the cutters. "Stoop – chop – straighten – lop – stoop – chop – straighten – lop" They quit after one week.

Image KY collection cigarette card

To the world at large, Jack's career appears aimless – a milkman for four years after leaving school, an assistant steward on a home trade tramp steamer for two months, a fireman on a foreign trade vessel, a deserter, a cane cutter for a week, a stockman for a week and a swagman for two weeks all by the age of 18.

Stockmen. Jack and friend tried being cowboys, but found the work arduous. The station owner would not pay Jack the 30/- (shillings) a week he demanded, so they parted company after only one week.
Image KY Collection

Now in August 1910 he had become a coal miner in New South Wales, an occupation he could easily have followed at home in Shields which had three collieries within the borough boundaries. Perhaps coal mining in Australia could match his expectations?

The story of Jack's forefathers, the Kirkpatricks, the Simpsons and the Hosgoods is one of ambitious single-minded men who in spite of humble origins and minimal education, reached near the top of their chosen careers. Jack does not appear to have inherited the ambition genes, but he did inherit the single-mindedness of his successful forebears. His letters reveal he was far from aimless and he had indeed one overriding purpose in life. His migration to Australia was mercenary rather than from any heartfelt attraction to the country. In a letter dated 29th September 1910 Jack stated:

> *"You will never be dependent on any son-in-laws for anything if I can help it, now if only you had a lodger and Annie working and the ten bob a week that I send you, I don't consider you would be doing too bad"*, and on the 1st October, he stated, *"Well Mother, I don't care about writing unless I have something to send with it."*

Jack's whole purpose in life was to send his Mother, ten shillings a week and thus ensure her financial security. He was absolutely devoted to his mother, perhaps to the point of obsession. He had been brought up and probably spoilt, virtually as an only son by Sarah who had lost two 'James's' in infancy and also her firstborn Alfred through estrangement. Jack's actions, when judged in the light of his declared objective, make sense and demonstrate he was far from shiftless.

A milkman's remuneration was too small; as steward on the HEIGHINGTON, he allotted half his wage to his Mum, likewise he allotted half his wage as fireman on the YEDDO (£2 a month, close to his target of 10 bob a week); he joined the YEDDO intent on reaching Australia where he had heard wages were higher than in the old country; one letter indicates premeditated desertion; at cane cutting the money was so small; on the cattle station the boss offered *"to give me one pound, but I wanted thirty bob and he would not give it to me, so I told him to keep his quid and get somebody else"* said Jack. Employment in Australia so far had failed to meet his expectations. Maybe coal mining in New South Wales would pay enough so he could send his mother that ten shillings a week.

Wearing the new clothes that had cost him his last few shillings, Jack started his career as a miner at Coledale Pit on the nightshift on 1st August 1910.

His pay was eight bob (shillings) for a nine hour shift. After a fortnight, he sent an apologetic letter explaining:

> "*Now Mother, I am sending you 15 bob this pay as I only had seven shifts for the fortnight, which after paying 2 pounds for board, and paying ....(word illegible) for my fags, I am just about cleaned out.*"

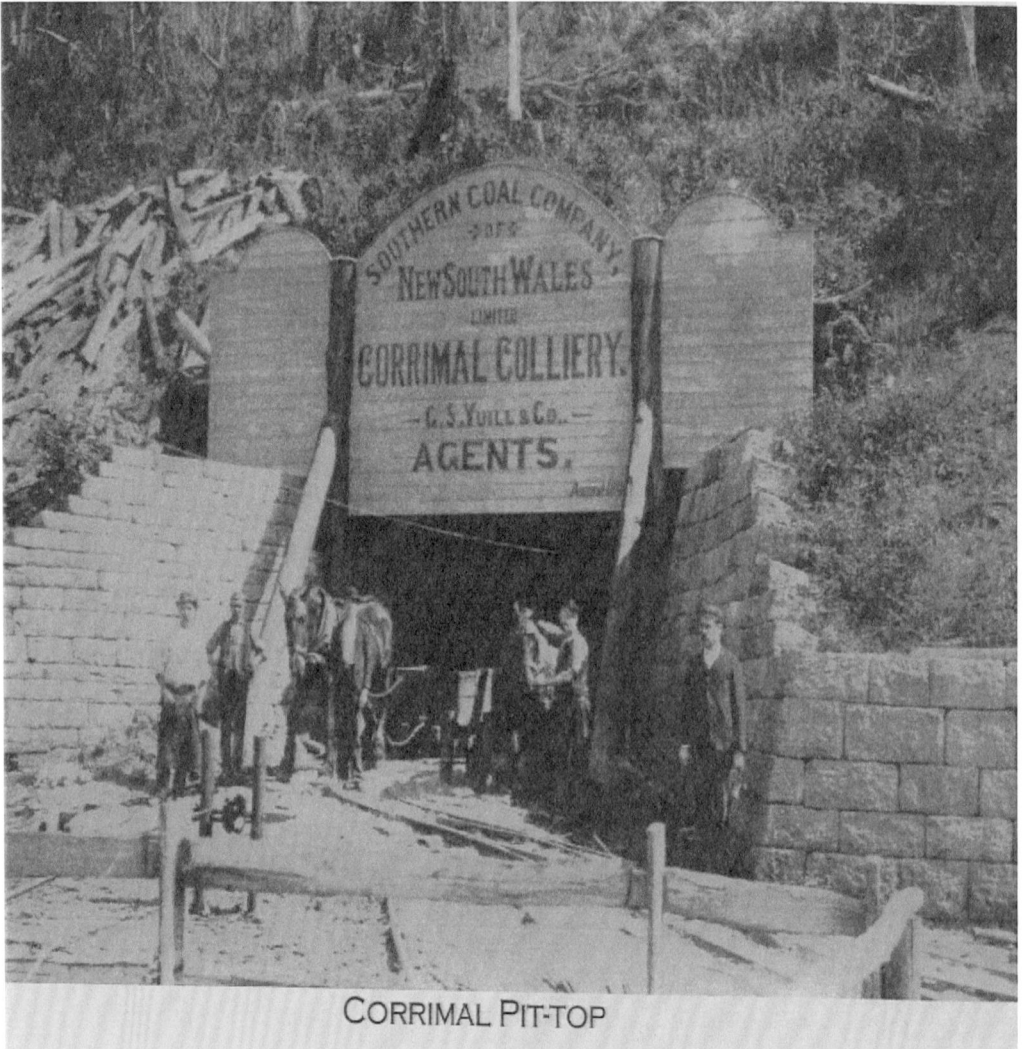

CORRIMAL PIT-TOP

Coal mining N.S.W. Coledale, Corrimal and Kembla. By 31st July 1910, Jack had reached NSW intent of making a living as a coal miner. He worked in all 3 mines but found the shifts, although well paid, were irregular.

Image courtesy of John Reay, Corrimal, N.S.W.

**2 of the miners cottages circa 1900
Midgley St Corrimal**

Miners cottages 1900. While working at Corrimal, Jack lodged with a South Shields couple named Parkes. He wrote home complaining. Wages might be high in Australia, but so was the cost of living. *Image courtesy of John Reay, Corrimal, N.S.W.*

Jack's seven shifts earned him £2.16.0, so if he paid £2 for board and 15/- for a postal order for his mother, he had only 1/- spare for his fags. In the same letter he enquired about his pigeons and his dog Lilly offering to send 7/6d to pay for her license. He goes on to tell his Mother:

> *"You should be out here keeping lodgers, you would make a fortune in a quarter less than no time for you would get a pound a week and they don't feed you too well either.*

It was not only the 'grub' that was 'crook' in his first lodging house. He could '*hardly get a drop of water to bathe with*', but these were not his only problems. His landlord and lady were not the most affable of people.

> *"...when the man and wife were drunk they used to scrap like hell, then he started with me and that put the tall hat together for he smote me across the head with the poker and put a cut in my head about an inch long. After that I sailed in then and you could not see anything tor dust for I broke a chair over his head and in tho struggle we upscuttled and broke a few things, so he got a summons out against me for assault – but as both him and his wife were drunk and I wasn't, the case was dismissed."*

This letter is undated but must have been written in the second half of August 1910 by which time he had found new digs with the Parks Family in Midgley Street, Corrimal. They were South Shield's people – *"a good lodge"* he tells, *"with plenty of hot pies and onion puddings."*

With his next letter dated 29th September 1910, Jack sent a Postal Order for a quid – one pound. This was followed quickly by another letter on 1st October. He had been paid off from Coledale Pit for 'slackness' of trade, and for *"3 weeks I have been knocking around the best way I could until I got a start at South Bouli mine"*. Employed on the night shift all the time on stonework, he earned 8 bob for a nine hours shift. However, he was finding there was a corollary to high wages - a high cost of living.

> *"Now mother"*, he says, *"you will be saying he is doing well but what a mistake the people at home make. They hear they make good money out here, true, but what is the good of it, if you have it all to pay away"*.

Jack was having trouble making ends meet. *"I work for about 2 pounds and 2 shillings a week and that is not constant, it is very seldom the pit works the full number of shifts."* From this he had to pay a pound a week for lodgings, *"you can't get them a penny cheaper and no washing done"*, - after which he was left with £1 2s.from which he sent his mother 10/- leaving him with 12/- a week to tide him over and to pay for his laundry, his fags and other living expenses. *"You will see I have not much left and I am about sick of it"*, he complains and says *"he is looking around for something better"*. Jack promises to write every fortnight and exhorts his mother to do likewise, reiterating the address of his South Shield's hosts; *"c/o W Parks, Midgley Street, Coxtons Estate, Corrimal, Elwarra, N.S.W"*. – the spellings are Jack's own version.

Keeping his promise, Jack wrote again on the 12th November, a lettercard to his sister Annie and a full letter to his Mother enclosing a Postal Order for £1. That same morning he received three letters from his mother, addressed to Coledale from where he had written on 31st July, thus giving a three and a half month turnaround time for news, and a 6-7 week transit time for letters in each direction - a far cry from the 21st Century when the author in County Durham can converse instantly by Skype with cousins in Wollongong, New South Wales.

There had been friction in the Kirkpatrick's household in South Shields, however Jack writes belligerently:

"I see you have given Sam (his brother in law) his marching orders, just like his dammed cheek to try to rule the roost, he would not have done it if I had been at home…… I also see you have given Antonio his notice to 'Git', but it was just like that pig to try and boss it when he got his chance. I wish I had been at home, I would have made the Russian Jew bugger dance a hornpipe on his arse, but never mind, better luck with the next lodger".

We do not know what Jack's mother said in her letter, but it certainly provoked a violent outburst of racism from her son, displaying perhaps the politically incorrect prejudices prevailing in a working class seaport at that time. Jack also informed his mother that he was moving lodgings as the Parks were returning to South Shields and had already sold the bed he was using.

A couple of weeks later, on the 27th November, Jack sent another letter enclosing Christmas cards and wishing he was *"at canny old Shields for the Christmas …….. to help you eat that goose……this place is so quiet, I can feel my whiskers turning grey."* He gives his new address as c/o J Heslop, Midgley Street, Corrimal and ends with his usual *"P.S, I am enclosing a PO for a quid."*

Fifty six years after his father jumped ship to try his luck in Victoria's goldfields, Jack disillusioned with coal mining, succumbed to the lure of gold.

At 14 Bertram Street, South Shields, Sarah had received her Christmas card from Jack, who, as promised had been corresponding diligently every fortnight for the previous two months. By mid- January 1911, she expected the next letter from Jack to drop through the letterbox. None came. With mounting anxiety she watched daily for the postman. January passed without a word and February was almost over before a letter in Jack's handwriting finally dropped through her letter box.

Jack's letter addressed from *'S.S. Corringa, Albany, West Australia'*, dated 16th January 1911, explained his silence. A week after sending his letter and Christmas cards, he quit Corrimal and went to nearby Mount Kembla, but only stayed for a week. *"It was a very quiet place so I took (off) and worked my passage across to Fremantle in Western Australia".* He must have arrived in Fremantle around Christmas time, though he makes no mention of the festive season. Jack made his way up country about 200 miles to Bullfinch.

"There has been a very big gold rush here, but all the good it done was simply to overrun the country with men right from Bullfinch to Fremantle and work was bad to get. There were some men working for three or four bob a day so that was no good to me" recorded Jack.

General Store at Bullfinch 1910. A new gold strike in Western Australia lured Jack away from N.S.W. He worked his passage to Fremantle, then made his way up country to **Bullfinch..** *Image Courtesy of Royal Western Australian Historical Society, and the State Library of Western Australia.*

S.S. Kooringa, owners McIlwraith McEachern, Melbourne. Jack enlisted as steward at Fremantle, 16th January 1911. He soon graduated to Fireman and eventually Greaser. *Image courtesy of John Reay, Corrimal, N.S.W.*

The days when a man could work his own claim with shovel and pan were long since gone. Gold was discovered in Bullfinch in 1910 sparking a boom for the town, but gold was now mined by corporations on an industrial scale. Unlike the 21st century, miners in Western Australia, were poorly paid. A strike for better pay by the Bullfinch miners in 1910 lasted six weeks, but judging by Jack's remark six months later, pay and conditions had not improved. A narrow gauge railway stretched from Perth to the town of Southern Cross, twenty miles short of Bullfinch – the line was extended later in the year, so Jack had to complete the final leg of his journey on foot. He may have been in Bullfinch from a week to a fortnight. Whether Jack swung a pick or wielded a shovel to earn his crust, he does not say. He does not tell us how he survived. He tightened his belt and went back to the coast again. *"I got the chance of a second steward's job on the Corringa, so I took it until I can get something better"* he wrote. He apologised for not sending anything with this letter as he was 'dead broke' and would not be paid until the end of the month. Jack had travelled a long way to meet another disappointment.

Jack was right back where he started when he first left home, aged 17, a second steward on a tramp steamer. He must have realised at long last that his only prosperous spells in Australia came when he was working his passage on-board merchant ships. These offered better pay, regular employment and the bonus of not having to pay for lodgings. Jack's service on the KOORINGA was to last two years and five months, first as steward, then fireman and finally greaser in the engine room. During this period he came of age literally and metaphorically. His letters show his conversion from 'Geordie' to 'Digger'—almost but not quite. They reveal the development of his social and political opinions; his view of marriage; a cooling of his relationship with his elder married sisters and their husbands; and his unwavering devotion to his mother and his 'kid' sister Annie!

The KOORINGA, a steamer, 3174 gross tons, built in Port Glasgow, Scotland in 1902, was registered in Melbourne to owners McIlwraith and McEachern Proprietary Limited. She plied her trade from the coal ports on Australia's east coast, across the Great Australian Bite and as far north on the west coast as Geralton. She was a regular caller at Newcastle, N.S.W., Sydney, Port Kembla, Melbourne, Adelaide, Albany, Bunbury, Fremantle and Geralton. The Kooringa's peregrinations made it difficult for Jack's mail from home to catch up with his at times.

On the 17th February 1911, Jack wrote from Bunbury, apologising for not sending any money with his previous letter as he was 'dead broke' and for only sending a PO for a quid with this letter as he had to *'buy duds again'*. (working clothes). He tells his Mum, he is *'filling out again'*, he is *'12 stone and 4 pounds'* and is *'getting an awful size'*. By the beginning of March, he was in the stokehole once more and from then on was able to send his mother £2 a month. While in Fremantle, he read that the directors who floated the mining company in Bullfinch were on trial for fraud in Perth. As time passes it became apparent Jack was an avid reader of newspapers and keenly interested in current affairs both in Australia and Shields.

In May he asked his mother to pass on a piece of sad news. *"Tell Mary Smith White that Adam Smith went down on the Younggala, an Adelaide boat which went down with all hands between Sydney and Brisbane – his father went down on a collier out of Shields"*. Jack gives no clues about who Mary and Adam were. Back in South Shields, Annie was working in a fruit shop and Sarah was thinking of setting up a shop of her own, but we are not told what type of business it was. Jack is quick to give her advice.

> *"I am very much afraid that you are in the wrong district to make a fortune for the people round there would rob 'Old Nick' himself if he gave 'Tick' (credit), and I suppose you will know that there is no hope unless you give the good old 'Tick'. I wasn't four years going round with the milk without finding out a little of their weak points".*

By the age of 17 Jack was already street wise. In the same letter he speculates teasingly about his beloved kid sister Annie. She was 17 and Jack 19 when this was penned.

> *"I often wonder what she is looking like. I suppose she will be like all tall young women of her age, Long, Lean, Razerfaced and all legs and wings, but never mind kid, things was never that bad but what they could not be worse".*

Annie, aged 17. *Image from* www.anzacday.org.au *courtesy of the late J.S.Parkin*

195

At the beginning of June, he received three letters from his mother and a postcard from Annie. He has a little moan in his reply to his mother that she never tells him how the shop is doing. He responds to the news of a friend's marriage with all the worldly wisdom of a nineteen year old.

> *"You were telling me that Jack Fenwick has got married. Poor Bugger, tell him I am sorry to hear it and give him my deepest sympathy. But tell him that he is silly to waste his time loading hay for his old man, he wants to keep his eyes open for a ship coming out this way, and get out with her even if he has to work his passage out, for it doesn't matter in which part of this colony he lands, he will get as much work as he wants, if he isn't frightened of a bit of hard work, if he does manage to ever get out here he could get his wife and kid out here for about a fiver and I am sure he would be better out here than slaving in that old louse bound country for a quid a week."*

Jack having conveniently forgotten the hardships he experienced in his first six months in Australia is now extolling the benefits of his new homeland and actively promoting migration from the *'old louse bound country'*. No one becomes a more fervent evangelist than the convert.

Writing on the 9th July 1911, a week after his 19th birthday, Jack sounds aggrieved:
> *"I have not received a letter from you for above two months. I am just wondering if you have forgot me altogether".*

*H.S.*Edward Street, South Shields. Jack's mother set up a business, against his advice, in the Tyne dock area. The Burgess Rolls for South Shields show she occupied premises on the above street in 1912/1913. Jack joked that her 'coconut buns' would be selling all over Shields. The enterprise evidently, was not a success.

196

Jack asks again how the shop is doing and speculates that in a short time he will be hearing 'of all the horses and carts that are running about with your famous '*Cockonut Buns*'. He also asks his mother to send a photo of 'Lil' his Yorkshire Terrier, as he wants to show it to the donkeyman on the ship who is also from South Shields. A mate on board the Kooringa has asked if Jack will go out with him across to Vancouver, British Columbia, but he is undecided.

There is some mystery about Sarah's shop and the fate of the dog Lil. Tom Curran, who had contact with a son of Annie in England, and her sisters in Queensland, states that Sarah did not open a shop, and also that Lil had died of poisoning. (*Across the Bar, 1994 p98-99*) Why was the family reluctant to tell Jack the facts? However the Burgess Rolls for South Shields, contradict this story and show Sarah occupied premises in H.S. Edward Street in 1912 – 1913, two streets away from the family home in Bertram Street, apparently in a shop selling home baking. Perhaps the shop had not been a success, as Jack had prophesied, and Sarah was reluctant to admit he was right and she was wrong.

Victoria Quay Fremantle circa 1906

Postcard KY Collection

Flinders St and Custom House, Melbourne

Jack's next letter was sent from Fremantle on the 21st August on arrival from Port Kembla. The trip across the Great Australian Bite took 20 days instead of the usual 14 days because of severe storms. The Kooringa lost two lifeboats and Jack adds in a matter of fact note *"the second cook was washed overboard and drowned"*. Life in the merchant navy was every bit as hazardous as in the coal mines, but tragedies at sea were remote and did not command the same publicity as mining disasters.

There were no letters on file for September and October. The next is dated 8th November from the Kooringa, Adelaide, and Jack is now thinking of Christmas. He tries to impress on his mother and Annie, how different Christmas in Melbourne will be. *"About 125 degrees of heat… and that is in the shade"*. With this letter he sent his mother a couple of extra quid…. *"for your Christmas Box"*, and in a P.S. he mentions a Postal Order for a quid for Annie. He sent no Christmas greetings to his older sisters Peggie and Sarah, and their children.

Jack's final letter of the year sent from Fremantle on the 7th December was very brief, enclosing a Postal Order for a quid. Over the course of 1911, Jack sent home £25 to his mother and £1 to his sister Annie. He was sending home about 40% of his earnings.

The Kooringa arrived in Melbourne from Bunbury on the morning of the 7th January 1912, when Jack found a pile of correspondence awaiting him, two letters from his mother, two from Annie and three newspapers. He replied that same day saying he was sorry that they had both spent a very quiet Christmas. His Christmas had not been quiet as he explained.

> *"We left Kembla, N.S.W. about Xmas eve for the West, of course we had a good dinner. We had goose and Plum Pudding and Brandy Sauce and we drank each other's health quite a number of times until each man thought he was Jack Johnson, champion of the world.* (Jack Johnson won the world heavyweight boxing championship in Sydney, Australia on the 25th December 1908, becoming the first African American to win the title. Before a crowd of 20,000 spectators, he defeated a white Canadian, Tommy Burns. The police fearing a riot, stopped the fight after 14 rounds.) *then my mate suggested going over and having a fight with the sailors, of course that was hailed as a noble idea, and as the sailors were feeling a bit lively themselves from sampling the bottle too much, things went pretty lively for the next half hour, you couldn't see anything for blood and snots flying about until the Mates and Engineers came along and threatened to log all hands forward. We all had trophies of the fray and someone bunged one of my eyes right up and by the look of my beak someone must have jumped on it in a mistake when I was on the floor, but as they say 'alls well that ends well' so I suppose it must be for both my eyes and my nose are alright now, so that is the way I spent Xmas."*

One wonders what a nervous mother thought of her son's escapades. With this letter Jack sent a photo taken on the wharf by an amateur photographer one evening as he and his shipmates were going for a swim before tea. He apologised for the quality of the photo as *"the sun was right in our eyes and I wanted a haircut badly".* This photo survives in the AWM archives.

Jack on the right, and his mates on the wharf at Bunbury. This photo was sent home to his mother in February 1912. He wrote "We knocked off in the engine room at 5 o'clock, we were going along the wharf for a swim before tea" He apologises for photo, "The sun was in our eyes and I wanted a haircut badly".

Image Courtesy of the Australian War Memorial   (AWM P01446.001)

Jack's next letter was dated 10th January, only three days later, from Fremantle. Could the Kooringa have covered the distance from Melbourne to Fremantle in that time, or are Jack's dates wrong? He gives a vivid description of the conditions in the stokehole.

> *"We lay off Melbourne for about 2 hours on Boxing Day, we had to call there to pick up an old three masted Barque that they used in Melbourne for keeping coal in as they were sending her to Fremantle for our Company, we had to tow her round to Fremantle, and it made it pretty heavy for us chaps down below, for she (KOORINGA) is heavy enough for us to fire without having a great big hulk to tow, and at the very hottest time of the year. We have been working with as far as 135 degrees of heat in the Stokehole, there is none of us sorry to get a spell of four days and then we will be off again for another 15 days run East."*

200

No one could accuse Jack of being indolent. He took pride in his work in spite of the infernal conditions in the stokehole, and in his physique which enabled him to pursue his calling as a fireman. He regularly checked his weight, around 12 stone 4 pounds and reported the results to reassure his mother of his good health. When serving in the army, Jack may have skived a bit to avoid senseless drills, but then which serviceman has not done likewise? He concludes his letter with a résumé of the remittances sent in 1911, amounting to £25 to ensure that his mother had received every one, a practice which became a ritual in his correspondence.

The KOORINGA docked in Newcastle on the 1st March 1912 and Jack wrote that day opening with one of his favourite phrases when he had not written for a few weeks. *"Just a line to let you know I am still alive and kicking and in the best of health"*. Before sailing for Newcastle, the ship had been laid up in Melbourne for 16 days during which time Jack had bumped into a man from South Shields, called Jack Waters.

"You know his mother lives in our old house in Corbridge Street", Jack reminds his mother. Waters, a donkeyman on a Port Line boat boasted how well his three sons were doing and says Jack, *"he told me he was second engineer on the old SOUTHMOOR with my father…. He is a hell of a liar"*. Jack's father, Robert Kirkpatrick served as 1st or 2nd Mate on the SOUTHMOOR from March 1888 to March 1897. The crew lists for the SOUTHMOOR have been checked and Mr Waters did not serve on the ship as engineer or in any other capacity along with Robert Kirkpatrick. Waters however must have known Robert Kirkpatrick fairly well even though they never served together on the SOUTHMOOR as it was 15 years since Jack's father had left the ship. Jack's judgement of Water's veracity was sharp and shrewd.

> *"he must have thought I had been out here ten years instead of two and did not know his sons. He is a bigger liar than Tom Perry"* (an old legendary Jack Tar who was expelled from Hell because he was a bigger liar than Satan himself. He was condemned to roam the seas until he learned to tell the truth).

Jack was evidently keeping himself informed about current affairs in Britain and South Shields and he says: *"I got those Gazettes and Xmas papers"*; the Shield's Gazette is still in print today. Jack also mentions meeting Shields men form a ship called the WEAR, but he did not know any of the men on her. *"The firemen are all Shield's men, but they belong to the low end of the town".* Jack presumably met visiting seamen congregating in the Seaman's Missions, which provided accommodation and leisure facilities in major ports across the world. Jack warned his mother she would probably get a visit from Mr Waters on his return to Shields.

Seaman's Mission, Melbourne. A place of relaxation for Jack, a place where he might bump into seaman from home, and a place where his mail could be directed.

Image KY Collection

Jack next wrote from Albany on 1st April 1912. This letter was short and included a postal order for £3 and a postcard of the KOOMBANA, a passenger boat built on the Tyne that had gone down off the Australian coast with 147 people on board. Sarah, like every merchant seaman's wife was only too aware of the perils of the sea and had lived with the dread of bad news throughout her 30 year relationship with Robert Kirkpatrick. Now her beloved son was facing similar dangers.

The next letter from Jack is headed S.S. KOORINGA, Bunbury on the 4th April. Not for the first time is the dating of Jack's letters problematical. In this letter he mentions he has seen that *"the Titanic has went down with above 1000 people".* The Titanic sank around 2.30am on the 15th April; about 700 survivors were picked up from lifeboats by the CARPATHIA after day break on the 15th and the magnitude of the disaster only became clear as the day progressed. The Australian press could not have published the news before the 16th and the KOORINGA would have to be in port for Jack to see the newspapers. In spite of the anomaly with dates this is one of Jack's more revealing letters, reproduced here in full.

"Dear Mother,
I have just received your letter 4 days ago in Geraldton and a paper and PC from (?) I am glad to hear that you and Annie are keeping well. I see that the miners have started work again and by the accounts in the papers out here they have not got what they came out for. It is damned hard when you come to think of it the way they have been treated. It is a pity they had not waited for another two or three years until they had plenty of money in their union so that they could have carried on a bit longer. Then the government would have forced a settlement one way or another but then it will all ways be the way in that louse bound country, it is not like Australia for we have not got any House of Lords where a lot of empty headed fools have the right to throw out any bill no matter how much benefit in would to the working classes just because their fathers sat there before them. But then England has always been like that and always will be until the people do away with the Lords. Look at the railways at home for instance, they all belong to private companies that pay very large dividends every quarter through having the men with constant jobs work ten hours a day for the huge sum of 1 pound, one shilling a week, then other people think that they are very well paid, the Government workers on the railway out here were growling about a rise of wages so they went to Arbitration Court and the award they got was that no man that was working for the Government connected with the railways, the least he could work for was 9/- per day and of course paid higher wages according to your job. Now on the N.E.R. at home a porter gets 22 shillings a week one week and 18 shillings the next and if he is extra civil to the passengers he might if he has got a bit of good luck he might get a stray threepenny bit so you will see the difference between the two countries. The working man out here votes for a labour Government out here but the man at home has not got the sense for that. He must go and vote for the first big Liberal capitalist that puts up for the seat. Now Mother hope that you and Annie are keeping all right and that Annie is still liking her job. I am not looking to well myself for I went greasing a couple of months ago and I don't think that the engine room agrees with me. I have lost

about 4 pound in weight since I started so I think that I thrive better on the hard work in the Stokehold, off course it is a very light job. I have got a responsible job to but I am thinking of turning it in as it does not suit me. I see the Titanic has went down with above 1000 people. Now mother I will now conclude so with love to you and Annie ,I remain
Your Loving Son
Jack
PO for 3 quid

Jack pulls no punches in condemning the British political system, in particular the House of Lords. He even regards the Liberals as capitalists, although the Liberal Prime Minister, Asquith had already threatened to abolish the House of Lords when they voted against his budget introducing a universal old age pension for men. The young lad who went to sea on the HEIGHINGTON two years earlier was keen to go sightseeing in Genoa and Tunis. By 1912, he had developed a keen interest in politics and trade unionism, and was following closely the course of industrial disputes in both England and Australia. Having been reared, educated and employed in the Tyne Dock area, the working class end of South Shields, he could not be anything other than a labour supporter, diametrically opposed to the stance of his first biographer Sir Irving Benson, a knight of the realm, a Methodist minister and a pillar of the establishment. In his 1965 biography "The Man with the Donkey", Benson carefully edited out Jack's (then) radical views as well as his bad language. When this letter was written Jack was now a 'Digger', one hundred percent.

At the same time as he wrote to his Mum, Jack sent a humorous postcard to his sister Annie repeating the erroneous date "4-4-12", and referring to the Titanic disaster. His blind spot with dates is puzzling. In the card he mentions *"We had a big wreck out here where I am. I sent you the photo of the KOOMBANA last month, I had a good few friends in her, 147 went down in her".* The KOOMBANA was lost totally in a cyclone on the 20th March 1912, north of Port Hedland. The Kalgoorlie Western Argus of the 9th April 1912 published a list of passengers and crew, amongst whom was a fireman C. Anderson. When Jack deserted from the YEDDO in 1810 one of his fellow deserters was a 'J. C. Anderson', perhaps one of the friends he referred to.

By 3rd June, the KOORINGA was in Newcastle. Jack acknowledged receipt of a letter from his mother, two postcards from Annie and a postcard from his elder sister Sarah with three photos in it. *"I was surprised when I got it* considering that I have been out here two years and that is the first PC I have received from Sarah." Jack learned from his mother's letter that she had tried to send him a photograph of his father, but her letter had been returned. The photograph of Robert Kirkpatrick would have been a rare find – what a pity it did not survive. Jack enjoins his Mother to send his letters to S.S. KOORINGA, c/o McIlwraith, McEachern, Fremantle. "I would have answered Sarah's PC but I don't know her address, so give my respects to Sarah and Sam", he adds and finishes with his usual "P.S. I am enclosing PO for 3 quid". The family tiff with Sam, two years earlier has been forgiven and forgotten apparently.

In a brief note dated 12th July 1912, Jack tells his mother to stop sending the 'News of the World' (a weekly paper popular at one time for printing salacious reports from the courts). "I can get them in the shops here every week". The News of the World was still in circulation until July 2013 when, after a span of 168 years, it was closed by the Australian proprietor Rupert Murdoch amidst a phone hacking scandal.

The KOORINGA was at Geralton on the 9th August. After the usual pleasantries, Jack mentioned reading in the Gazette about Louis Haliday getting killed. "I knew him well. It is pretty hard luck him getting killed for he was a good sort of chap". He then tells his Mother "I met a fellow called Cockburn in Fremantle, he has just come out, they used to live beside us in Eldon Street". His letter goes on, "Now Mother, I think I will leave the KOORINGA when we get East again, because the greasing is knocking me up. I have (been) getting very thin and as pale as a ghost, I weigh above eleven stone and a half now, I can't eat, I have lost my appetite, for when I was firing I could eat like a horse for the KOORINGA is a pretty heavy firing job and very hot, so I think I will have a month's rest and then look for another firing job." This slightly worrying news for Sarah was accompanied by the usual P.O. for three pounds.

In his letter headed 1st September 1912, S.S. KOORINGA, Adelaide, Jack makes no mention of his loss of appetite, or whether he is greasing or firing in the KOORINGA. Once more however he is on his political platform and speaks with some passion, even talking about 'revolution' in England.

"Dear Mother,
Just a line to let you (know) that I received your letter this morning. I am glad to hear that you and Annie are keeping well and that things

are keeping all right at home. I see by the papers out here that the dock strike has not been settled yet and I see that the railway men who get 24 bob a week have got a rise of 3½ per cent. I suppose that they must have caught the owners when they were drunk and in a generous state of mind to have got such a hell of a rise. I suppose that the railway men will be going about like Lords now that they have got a shilling a week rise but I suppose the Lords and Dukes will take it off them next year again as the expenses will be to big for them to pick up. That is just the style in the old country. Something like the Insurance Bill that is something else that will help to pay the men's wages with billets worth ten thousands a year. I often wonder when the working men of England will wake up and see things as other people see them. What they want in England is a good revolution and that will clear some of the Millionaires and Lords and Dukes out of it and then with a labour Government they will almost be able to make their own conditions. I am enclosing P.O. for 3 quid.
With Love to you and Annie from
Your Loving Son
Jack"

Jack's next letter was sent from the KOORINGA at Bunbury on the 15th October where Jack says *"we are loading timber here for Melbourne and Sydney"*. His mother's latest letter conveyed the news that his brother-in-law, Peggy's husband … *"Will Balneaves is on his way out here, Well I hope that he gets on for he is a good sort, too good for the likes of Peggy, don't you think so. I think if I was to get a wife like her I would be getting hanged inside of a year"*.

Jack is extremely harsh on Peggy. It seems tempers flared easily in 14 Bertram Street, South Shields. Reading between the lines one gets the impressions that Sarah and her daughter were very much alike in temperament, both volatile and hot tempered. Jack of course, only heard his mother's side of any family quarrel and of course, took her side.

A letter sent from KOORINGA, Port Kembla, New South Wales on the 3rd November was very short. He sent the usual 'three quid' and told his mother *"I am keeping pretty well but I am very thin, yet I don't seem to be getting my flesh back again at all"*.

Jack's final letter of 1912 was sent from Melbourne on the 12th December, after his ship was there a fortnight. Following the usual exchange of greetings and comments on the weather, Jack enquires:

> "*How is things looking at Shields, still the same old hum-drum style I suppose. I think I will leave the KOORINGA after the New Year and go across to the New Zealand Coast, and (I am) getting tired of this side so I think I will have a change".*

This is the first indication that the attractions of Australia are waning a little. There has never been any hint from Jack of finding a girlfriend and settling down. Jack was about "*to have a change"* in 1913, but not as he wished. He would not go to New Zealand and his health and fortunes would suffer a downturn.

His first letter home in the New Year written on the 11th January, found Jack still on the KOORINGA at Bunbury. *"The weather out here is terrible hot, yesterday the heat in the engine room was 125 degrees"*, he tells his mother, then states he is sending a postal order for three quid, *"the last one for 1912".* Jack had sent 12 postal orders for three quid and is insistent his mother confirms receipt of "*the 36 pounds all right".* His use of calendar dates may have been lackadaisical, but his book-keeping was totally accurate.

A month later he was still on the KOORINGA, writing from Port Kembla. The ship had been lying in Sydney for a week. "*I took three days off and me and my mate had a good time in Sydney and we missed our passage from Sydney to Port Kembla".* Jack does not elaborate on what constituted '*a good time',* and his spree probably cost him a train fare from Sydney to Port Kembla to catch up with the ship.

By the 14th March, the KOORINGA had returned to Port Kembla. There Jack wrote what must have been a worrying letter to a fretful mother. His next port of call was to be Melbourne, "*where I think that I will leave for I am not keeping too good. I went to see the doctor in the West and he told me that I was properly run down and needed a rest to put me right, so I will have to do this trip round West and then to Melbourne where I think that I will have a couple of months holiday, that is of course if the exchequer will hold out that long...... I feel properly rotten and I look more like a corpse than anything else, of course that is the engine room that does that, and I cant eat my grub like I used to, but for all that I am pretty heavy yet, for I am twelve stone, three pounds,"* - much the same weight as when he enlisted in the Australian Army in August 1914.

King Street, Sydney circa 1910   *Image KY Collection*

Through Jack's correspondence, a strong bond of affection for his sister Annie is very evident. Although Annie was only two years younger, he often addressed her teasingly as 'Kid'. On the 1st April 1913, he sent her a pictorial letter card showing eight views of Western Australia. Unfortunately the poor quality of the card prevents reproduction but the message is decipherable.

"1-4-13
SS KOORINGA
Fremantle

Dear Annie,
Just a line to let you know I am still alive and kicking. Now kid, I got the Muffler today and thanks very much, it was very good of you to remember me at Xmas, but nobody wears Mufflers out here, so I have put it away until I get home, then I will be able to wear it. I might be taking a run home someday if I can strike a ship handy, and see mother and you. By the way, Mother tells me that she is keeping very poorly, so Annie I hope that you are kind to her, for there is only you and her, so be good to her while you are at home, for if you ever happen to be knocking about on your own, then's the time that you

208

will miss her. Now Annie, how are you keeping, and do you still like your job, you have been a long time there. I am sending you a PO for one pound in Mother's letter, so it will be some pocket money for race week. Now kid, these are views of West Australia, so give my love to mother and with love to yourself, I remain your Loving Brother, Jack".

The state of Sarah Simpson's health was now causing Jack some concern. This is the first time since coming to Australia that Jack talked of returning home, after an absence of three years. A month later, Jack sent a postcard to Annie, with a view of the 'Beach Esplanade, Newcastle', crowded with Edwardians in summer dress. The card is very reminiscent of the beach scenes at South Shields. Jack asks *"how are things looking at Shields, still the same I expect, I suppose things have not changed a bit since I left".* Jack's thoughts are obviously turning more and more to home.

In a letter Jack wrote from Newcastle on the 1st May to his mother, we learn that his brother-in-law, Will Balneaves, Peggy's husband had emigrated to Broken Hill, Australia. *"Well send his address in your next letter for I would like to meet Will for he is a decent fellow"*, Jack wrote. It seems he was on friendlier terms with his brother-in-law than his sister. The 1911 UK census shows that the Balneaves lived in Spennymoor, a mining village six miles south of Durham City. Will was aged 34, and a photographer, Peggy now calling herself Marguerite, was aged 29, and their children were Martha aged 9, John aged 8 and George was aged 5. Will had emigrated to Broken Hill, an isolated mining town, 680 miles west of Sydney and 310 miles north east of Adelaide, an unlikely destination for a photographer from Durham. Marguerite and the children did not sail for Australia until 1st March 1916, their migration perhaps hampered by the outbreak of war in 1914 and a consequent shortage of shipping.

Jack's next letter signalled a major change in his life. After nearly two and a half years on the KOORINGA, he wrote on the 11th June from 616 Bourke Street, West Melbourne and told his mother:
> *"I have left the KOORINGA and am having a spell ashore in Melbourne. I left the KOORINGA last week and I have been laid up with influenza between the West and Melbourne, so I finished up when we got in, but I am beginning to fell all right".*

With the letter he sent a PO for ten pounds so his mother would be *"all right for the next three months".* Jack promised to get his photograph taken before leaving Melbourne as he was approaching his 21st birthday on 2nd July 1913. His recuperation however took longer than expected.

Studio Portrait of Jack, taken in July 1913 in Melbourne to mark his 21st birthday. He wrote on the 11th August 1913. "I got my photo taken before I laid up. I am sending you and enlargement and three small ones." An enlargement currently graces the sign of the Kirkpatrick pub (former Marine college), Ocean Road, South Shields.

Image Courtesy of the AWM PO1446.001

Sarah was left in suspense for two months, worrying about the health of her beloved son as he did not write again until the 11th August, by which time he was staying at 303 Raglan Street, Port Melbourne.

"Well Mother, I had six weeks holiday after leaving the KOORINGA and I was going to go to sea the next week when I got a very bad dose of cold. I have been in bed about a month and am just beginning to get about again. It has given me a shaking I can tell you for I am as weak as a rat, I was about 12 stone six before I was sick, and I have lost about 8 pounds in weight, I look properly consumptive. I got my photo taken before I was laid up. I am sending you an enlargement and three small ones. Well mother, I hope you and Annie are keeping all right and things are going all right at home for I cant send any more money until I start again for I am dead broke. I hope to be able to start again about next week. If I feel strong enough for a man don't want to be feeling so very weak to be firing on this coast now that summer is coming once again, so with love to you and Annie,
I remain,
Your Loving Son
Jack"

Jack's illness sounds much more serious *'than a bad dose of cold'.* It is a pity that he does not tell us what medical attention he received and who was the good Samaritan who tended him at 303 Raglan Street. It would be interesting to know who lived at this address and if it was a boarding house or private home. During his mining days in New South Wales, he told his mother quite a lot about his landlords and landladies. His letter is surprisingly short after an interval of two months. Poor Sarah had to wait even longer, over four months, for the next letter from her now not so dutiful son. He sent only one more letter that year dated 31st December 1913 from the SS TARCOOLA, Port Pirie, South Australia. He opened with the usual greeting:

"Dear Mother,
Just a line to let you know that I am still alive and kicking. Well Mother you will be wondering why I have been so long in writing, well things have been bad with me this last few months so it was no good writing as I had nothing to send, I am firing in this ship, she is a pretty fair job, but I am in pretty good trim just now and I feel as fit as a fiddle, I was weighed last night and I went 12 stone 5 lbs so that I am

in pretty good nick for to be working in the stokehole, for I have no soft fat on me…..I believe you have been keeping poorly lately, I wish I could send you some of my good health, but I suppose the winter is just as miserable as ever in the old country, Now I am sitting under the shade of the forecastle head and the heat is about 105 degrees in the shade for it is the middle of summer here now. I met a chap named Jackson here in Pirie last trip, he is working as a bricklayer in the smelting works and his brother is a cook on the Prophet. I was with them both last night, they used to live in the same lane as us in Frederick St. you know there mother."

The tone of Jack's letter shows he had recovered his appetite, health and ebullience, but only two letters sent home in six months? Was there something he was not telling his mother? Jack acknowledged receipt of all his mother's letters and Christmas cards from Annie and sister, Sarah Christie, but no mention is made of Peggy. If Peggy was still 'persona non grata' at Bertram Street, and with her husband in Broken Hill, she must have had a lonely Christmas. Jack Jackson would become a mate of Jack on his next ship the YANKALILLA.

The frequency of Jack's letters did not pick up in the New Year of 1914. His first dated 1st March was sent from the SS YANKALILLA, Sydney. He went onto explain:

*"Just a line to let you know that I am still alive and kicking. I wrote you a letter a couple of months and sent you three pound. I expect that you have got it by now. (*He does not apologise for not writing January or February) *I had a row with the chief on the TARCOOLA and I finished up and I was out of work for three weeks before I joined this one".*

Jack talked at length about a man mentioned in his previous letter, a bricklayer called Jackson who was, thanks to Jack, working as a trimmer on the YANKALILLA. His final paragraph was very telling.

" It is four years since I left home, how the time does fly, but if I can hang this ship down for another twelve months, I will have a run home, I am beginning to get tired of this country, I think I would be just as well sailing out from home, for the money is getting bigger at home, and the money goes out sharp here."

212

After four years, Jack's love affair with Australia had petered out and the old 'louse-bound country' with its Dukes and Lords did not look so bad after all. A letter sent by Jack on the 9th April 1914 from the YANKALILLA at Melbourne is longer and more informative than the previous two. His correspondence was evidently having difficulty catching up with him, so he reminds his mother to send everything to the Seaman's Mission at Stockton, Melbourne. He sent his thanks to Annie for sending him his favourite cigarettes, Woodbines. Jack Jackson was still trimming to him and getting on all right.

> "*I was showing him around Melbourne last night, he was surprised to see such a fine city for Newcastle on Tyne is not a patch on Melbourne. That's the worst of you people in the old country, you all seem to think Australia is all bush land but there are finer and more up to date cities out here than a lot of the cities at home*".

Well said Jack. Architects and town planners in the new dominions had the space to work with and were unhampered by a legacy of cramped streets and ancient buildings dating back centuries. Jack tried to correct a patronising and insular view that persisted in the UK for a long time. The feud with Peggy was still raging however.

> "*Now you were telling me in your last letter you had had Peggy staying with you. Now mother, why don't you have a bit of sense about you, and keep her out of your house, you should know by now that whatever you did for Peggy, she would not have a good word to say about you even if you gave her your all, and as regards her talking about you, you can tell her I will ring her neck if I get home before she gets away*".

Sarah had asked Jack if he had seen Will Balneaves. He had not. "*If he wanted to get in touch with me, he could easily have got my address from you, but he has never wrote to me so I have not wrote to him. It is very strange, he has not been able to get Peggy and the kids out before now, for I know lots of fellows who paid half the fare, and paid the other half after they got their wives out and they have been out inside of three months of making the application in Melbourne.*" Will Balneaves, it seems was in no hurry to be re-united with Peggy.

Jack ended by re-affirming his intentions. "*I am going to be home about June next year if I can save up a few quid by then*". This letter had the usual PS with a money order for three quid.

Sarah Simpson's lot was not a happy one. Her relationship with her eldest daughter Peggy or Maggie as she had been christened was bitter and fractious. Peggy was the only surviving child from Sarah's time in Leith, and an affectionate relationship with her daughter would have made life so much happier for her. Moreover the correspondence with Jack tells us Sarah was often 'poorly'. The news that her only son was coming home after an absence of four years must have brought joy to Sarah's heart. Sarah's situation is all the more poignant as we, the readers, know the end of the story.

Jack wrote to his mother again from the YANKALILLA on the 5th May from Port Pirie. He was sorry to hear that she had been poorly; he asks her to tell Annie he has received her letter and the Gazettes; he had also received a letter from Customs and Excise in Sydney saying they were holding a box for him, (The box of cigarettes sent earlier in the year by Annie) and he then indulges in a bit of nostalgia.

> "*I am going to try and hang this ship down for another eight or nine months then I am coming home, so see and start looking your best for next year, for I am getting sick and tired of knocking about out here, and you know the old saying that 'every bird likes its own nest Best', so you can look for me next year even if I land home broke*".

Three weeks later, on the 30th May 1914, Jack wrote again from the YANKILILLA in Melbourne, following receipt of a letter from Annie, who had enclosed a photograph of herself. Annie had also told Jack that Peggy had been stirring matters at home, claiming that Jack had been writing to her. This claim provoked an indignant reply from Jack to his Mother.

> "*The only letters I have wrote to the old country since I left, were to you and Annie, for I have not even answered Sarah's letters and for all the love I have for Peggy, it would not be worth the trouble of wasting good writing paper over her. I wrote a couple of letters to her when I was on the Heighington and that was the only letters that I wrote in my life to Peggy, and the only ones that I am ever likely to write to her.*"

There was no sign of peace breaking out in South Shields.

Jack's final letter as a civilian, sent shortly after his 22nd birthday on the 6th July 1914 from the YANKILILLA in Newcastle, was very brief, and he apologised for writing in pencil as he had no ink. His main concern was his mother's health and wellbeing. He sent a P.O. for three quid, making fifteen in total since joining this ship. He exhorts his mother, *"I will be home next year, so see and be looking your very best for next year.*

Woodbine Cigarettes, an essential in Jack's life. Jack added a PS to a letter in July 1914, "Tell Annie he got the box of fags alright, also the fags in her letter, and thank her for being so kind." The 5 packet cost 2 pence, the 10 packet cost 4 pence. Jack had to collect his fags from the Customs House in Sydney.

Image KY Collection

In his P.S. (Jack liked post scripts and almost every letter had one) he asks his mother to tell Annie that *"he got the box of fags alright, also the fags in her letter, and thanks her for being so kind".*

Eight days before Jack's 22nd birthday on 28th June, an assassination took place in the streets of Sarajevo. A 19 year old Serbian nationalist, Gavrilo Princip, stepped into the road and shot the heir to the Austrian throne, Archduke Franz Ferdinand and his wife, Sophie, the Duchess of Hohenburg as they passed in an open car. If the event was reported in the Australian newspapers, it did not register with Jack. However those shots ignited a fast burning fuse. By the time the YANKILILLA and Jack returned to Fremantle in August, Britain and her Empire had declared war on Germany and her allies on the 4th August. 'It would be all over by Christmas' was the widely held view. No one could imagine the horror as millions of men were killed and maimed over the next four years which would be known infamously as the GREAT WAR.

Primary Sources

Crew Agreements for HEIGHINGTON and YEDDO - Maritime History Archives, Newfoundland
J. S. Kirkpatrick's Letters - Australian War Memorial, Canberra, AWM DRL/3424
Burgess Rolls 1912 – 1913, South Shields Library
UK Census 1911, South Shields, Spennymoor and Newcastle

Chapter 10

No. 202 PTE. SIMPSON, J.

The next letter in the Australian War Memorial files was written by Jack from the Y.M.C.A. Military Tent, Blackboy Camp, Western Australia and dated 13th September 1914, the Australian Medical Corp. On 23rd August in Perth, Captain D McWhae had found Jack 'fit for active service' and on the 25th August, Jack completed his attestation paper at Blackboy Camp, 35 kilometres from Perth.

"Dear Mother,

Just a line to let you (know) that we are still in camp yet. We are expecting to get orders to hand at any minute, for the Old Country. I left you 4 Shillings per day out of my pay. We are only to have 5 shillings per (day) and one Shilling per day deferred pay. They have chopped our wages down one shilling per day. So you can take two Shillings for yourself and put two Shillings per day in the Bank for me when I come home from the war. I will be having a good holiday. I have made an order for my wages to be made payable at the Commonwealth Bank in London, so that you will have no difficulty in drawing your money. Now mother, I wrote to the Mission at Stockton and asked to have my letters all forwarded on to my home address at Bertram Street. Now there will be one important letter that I want you to take of for me. There are some Tickets in the letter for the Tasmanian Lottery and I might have a prize in my Numbers, so take care of them till I get home. Now Mother, I wrote to you last week telling you about that three pounds that the Post Master at Stockton was forwarding onto to you. Now Mother, I think that I will now draw to a close hoping that this will find you and Annie in good health as it leaves me at present, and with love to you and Annie.

I remain

Your Loving Son

Jack xxxx"

Jack at Blackboy Camp. When Sarah wrote on 3rd September she didn't know Jack had jumped ship once more, and was already training at Blackboy Camp near Perth, in Western Australia, as No 202 Private John Simpson, a stretcher bearer in 'C' Section, 3rd Field Ambulance A.I.F.
Image courtesy of the A.W.M. AO2827

Tantalisingly the letter which he wrote a week earlier is missing from the archive. It might have explained why he decided to enlist in the Australian Imperial Force. The letter dated around the 6th September was written shortly after he joined up, and would have informed his mother of his new address, why he had joined up and why he was using the name Simpson. No letter around this date is quoted in Tom Curran's book "Across the Bar" or Graham Wilson's book "Dust Donkeys and Delusions" although both authors researched the letters thoroughly. Perhaps it was lost or misfiled when in the possession of Sir Irving Benson. Did Jack enlist out of a sense of patriotic duty, or in order to get home to his mother and sister? He had no great love for what he had called a 'louse bound country', nor for its political system and its Dukes, Lords and Capitalists. He had been promising his mother and sister Annie, that he was coming home to "canny ould Shields", however.

In his letter of the 13th September, Jack mentioned he had left instructions with the Seaman's Mission at Stockton to have his letters forwarded to his home address at Bertram Street, South Shields. As a result, two of Sarah Simpson's letters to her son were returned and survive in the Australian War

Memorial collection. These were dated August 17th and September 3rd 1914, some 6-8 weeks before Sarah knew that Jack had enlisted in the Australian Imperial Force, as it generally took 6 weeks for Jack's letters to reach his mother. War had broken out on the 4th August and Sarah's letters show the effect on the minds of the civilian population in Britain. As the German Army smashed through Belgium, atrocities were committed when men, women and children, even priests were executed. When news of these events was published in the press, anxieties gripped the country. These were fuelled further by propaganda and the fear of invasion was palpable. Spy mania spread like wildfire and everyone of German origin became suspect, even naturalised citizens. Eventually all were rounded up and sent to internment camps. Many innocent people were victimised groundlessly. Sarah's letters reflected the feelings of the masses at this moment in time.

WE'RE DOING OUR DUTY
The Pier
FOR KING AND COUNTRY AT SOUTH SHIELDS

"We're doing our duty". War was declared at 11pm on the 4th August 1914. Men flocked to the colours. Sarah wrote to Jack on 3rd September 1914 "Shields is full of soldiers and territorials... I am thankful your far away from hear now". She didn't know that Jack had already enlisted in AIF a week earlier.

Image KY Collection

The German Seaman's Mission in South Shields was closed for the duration of the war and the Pastor was interned. German ships in Tyne Dock were impounded and seamen interned. The Mission Building was converted to a hospital manned by V.A.D. staff (Voluntary Aid Detachment). Conversely about 150 Shields seamen were detained in Germany.

Image KY Collection

SOUTH SHIELDS, ENGLAND Deutsches Seemannsheim

Her second letter dated September 3rd 1914 illustrates this little known aspect of war on the home front.

September 3rd 1914
14 Bertram Street,
South Shields

My dearest Jack,

Only a few lines hoping that you are still keeping in good health as this leaves me at present, but Jack, England is in terrible trouble with this awful war. God knows how it is going to end, it is awful to think about it. The people here are terrified for if the Germans got into England they will stick at nothing, look at the terrible atrocities that they have committed in Belgium, and they will do worse here for they hate the English for taking the part of France, we have been waiting for news since Sunday but there is nothing yet. I can tell you it's making the people very anxious. We have already lost about 6000 soldiers and God knows how many poor souls will have gone by now. What a lot of young fellows are enlisting. Shields is full of Soldiers and Territorials. They are guarding all the principal places and this place is full of German spies. I heard today that Fisher of the pork butchers shop in Frederick (Street) has been caught sending carrier pigeons to Germany. What do you think of naturalised British, they want hanging, it's too good for them, they should be rosted alive, the traitors, and make an example of them. Our Navy had a Battle with the Germans and they sunk 5 of their ships, but we hope our fleet will be able to keep the Germans out of England. My dearest Jack, I am thankful that you are away from here now, but I hope that this war will soon be over and things go quietly again for its terrible to think of what might happen but we will just live in hope and trust for the best. I sent you some papers last week and am sending some just now so I hope that you will get them, but they will be stale news when you get them for you get all the news in Australia, but Australia is responding handsome to help England out. All countries are doing the same and good luck to them for they think that England is fighting a just cause. I wish to God the right should win. Now my dearest lad, I wonder if this war will keep me from seeing you again. I hope not, but I will live in the hope. Now my dearest son, I will have to stop for I am broken hearted and cannot settle. I am worried to death and cannot help it. Now with love and best wishes from your ever loving and affectionate Mother

Good night and God bless you and take care of you. xxxxx Write soon for I feel crazy.

It is impossible to read his mother's letter and not feel tears of compassion welling up inside. We know, but she did not, that Jack was already a soldier waiting to join this 'terrible war'. We also know the end of the story.

Jack wrote again on the 14th October from Blackboy Camp. He was expecting to leave any moment. The transport and war ships were in Fremantle, but the departure of the 20,000 contingent was delayed, Jack thought, by the presence of six German warships in the Pacific Ocean. He was well informed. The destination of the Australian Imperial Force was expected to be Aldershot in England before going to the war in France – *"So I will be able to come up and see you and Annie pretty often before we go to the front"*. He gave his mother an address to write to:

Private Jack Simpson, Number 202, C Section, 3 Field Ambulance, Australian Army Medical Core, 1st Australian Contingent, England

Sarah Simpson's emotions must have been in turmoil. She was going to see *'her dearest lad'* after an absence of 4 years, but he was on his way to the trenches in Europe.

Jack had no time to write further before 'C' Section, 3rd Field Ambulance marched out of Blackboy Camp to board their transport the SS MEDIC at Fremantle. At 6.25am on the 1st November, the ANZAC armada put to sea, in spite of the continuing presence of German raiders in the Pacific.

SS Medic built in 1899 in Belfast for the White Star Line for their Australia run. She also served as an Australian troopship during the Boer War.
Image KY

WHITE STAR LINE.

TWIN-SCREW S.S. "MEDIC," 12,222 TONS.

Sinking of the German Cruiser, EMDEN. The First Contingent of ANZACs sailed from Fremantle on the 1st November 1914. The EMDEN, a threat to the convoy was engaged by HMAS SYDNEY and sunk off the Cocos Islands – Australia's first triumph of the war.
Image KY Collection

H.M.A.S. SYDNEY & MELBOURNE SINKING THE GERMAN CRUISER EMDEN

On the 9th November, the radio operator at a British Wireless Station on the Cocos Islands managed to get off a signal that he was being attacked by the German cruiser EMDEN. The Australian cruiser HMAS SYDNEY was detached from the convoy and caught the EMDEN like a sitting duck at the Cocos Islands. The SYDNEY found the EMDEN at anchor and after a brief 25 minutes of action, the EMDEN was sunk. The SYDNEY returned in triumph to her convoy duties. Australia had notched up her first victory of the war. Legend has it that the troops on board SS MEDIC rushed on deck when the news came, leaving their pannikins of beer on the mess table. When 'C' Section returned to the mess they found Private Simpson had remained behind and emptied all their pannikins – a tale perhaps exaggerated over time.

H.M.A.S. Sydney returning home victorious

Image KY Collection

The convoy with the First contingent of the Australian Imperial Force (AIF) reached Alexandria at the Mediterranean end of the Suez Canal on the 9th December where disembarkation commenced. To the disappointment of Jack and many other Brits in the AIF, they would be continuing their basic training in the Egyptian desert around Cairo, rather than at Aldershot in England. Quite simply there was no accommodation for the Australians in England. As a result of Lord Kitchener's appeal for volunteers 'Your Country Needs You', men were joining the colours at a rate of 20,000 a day during August 1914, culminating in a peak of 33,000 in one day in September (as much as the first and second Australian contingents combined). A Canadian contingent already in Britain were still living in tents on Salisbury Plain in December while huts were being built, and were drilling in rain, mud and cold. Perhaps the desert in Egypt was slightly less uncomfortable.

CAIRO—NEW ZEALAND TROOPS PASSING CAMEL STREET, 23RD DEC., 1914.

SERIE No. 1218-4

New Zealand troops passing through Cairo. The ANZACs progress to the Great War halted at Mena Camp, Cairo, Egypt. There was no room for them in Britain where barracks and training camps were overwhelmed with volunteers. Jack wrote home from Mena 20th December 1914.

Image KY Collection

Captain McWhae, with the men of 'C' Section, having travelled from Alexandria to Cairo by train and tram, arrived at Mena Camp about 11.14pm on the 12th December. Jack Simpson wrote his first letter home from Egypt on the 20th December 1914.

Dear Mother,

Just a line to let you know that we arrived in Cairo last week. We were 42 days on the trip and we had a very fine trip through. We are camped about ten miles out of Cairo at the entrance of the desert you can see nothing but sand, sand, sand. We have got two pyramids about 300 yards from our tents. It is a terrible long climb to the top of one of the pyramids. There is 100,000 troops in this camp that is with English troops and Indians. They are expecting the Turks to advance on Cairo they are building a light railway across the desert to reach Cairo. I wish that they would hurry up and come for everybody is getting impatient to have a brush up with the Turks. I am afraid that when they do come they will get a pretty hot reception, when they do come they will find everybody ready for them.

Now from the 25th October you should be drawing 2 shillings a day I am getting 6 shillings per day, 5 shillings per day and one shilling deferred pay and I am drawing one shilling per day for pocket money and am leaving you 2 shillings per day to you. Now I am having 2 shillings per day to my account in the Commonwealth Bank in London. The grub in this camp is very bad. We have to buy nearly as much as they would think that they were feeding a lot of sparrows instead of hungry men.

Now Mother I hope that you and Annie are keeping well for I am in the best of health. It will soon be Christmas and a pretty miserable (one) here by the looks of things. Now mother I think I will draw to a close hoping that this will find you and Annie in the best of health and with love to you and Annie.

I remain
Your loving son
Jack

Jack wrote again on Christmas Day and had not yet received a letter from home. His morale was low, reminiscent of his first ever letter home when he sailed on the HEIGHINGTON four years earlier.

Dear Mother,

Just a line to let you know I am still in Cairo. It is Christmas Day. I was looking forward to spending today in Shields but I was doomed to be disappointed. I would not have joined this contingent if I had known they were not going to England. I would have taken a trip home and had a holiday at home and then joined the army at home and went to the front instead of being stuck in this ungodly hole for all that you can see is sand and drill from morning to night and the grub is very poor and not half enough of it. I have lost about a stone in weight since I joined the contingent for when I joined I went 12 stone 7 pound and I don't go near 12 stone now. What sort of Christmas did you have at Shields. I suppose that everything is pretty quiet on account of the war.

Now Mother when we left Australia I made out a form for to leave you two shillings per day all the time that I am in the Australian Army. I hope you are drawing it all right and I am having two shillings per day put into my account in the Commonwealth Bank in London, and I am drawing one shilling per day pocket money, and I have to spend it all on grub for we don't get enough to eat. You will be drawing your money through the commonwealth Bank in London so I hope that you are drawing it all right. I made it over to Sarah Simpson as I am in the name of Jack Simpson here in the Section. I hear we are likely to move from here in about six weeks time, and whether we are to go to England or to the continent I cannot tell you. But I hope that we go to England for I would give anything to have a run up to Shields to see you and Annie before I went to the front. I see by the papers that the Germans have killed lot of people in Hartlepool; they were pretty close to Shields. I hope they don't get as near again for I would not like to see poor old Shields knocked about by the Germans, but they will have to pay the piper for it all in the long run. I would like to have the pleasure of putting a bullet through the dammed old Kaiser for he is the start of the lot. But it is just as well for it to happen now, for it had to happen sometime. Now mother, I hope these few lines will find you and Annie well as it leaves me at present, so with love to you and Annie.

I remain, your loving son
Jack

Depose G.L.

Australian Horsemanship
in Egypt

Australian Horsemanship in Egypt.   When not drilling and marching, the ANZACs enjoyed the flesh pots of Cairo. They had 5/-(shillings) per day to spend, compared with the British Tommy who had 1/-(shilling) per day. The writer of the card stated this form of transport back to camp cost about a shilling.

Image KY Collection

Arrival of mail at Mena Camp. Every ex-serviceman will tell you that the arrival of mail from home was the highlight of the day. The lucky found a quiet corner to read and re-read their letters; the unlucky returned to work in disappointed silence.

Image Courtesy AWM PS0660

Jack instructed his mother Sarah, to use her own name 'Simpson' when drawing her allotment. In the 1911 Census, Sarah signed her name as 'Kirkpatrick'. It seems likely that Jack was still unaware that his parents were never married.

On 16th December 1914, a misty morning, German cruisers fired upon the town of Hartlepool on the north east coast of England, some 30 miles from South Shields. A piece of shrapnel stopped a bedroom alarm clock at three minutes past eight am. The people panicked in fear of an invasion; 500 people were injured and 152 men, women and children were killed, the first civilian casualties of the war in Britain. The attack did not herald invasion, however, but was an attempt to draw part of the British Grand Fleet into the open. Admiral Fisher did not rise to the bait. The British North Sea Fleet remained in its safe anchorages in the firth of Forth and at Scapa Flow in the Orkneys.

Jack, aggrieved at being bogged down in Egypt, wished he had gone home first and then joined up to have a crack at the Germans. If he had, he would not have been able to provide an allowance for his mother. The British Tommy was paid only one shilling a day compared with the generous five shillings a day paid by the Australian Government to their recruits.

Jack's next letter, dated 3rd January 1915, tells us that the mail from England had finally caught up with him.

> *Dear Mother,*
> *Just a line to let you know that I received your Christmas cards and one from Annie. It was very kind of you both to send me Christmas cards and I got them yesterday morning. I am glad to hear that you and Annie are keeping well for I am keeping well enough here considering the grub we get but I have lost a good bit of weight since I first joined the contingent. I am sorry that there is not much news to tell you from here for life is pretty much the same day in and day out and it is just the regular routine of work of the army marching and drilling.*
>
> *It is not a bad sort of life taking it all together and at any rate it is a much easier life than working one's life in a stokehole but everybody is wishing they would make a move out of this place either to England or the front. I would like to have a month in England before*

we go to the front. I see that there has been another English
battleship lost in the Channel that is a bit more that the British will
have to take out of Germany's hide for she knows it is only a matter
of time with her. I see by this morning's paper Australia is going to
send another 100,000 men. I am not surprised for men were just
simply going mad out there to go to the war. There was many a man
envied us first contingent men for being so lucky to get off to the war.
Well Mother I think that I will draw to a close now with love to you and
Annie (etc.)

At this date, the AIF still expected to go to England or more likely the
Western Front. On January 2nd 1915, the British Government received a plea
for help from their Russian ally. The Turks with whom the Germans had
carefully cultivated an alliance before the war, were attacking their traditional
enemy, the Russians vigorously in the Caucasus region. The British War
Council, persuaded by Winston Churchill, First Lord of the Admiralty, agreed
on the 13th January to send the Royal Navy through the Dardanelles, the
straits connecting the Mediterranean to the Black Sea. With one master
stroke, the Allies could capture Constantinople; take Turkey out of the war;
open a supply route for war materials much needed by Russia; open the
gates into the Mediterranean for Russia's Black Sea Fleet; and pave the way
for a second front against the Austrian Empire. The Ottoman Empire
(Turkey) was known as 'The Sick Man of Europe'. As a military power she
was third rate, Churchill declared. The Navy with its 12 and 15 inch guns
would wipe out the Turkish forts in the Dardanelles and sail directly through
to Constantinople forcing the Turks to surrender. The army would not be
needed he told Field Marshall Lord Kitchener and the War Council. The
forces training in Egypt would still be available for service on the Western
Front, Churchill assured the War Council.

When Admiral Jackie Fisher, head of the Navy learned of the proposal he
was appalled, but his political boss Churchill would not allow his objection to
be expressed to the War council who therefore assumed the plan had full
naval support.

Jack had time on his hands for letter writing and another followed on the 10th
January. He reassured his mother that the German Navy were unlikely to
repeat the attack on England's north east coast. He did not have much news
he said but he did ask:

"What did the people at home think about the Sydney sinking the Emden. The Sydney belonged to the Australian Navy and was escorting the first contingent from Australia to Columbo, with five more Australian warships, when she left us one morning and when she came in sight again we heard that she had sunk the Emden. I can tell you things were pretty lively aboard all the ships in the convoy, there was 38 liners transporting us to Egypt. We had a pretty lively time on the Medic the day the Emden was sunk, the Medic was the transport we were on. The old Colonel called beer for all hands on board and we all drank to the health of the Sydney pretty deeply."

Jack of course says nothing to confirm the reports that he stayed below while his mates went on deck, and that he emptied their pannikins of beer.

Following receipt of the letters from his mother and Annie, Jack wrote again on the 17th January. He was sorry to hear that Sarah had not drawn any of the money he made over to her, but he says *"I am going to see my colonel as soon as he comes into camp today to see if he can sub me a few quid to send to you."* He had only a shilling a day to himself. Sarah should have received about 8 pounds accrued form the 25th October 1914. He blamed the mess up on the fact the first contingent landed in Egypt where there was no Commonwealth Bank, and he told his mother *"not to worry – for it will all come to you eventually ……….. As soon as I get things fixed up with the paymaster."* The notion of Jack approaching his Colonel for a sub is almost unthinkable. Was the AIF really so classless that a private could think of borrowing from his Colonel?

Jack also replied to Annie's letter on the same day. Most of the letter is devoted to banter. He teases her about *"turning down your sailor boy… after such glowing accounts in your last letters … My word women are such strange animals…. they are like the wind, very changeable, …… and he actually drank beer, well he must be a brute."* Annie must have proposed sending Jack a new watch, but he tells her not to *"for there are 99 chances out of a hundred I will not get it….Keep it until I get home."*
Annie's sailor boy however was not deterred and three years later Annie and he were married, though Annie ignored the advice from her late brother to marry a Fireman rather than an Able Seaman. His story, coming later, is also an interesting one.

The need to sort out his mother's allotment was pre-occupying Jack's mind. He followed up with another letter on the 24th January from Mena Camp. He explained that he had not been able to get a sub from his officer, but he had made out and signed a form for a Bank in London, *"but they want a copy of your signature….. I am making the order payable of 2/- per day from the 25th October …. Don't forget that I made the order payable to my Mother – Sarah Simpson, so the sooner that you write and tell me that everything is fixed up and drawing the money, the better pleased I will be. I have not received your parcel yet but I suppose I will get it later on."*

The AIF seems to have had problems with its paperwork and administration systems – not surprising for a new army that had no military history and no experience of going to war on the other side of the world.

Jack wrote three days later on 27th January. He was in the best of health, still in Mena with no signs of moving. There had been some fighting on the Suez Canal with the Turks and two battalions from the contingent had been sent down there. On money matters he says:

> *"I told you last week my officers had sent a form to Sir George Reid to see about my money paid over to you. I have wrote to the Manager of the Commonwealth bank in London today so you might be able to draw the money all the quicker….. write straight away to the Manager of the Commonwealth Bank in London and if necessary show him this letter and I think that you should be able to draw the money all right".*

One has to admire Jack for his persistence and determination to see his mother alright financially. Sir George Reid referred to in Jack's letter was none other than the Australian High Commissioner in London, and a former Australian Prime Minister for a short spell in 1904-1905. Jack had no qualms about going right to the top to resolve his problems, be it the Colonel or High Commissioner.

On January 28th, at a War Council meeting, Churchill allayed the anxieties of those council members with reservations about his plan by giving an undertaking that naval operations would be called off if serious obstacles were encountered.

Jack's pen had never worked so hard. He wrote again on the 30th January. He was pleased to hear: *"....that Annie had got such a fine job. I suppose that there will be no flies on her now seeing that she is a lady clerk. I hope that she likes her job for it is a nice easy one, at any rate there is no hard work attached to it. I am sorry to hear that the Germans have got the people so scared at home...... but I suppose that the English will have their turn soon for they will be sending about a million fresh men to the front this year then the war will start in earnest."*

According to Jack everyone in Egypt was fed up with the daily routine of camp life, drill and rout marches. *"There are nearly two hundred thousand troops in Egypt altogether and all of them looking most heartily forward to the coming fray and hoping that the Turks will hurry up across the desert and show themselves. Now Mother, I received your hamper the other day, and we had the loaves (fruit loaves presumably) for tea at our Mess Table, the boys were full of praise for your loaves for I told them that you baked them yourself..... Now Mother, I made out a form this week for Sir George Reid about that two shillings, so then he will hurry the Commonwealth Bank up and see that you draw your money every week regular".*

(Fruit loaves' presumably as bread loaves would not have lasted the journey).

Jack had a break from letter writing until 14th February when he took up his pen again to acknowledge receipt of newspapers and letters the previous day from his mother and Annie.

He passed his opinions on the loss by the Germans of the Blucher, their most powerful cruiser, sunk by a British squadron in the North Sea on the 24th January. The Germans were trying to repeat the raids made at Scarborough and Hartlepool the previous year. Jack then reported on hostilities in Egypt.

> *"There was a bit of fighting down on the canal last week. They let the Turks come right up to the Canal and start building a bridge across when the artillery opened fire and blew the Turks and the bridge to pieces and took a lot of prisoners there are about 500 Turkish prisoners in Cairo. It was our Indian troops that were stationed at a place where the Turks tried to cross and you can guess that they gave the Turks more than they could do with.*

Now Mother I don't know when we will be making a move from here but the second contingent has arrived in Egypt... I heard that the first contingent is likely to go to Marseilles about the back end of March but you cant believe anything you hear in this place We hear such a terrible lot of rumours. But the sooner they make a move the better we will all like it for this is a dull place and if we went to France we might get a chance to run over to England when it comes our time for furlough. Now Mother I see by your letter yesterday that you have not drawn any money yet but as soon as Sir George Reid gets that letter which my officer sent him you will be able to get the money through him and you will be able to get all that is due to you in a lump sum. Now Mother I will draw to a close..........."

Jack was still hopeful of going to France but the next day 15th February his destiny and that of the ANZACs was decided at the War Council meeting in London. The members were stunned when an Admiralty War Office staff memorandum was read out to them – *"A naval attack on the Dardanelles was not a sound proposition, unless undertaken as a joint amphibious operation. A large military force was considered essential to assist in the assault from the outset or at the very least to be on hand to seize and hold ground won, once the forts had been silenced."* Now for the first time the War council was made fully aware of the Navy's true appreciation of the situation. Churchill claimed that this had come to him as a revelation, although he had known full well the views of Lord Fisher for a fortnight. Four days later on February 19th, Churchill informed the Council it was no longer possible to abandon the naval attack on the Dardanelles. A setback would be a serious blow to Allied morale, whereas victory would be a turning point in the war. Churchill insisted on the participation of British troops with a typically Churchillian phrase, *"to reap the fruits of victory."*

At a further meeting on 24th February, the War council agreed to send a force of 130,000, in spite of objections from Kitchener, on the grounds that Britain could not be seen to lose face politically and militarily. A force sufficiently strong to defeat a third rate power like turkey had to be sent. The plan for the Dardanelles was widely published in the press, and the British public were eagerly following the progress of the fleet. The Turks were equally interested in the news which gave them two months to increase their troops in the Gallipoli peninsula from one division to six divisions (84,000 men) and to fortify potential landing sites with machine gun posts and artillery emplacements. Churchill's manipulation of the War Council provides a master class in political machination.

Jack sent a hasty letter on the 28th February.

> *"Dear Mother*
> *Just a line to let you know we are leaving Egypt today, I don't know where we are bound for but I hope it will be England or France. Now mother you will have to excuse short note as we are all in a hustle and bustle to get the transport waggons packed and leave this afternoon, so with love to you and Annie.*
> *I remain*
> *Your Loving Son*
> *Jack"*

Ironically the Turks knew better than Jack where he was going. Around the same time Jack sent a Field Service Postcard to his mother but the date stamp is illegible.

> *"Dear Mother*
> *Just a note to let you know I am keeping in the best of health. I received your letters and papers. I have had a letter from the Bank in London and I have got to write to Perth so that you will be getting the money all right soon. With love to you and Annie.*
> *Your Loving Son*
> *Jack"*

This was Jack's last reference to *"that two shillings a day"* he had allocated to his mother. Apparently Sir George Reid's intervention was successful thus relieving Jack of one worry.

At home in South Shields, Sarah and Annie had an anxious wait of about six weeks for another communication from Jack. Meantime they read the newspapers avidly for any information they could find about the Australian Imperial Force. When a card did arrive it told them little. Third Field Ambulance, C Section sailed from Egypt on the transport ship MALDA arriving at Mudros on the Greek island of Lemnos on the 9th March, about 60 miles from the landing ground at Anzac Cove. Much of the next seven weeks was spent on board the MALDA as the 3rd Field Ambulance practised disembarkation and landing drill, but Jack could not tell his mother any of this. His card written on 14th April simply said:

> "Dear Mother
> Just a line to let you know I am keeping well. We are still at anchor yet. I can't give you any news as the censor will not pass the card. Hoping that this will find you and Annie well, so with love from you loving son Jack."

3rd Field Ambulance, Jack's Unit. For 7 weeks at Lemnos, the Field Ambulance practiced disembarking, and transporting their gear and casualties in the landing boats. Jack possibly, lying with hands behind head?

Image Courtesy of AWM PO2902.001

Practice Landing at at Lemnos, a Greek Island in the Aegean Sea. Jack left Egypt on the 18th February 1915, not knowing where he was going. By the time the invasion forces reached Lemnos, 60 miles from Gallipoli, they knew their enemy would be the Turks.

Image Courtesy of AWM PS1447

Sarah and Annie would have read in the papers that the British and French fleets suffered a humiliating defeat on the 18th March when 18 battleships, 12 cruisers, 22 destroyers and several minesweepers failed to force the entrance to the Dardanelles. The Turks lost four guns (out of 180) and 40 men were killed, compared to a loss by the allies of six battleships (3 sunk and 3 crippled) and around 700 sailors killed. Churchill was furious but Sarah and Annie had the comfort that Jack was still alive and well. The Turks very unsportingly, had heavily mined the passageway through the Dardanelles.

Two days before the landings, Jack wrote his last letter home on the 23rd April 1915.

> *"Dear Mother*
> *Just a line to let you know that I am still keeping well. We did not go to ……..(censored) as I expected. I have not had any letters from you for nearly a month. Just address your letters to Egypt same as before and they will be sent to me here. I can't tell you where we are for the censor would cross it out, but you will be hearing about the Australians as soon as we make a start, hoping this finds you and Annie as it leaves me at present.*
> *With love from your loving son*
> *Jack"*

Such was the delay in the post that Sarah Simpson did not receive this letter until the 19th May, the day Jack's life ended.

The Shields Gazette of Tuesday 27th April gave Sarah and Annie their first inkling that the British Forces had made a start quoting a press bureau report that *'large forces had landed (in the Dardanelles) under protection of the fleet.'* This was followed on the 29th by a brief paragraph stating that allied troops were steadily advancing – not much information to ease the mind of an anxious mother. On the 1st May, the Gazette published a longer report issued by the War Office at 3.30pm on Friday 30th April.

> "THE DARDANELLES
> Colonials at Grips with the Turks.
> GOOD PROGRESS MADE
> *The following statement is issued by the War Office and the Admiralty on the progress of the operations in the Dardanelles from April 25th to the 27th.*

235

The disembarkation of the army began before sunrise on the 25th. Six different beaches were used and the operation was covered by the whole fleet. The landing was immediately successful on five beaches although opposed with vigour by a strongly entrenched enemy in successive lines protected by barbed wire entanglements in some places 50 yards wide and supported by artillery.

On the sixth beach, near Sedd el Bahr, the troops could not advance until the evening when a fine attack by British Infantry from the direction of Cape Tekeh relieved the pressure on their front. The arrangements for the landing had been concerted in the utmost detail between the fleet and the army."

Sarah scanned the report quickly looking for word of the Australians.

"The result of the first day's operations was the establishment of strong British, Australian and French forces at three main points, namely the Australian and New Zealand troops on the lower slopes of Sari Bahir to the north of Gaba Tepe, the British troops at Cape Tekeh, Cape Helles and Morto Bay, and the French force on the Asiatic shore at Kum Kale. After a gallant attack towards Yeni Shehr during the afternoon of the 25th, strong counter attacks by the enemy began and hard fighting took place. Meanwhile, the disembarkation of the army proceeded continuously favoured by good weather. Meanwhile the Australian and New Zealand troops at Sari Bahir who had pushed on with utmost boldness after landing on the 25th, had been engaged almost constantly with the enemy who made strong and repeated counter attacks which were invariably repulsed. The Australian and New Zealand troops fought with fine spirit and determination.

Early on the morning of the 27th, a fresh Turkish division was launched against Sara Bahir preceded by heavy artillery fire. A hot engagement followed. The enemy came on boldly time after time, but the Australian and New Zealand troops defeated every attempt and by 3pm had resumed the offensive.

On April 28th and 29th, the Allied forces rested and improved and consolidated their positions; and continued the disembarkation of stores and artillery. All counter attacks by the enemy which were incessant on the 28th, but weaker on the 29th, were repulsed".

When Jack wrote his letter of the 23rd April he was on board the transport ship DEVANHA, anchored off Mudros harbour on the Greek Island of Lemnos. The harbour was packed with an armada of ships of every size and description ranging from the small cutter which sped in and out collecting the mail, to a giant Russian cruiser, the ASKOLD, with five funnels nicknamed by the lads as the 'Packet of Woodbines'. The previous day, the 22nd April, Kenneth Fry, bearer officer of B Section (Curran 1994) recorded in his diary:

> *"At 8.30am McWhae told of practice embarkation into the torpedo boats (destroyers). RIBBLE alongside. Crawled down the ladder, men packed forward. Put off 50 yards then practised getting into the tows (rowing boats).'*

The 3rd Field Ambulance had been practising this drill for weeks. The reality was very, very different.

THE LANDING

The day after Jack wrote his final letter, 24th April, the DEVANHA and the rest of the invasion fleet weighed anchor and sailed for the Gallipoli beaches. At 11pm the convoy halted, and the destroyer RIBBLE pulled alongside. By 11.55pm the first part of the drill was complete and with the troops packed on deck, RIBBLE sailed on. The 3rd Brigade, supported by the 3rd Field Ambulance, had been selected as the covering force, and would be the first Australians to face the Turkish fire. At 1am on the 25th April, RIBBLE halted once more and the infantrymen of the 3rd Brigade, loaded with 200 rounds of ammunition, 3 days rations, full water bottles, rifle, bayonet and back pack began clambering down the rope ladders into the tows. A tow consisted of 3 lifeboats roped one behind another, pulled by a steam launch. By 2,30am loading was complete. At 3am the moon set. At 3.30am, the tows cast off and headed for the darkened beaches, timed to land at 4.30 am, just before dawn.

The bearers of the 3rd Ambulance, comprising of 3 officers, 3 NCOs, and 27 squads of four men carrying stretchers, with all available water bottles and surgical haversacks, were scheduled to follow in the second tow. As they waited they were already in the firing line. Captain McWhae on board the RIBBLE recollected:

> *"We waited our turn taking whatever cover we could on deck. The destroyer was under fire, several men were wounded. The rowboats returned......... we entered them under heavy fire. Then we rowed to the shore under a frightful fire...... Machine gun a few hundred yards north, near Fisherman's Hut...... the rowers showed great bravery. During the landing the bearer section of 3rd Ambulance lost 3 men killed and 14 wounded."*

The landing was opposed by severe machine gun and rifle fire. Casualties were heavy. At first the ambulance sections were pinned below the low cliffs, unable to attend the wounded strewn on the beach or struggling in the water. Sometime after dawn as the infantry drove the Turks from the ridges above the beach, the hail of bullets eased off; red cross flags went up at the collection points on the beach and the frantic work of the Field Ambulance teams began, though still exposed to shrapnel fire. By the second day, the Ambulance teams were suffering a shortage of stretchers as the wounded were evacuated to the hospital ships.

No 202 Private John Simpson Kirkpatrick, assisting an unidentified British Soldier.

Image Courtesy of AWM JO6392

No 202 Private John Simpson landed unscathed and carried stretchers all day on the 25th April with the other bearers. On the second day, Sergeant Hookway, reported him absent from the unit, but later he was found in possession of a donkey, working on his own initiative bringing in the wounded, his response to the lack of stretchers perhaps.

Contrary to British propaganda, the Turks defended their shores ferociously. By the 5th May, the ANZACS held a parcel of land only 1.5 kilometres from north to south and 0.5 kilometres at its widest – a position that remained unchanged for the rest of the campaign. During the period 25th April to 5th May, daily casualty rates were at their highest, tailing off for a spell thereafter as both sides dug in and consolidated their trench systems.

On 14th May, ADMS Howse, the senior medical officer signed a report on the actions of the medical personnel from the day of the landing to 1st May 1915. The report was submitted to 1st Division Headquarters where it was annotated as having been seen by General Bridges. In the report, Howse drew attention to the actions of a few specific individuals. He wrote:

"I cannot speak too highly of the work carried out by the Bearer Sub-division of Nos.1,2 and 3 Field Ambulances. They worked incessantly for 48 hours and on many occasions assisted the Regimental Stretcher Bearers in removing wounded men from the firing lines. The following names are submitted for consideration for Mention in Despatches as representative of the work done by personnel of AMC, 1st Australian Division, and attached:

No. 3 Field Ambulance

	Captain	*H.K. Fry*
No.9	*Sergeant*	*Gunn W*
167	*Sergeant*	*Hookway O.R.*
151	*L. Corp.*	*Farnham*
178	*Private*	*Rosser C.H.G.*
225	*Private*	*Watts H.T.*
202	*Private*	*Simpson J.*

(Letter ADMS Howse, 14th May 1915 (AWM 25 367/33)"

In the controversy as to whether Simpson Kirkpatrick should have received a gallantry honour in addition to his MID, it is important to note that the MID was granted for work in the first 48 hours and for assisting the Regimental Stretcher Bearers in bringing in wounded men from the firing lines (not a task of Field Ambulance Bearers according to the manual). A MID does not carry any citation spelling out the actions which earned the award. This is a pity. Sometime in that first two days when the fighting was at its most chaotic, Jack Simpson's conduct singled him out from the crowd, not for commandeering a donkey, but for displaying outstanding gallantry in bringing men in from the firing lines. This is confirmed in later testimony from his colleagues.

After the 5th May, when the battle lines stabilised, the Ambulance bearer sub-divisions reverted to their prescribed role of ferrying the wounded from the front line First Aid Posts to the Casualty Clearing Stations on the beach.

Jack however, continued to act with his donkey as an independent unit, and for the next two weeks became a familiar sight toiling up and down Shrapnel Gully. His independent action was condoned by his N.C.O's and officers who recognised the value of his work. Some detractors have claimed his work was no more valuable or no braver that that of the other bearers running the gauntlet in Shrapnel Valley. This claim ignores some crucial facts.

No. 202 Private John Simpson Kirkpatrick working with his donkey in Shrapnel Gully. On the morning of 19th May, Jack setting off with a passenger from the head of the gully was killed by a shrapnel ball (or bullet).

Image Courtesy AWM A03114

One man who did appreciate the service provided by Jack and Murphy wrote home from hospital in Alexandria.

"They took me to a dressing station where I was bandaged up and they said I could either go down to the beach on a donkey or wait till night. As it was 12.30, I preferred the donkey. I am glad I did, although I suffered some pain, but was on the operating table aboard ship by 3pm."

**Quote from a soldier in the 15th Battalion,
courtesy of Grant Malcolm, of Western Australia**

Grant Malcolm has made an in-depth, meticulous search of diaries, memoirs, letters and reports, referring to the 3rd Field Ambulance's operations at Anzac Cove and makes a very telling statement.

"The other 3rd Field Ambulance stretcher bearers were only on duty in Shrapnel Valley one day of every three, and then when the Turkish fire down the valley became too hot, they worked only at night. Simpson and his donkey, on the other hand, "worked all day and night throughout the whole period since the landing," according to eye witnesses Colonel John Monash, and Reverend Gillison, who succoured the wounded in the valley, wrote three weeks after Simpson's death how "he made as many as 16 trips on one day, caring nothing for shrapnel or snipers." So, whereas other stretcher bearers worked every third day in Shrapnel Valley, Simpson worked every day, sometimes long into the night. At any time he could have given up his work with the donkey and gone back to his unit where he would have been stretcher bearer one day in every three. He chose to continue his perilous work up the valley daily where, "the help rendered to the wounded was invaluable," as Monash wrote.

That Simpson went out when others found the fire too hot has long been part of the legend, courtesy of the CEW Bean despatch."

On 9th May, Jack snatched a few moments to fill in a 'Field Service Card', a pre-printed card giving the writer simple options to delete or leave. Addressed to his mother at 14 Bertram Street, South Shields, it conveyed his last message home.

"I am quite well.
I have received your letter dated March.
Letter follows at first opportunity.
I have received no letter from you lately.

Signature only – Jack Simpson 3rd Australians
Date, 9th May.

By the time the card reached home, Jack was already dead.

For another 10 days, Jack continued with his solo mission in a manner which won the admiration of all who observed him, officers and others ranks alike. His demeanour was described variously as cheery, whistling, singing, joking and contemptuous of danger. Was he brave or was he fearless – the two qualities are different?

The Turks launched a heavy attack on the ANZAC lines the night of the 18th/19th May. There was much work for the bearers the following morning. Jack had just picked up a passenger and was starting his descent, when his luck ran out. He was hit in the back by a bullet (some accounts say a shrapnel ball) which passed through his heart. Some of his mates placed the body in a nearby dugout from where they took him at 7 o'clock that evening to be buried at Hell Spit Cemetery. His passing was noted in a number of diaries by his colleagues. Here are just two instances.

> Sergeant J.E. McPhee, 19th May: *"Poor old Scotty Simpson killed by machine gun bullet in Shrapnel Gully this morning. Scotty Simpson will be much missed with his mates in Shrapnel Gully – his cheery face and droll ways known to a great many – particularly ambulance men."* **(Cochrane)**

Alfred (Chips) Adams, a close colleague of Simpson in 3rd Field Ambulance. They were in the same 36 man bearer section.

> *"May 19th Wednesday. Jack Simpson killed while leading donk and patients. J Fraser shot through wrist. Vic Master (sic) two bullets through thigh. Orders to sleep fully dressed and have to turn out for we are attacked by Turks (heavily) who are repulsed with terrible losses. Bury J Simpson in evening - large attendance.*
>
> *21 May. Make cross for Simpson, Hudson and Eccles and erect same on grave in afternoon….."* **(Malcolm.)**

Chip Adams survived Gallipoli but was killed August 19th 1916 at Pozieres on the Somme by a German machine gun. His diary was returned with his effects to his father in England who later donated it to the Australian War Memorial.

Perhaps the most unimpeachable witness to Jack's bravery was none other than Colonel John Monash (later Lt. General on the Western Front), commanding Officer of the 4th Australian Brigade who wrote to Divisional HQ on 20th May, the day following Simpson's death:

> "*I desire to bring under special notice, for favour of transmission to the proper authority, the case of Private Simpson, stated to belong to C Section of the 3rd Field Ambulance. This man has been working in this valley since 26th April, collecting the wounded, and carrying them to dressing stations. He had a small donkey which he used to carry all cases unable to walk.*
>
> *Private Simpson and his little beast earned the admiration of everyone at the upper end of the valley. They worked all day and night throughout the whole period since the landing, and the help rendered to the wounded was invaluable. Simpson knew no fear and moved unconcernedly amid shrapnel and rifle fire, steadily carrying out his self-imposed task day-by-day, and he frequently earned the applause of the personnel for his many fearless rescues of wounded men from areas subject to rifle and shrapnel fire.*
>
> *Simpson and his donkey were yesterday killed by a shrapnel shell and enquiry then elicited that he belonged to none of the AMC units with this brigade, but had become separated from his own unit and had carried out his perilous work on his own initiative.*"

The underlining is the author's addition. Jack Simpson Kirkpatrick was apparently fearless, a different kind of bravery. Most acts of gallantry are performed in spite of fear; they are performed from loyalty, from sense of duty, from honour, from an adrenalin rush, or even from a temporary fit of insanity as claimed by ADMS Howse who won a Victoria Cross in the Boer War for rescuing a wounded man between the firing lines. Jack's behaviour was not a one-off deed, but was sustained day in, day out for three weeks as he "moved unconcernedly amid shrapnel and rifle fire." Jack's bravery was a state of mind. "He knew no fear" observed Colonel Monash. Fear was lacking in Jack's character, a trait inherited from his seafaring father and grandfather perhaps.

POSTSCRIPT

Jack's behaviour in Shrapnel Gully was not the first time he had shown a lack of fear. When the Reverend Sir Irving Benson visited South Shields circa 1956, Jack's sister Annie took him to visit the 'Gut' in Tyne Dock, a cobbled ramp running into the river where horse drawn carts could be backed into the water for loading and unloading. The 'Gut' was a play area and when two small children fell in, Jack jumped in and saved them.

Mill Dam Gut c 1900, where carts would be loaded and unloaded from small boats. In 1956, Annie took Benson to see the Gut, the scene of Jack's first act of bravery when he jumped in to rescue two younger children.

Image South Tyneside images 0001639

In November 1933 when a statuette of Jack was unveiled in South Shield's Library, a boyhood friend of Jack was prompted to write to the Shields Gazette. He recounted how as a butcher's boy, he had to row out to a ship with a delivery of meat. Jack begged to be taken along. When on the water, Jack fell in and it took two attempts to haul him back into the boat. Jack's only concern was that his tabs (Woodbine cigarettes) were soaked. He was completely oblivious to the danger that he might have drowned. So is a lack of fear equivalent to bravery?

At the moment of his death, Jack Simpson Kirkpatrick was still a Geordie at heart. A few weeks later he would be resurrected in Australia's press as a Digger and a hero.

The Grave of No 202 Private John Simpson Kirkpatrick at Beach Cemetery, near ANZAC COVE. A Geordie Lad who gave his lifesaving wounded Australians.
Image KY Collection

Primary Sources
J.S. Kirkpatrick Letters. AWM 3DRL/3424, Australian War Memorial Archives, Canberra
202 Pte. Simpson J. Army Service Records. Australian National Archives

Secondary Sources
'*In The Shadow of The Man with The* Donkey' *(unpublished manuscript)* Grant Malcolm, W.A.
Report published 2013 – Tribunal inquiring into unresolved recognition for past acts of naval and military gallantry and valour. Chapter 15, Private John Simpson Kirkpatrick.
"**Across the Bar**", *1994. Tom Curran*
"**Simpson and the Donkey**" *1992, Peter Cochrane*
"**The Man with the Donkey**", *1965, Sir Irving Benson*
"**Gallipoli**", *2001, L.A. Carlyon*
"**Anzac to Amiens**", *1946, C E W Bean*
"**The Complete Victoria Cross**", *2010, Kevin Brazier*
South Shields Gazette, 1914

Chapter 11

EPILOGUE

Not for the first time, the A.I.F.'s administration systems let the Simpson/Kirkpatrick family down. Sarah Simpson and Annie Kirkpatrick received no immediate telegram, nor any letter of condolence from the A.I.F., to notify them of Jack's death. As a consequence they continued writing to him in the belief he was still alive. On 20th May Sarah wrote. On the 24th May Annie wrote, followed by another letter on 3rd June.

Shortly after Jack's Field Service card, written on the 9th May arrived at 14 Bertram Street, having taken approximately one month in transit. Annie responded on the 5th June, on behalf of herself and her mother who was too distraught to put pen to paper:

> "*Dear Jack,*
>
> *I just thought I would send you a few lines as the mail is leaving today. Isn't this card nice. So appropriate for you. It brought the tears to Mother's eyes when she read it. Mother is not keeping well at all. You are for ever in her thoughts night and day she is talking and praying for you safety. If only this cursed war was over and you safe beside us once more. But of course, it will have to be fought to a finish now. But it is cruel for men to be fodder for guns. I do wish I had been a man. I could have done something then. Recruiting is very brisk in S Shields. Now my dear Jack, I have not room for more, so with love and the best of wishes for your safely, from Mother and myself. I remain your ever loving Sister Annie xxxx*

Amongst Jack's documents in the Australian National Archives is a carbon copy of a letter gram sent to Military Commandant, Perth, (WA), presumably from the A.I.F. in Alexandria. It reads:

> *"KILLED IN ACTION TWO OUGHT TWO PRIVATE J. SIMPSON THIRD FIELD AMBULANCE RELATIVES RESIDE ENGLAND INFORMING DIRECT*
>
> *TRUMBLE*
>
> *23/6/15"*

From this we may infer that Sarah Simpson received the telegram dreaded so much by wives and mothers around the 23rd or 24th June – almost five weeks after her son's death. Annie's last two letters were returned unopened, with the word '*Killed*' pencilled on the envelope, a cruel way to receive the heart breaking news. The customary letter of condolence from the deceased soldier's commanding officer did not arrive. Eventually Annie addressed a letter to the 3rd Field Ambulance asking about the circumstances of her brother's death.

On September 2nd 1915, Captain Kenneth Fry replied to Annie:

"*Dear Miss Simpson,*

I am extremely sorry to hear that you have had no word from us about your brother. Colonel Sutton, then commanding the Ambulance wrote, I am practically certain, very shortly after the occurrence. (This letter may well have been lost at sea, through enemy activity). Colonel Sutton has now left us, and I was more in touch with your brother than the other remaining officers of our corps, so I am replying to your letter.

Your brother landed with us from the torpedo boat (destroyer)at daybreak on the 25th of April so taking part in the historic landing. He did excellent work during the day. He discovered a donkey… took possession and worked up and down a dangerous valley carrying wounded me to the beach on the donkey. The plan was a very great success, so he continued day by day from morning till night, and became one of the best known men in the division. Everyone from the General downwards seemed to have known him and his donkey which he christened Murphy. The valley at that time was very dangerous as it was exposed to snipers and also was continually shelled. He scorned the danger, and always kept going whistling and singing, a universal favourite. So he worked for three weeks. On the night of the 18th, as you will have read in the papers, the Turks made a heavy attack on our position. Early in the morning as usual your brother was at work, when a Turkish machine-gun played on the track where he was passing, the days of his almost miraculous escapes were passed, for he fell on the spot shot through the heart. He truly died doing his duty. We buried him that night on a little hill near the sea shore known as Queensland Point, Chaplain colonel Green of our division reading the service.

The work your brother did was so exceptionally good that his name was mentioned in orders of the day. We hoped that one of the military decorations of honour might be awarded him, as he fully deserved it, but unfortunately all who deserve cannot receive the special rewards. Mrs Simpson and yourself can at least take comfort that he gave his life in the performance of gallant and dutiful service that has been excelled by none.

I am enclosing with this letter a set of Ambulance Regimental Badges, which you have requested. Your brother's effects have been sent to the Base and will forwarded in due course to you.

In conclusion I wish to express the deep sympathy of our whole unit with Mrs Simpson and yourself in your sad bereavement. Believe me,

Yours sincerely,
H Kenneth Fry, Capt 3 Fld Amb.

Two of Simpson's mates, both serving in the 3rd Field Ambulance, have left accounts differing somewhat from the above and from each other. In the letter (AWM 93 417/20/35) from ex corporal A.R. Davidson to Major Treloer, War Memorial, Canberra , dated 28th March 1938, he stated:

"On the 19th May we were carrying from the top of Shrapnel Gully, Mahney, Gilles, Pratly and myself, we met Simpson and spoke to him. He asked Mahney how he was getting on. He always spoke with a definite brogue when speaking to Mahney (an Australian Irishman) and on this occasion added a ribald remark and we passed on. Forty yards further up the Gully he was shot, a machine gun bullet got him at his job. We wnt back and put his body in a dugout at the side of the track and carried on with our job. We went back for him about 6.30 and he was buried at Hell Spit the same evening, 19th May."

The letter from ex corporal Charles Love to the Sun Herald on 11th August 1965 stated:

"We lost a great many ambulance bearers in the landing, as well as many of the Battalion stretcher men, and the donkey saved the use of a four-man stretcher squad. About 10.30am on May 19th, as far as I can remember, I was with a squad travelling down to the beach. Murphy was just ahead of us. Johnny Turk sent over about a dozen shrapnel shells. We ducked for safety, but Murphy carried on. As we

*watched we saw Murphy stiffen and then drop. I ran forward and
another man and I picked him up and took him to the side of the
gully. A water party just behind us dropped their kerosene cans, and
we used their litter to carry him down to the beach. Then the doctor
put him on the table and began to tend to his wound. A shrapnel ball
had hit him in the back and went through his lung. On our return in
the afternoon about 3 o'clock we learned that he had died. As the sun
was going down on the beach, we stood round his single grave while
the Padre spoke of a wonderful and brave man."*

Captain Fry, as most commanding officers did, phrased his words
euphemistically to spare the next of kin from unnecessary hurt. Corporal
Davidson's account was written twenty three years after the event is matter
of fact and perhaps the more credible for that. Corporal Love's account was
written on the 50th Anniversary of the Gallipoli landing. It contains ostensibly
convincing detail, contradicting the traditional history that Jack was killed
instantly. Perception of events by witnesses can differ surprisingly, and of
course memories can be clouded by the passage of time. Three different
accounts, so there will always be doubt as to the circumstances of Jack's
death.

Sarah Simpson was at least spared the thought that Jack had suffered a
painful death. For her the tension, anxiety and uncertainty were over,
replaced by sadness and depression. Sarah was no stranger to grief.
Benson 'In Search of Simpson' stated "She had lost three boys with scarlet
fever and had a dread of losing him", - her only surviving son.

This statement is not entirely factual. Sarah did indeed lose her second and
third sons to scarlet fever, one in Leith and one in South Shields, but there is
no evidence that her first son Alfred Simpson, born in Edinburgh in July 1873
died of fever. Alfred was listed with Sarah in the 1881 census, aged 8, but
there is no death reported for him between then and the end of the century,
nor does his name appear in the Scottish Census Returns for 1891 and
1901. There is no mention of him ever in South Shields. At the time of the
family move in 1886, Alfred was 13 and may have opted to go to sea or
perhaps even join his natural father. He did not move to South Shields with
his mother and step-father. His disappearance from official records remains
a mystery. Sarah had however, lost an infant daughter to scarlet fever while
she was still in Leith.

Jack's service documents, held in the Australian National Archives, show it took six years to sort out his affairs. His allotment to his mother was paid up to 30th June 1915, the end of the month after his death. His Statement of Accounts was finally balanced on the 27th October 1915, showing an amount of £11.7/- "*due and paid*" – presumably to his mother.

Sarah Simpson, mother, next of kin and a widow was awarded a pension by the Australian Government of £2 per fortnight, payable from the 6th December 1915. On the 24th March 1916, a 'brown paper parcel' containing the effects of the late Private J Simpson, containing ' disc (identity), letters and postcards' was despatched to his next of kin. Sarah must have shed more than a few tears when she opened the parcel.

On the 18th January 1916, the Commonwealth Bank wrote to the Officer in Charge, Base Records Office, requesting a death certificate for Private J Simpson, so that they could give 'due consideration' to a claim from his mother Sarah Simpson, for the balance at credit on the depositor's account.

On 9th December 1915, a letter was sent from Base Records Office, Melbourne, to Sarah informing her that Jack's name had been promulgated in the Australian Military Order No 570 of 1915 "*for having performed various acts of conspicuous gallantry or valuable service during the period 25th April to 5th May 1915.*" The above letter was followed by another dated 10th April 1916.

> "*Dear Madam,*
>
> *I have it in command from his Majesty the King to inform you, as the next of kin of the late PRIVATE JOHN SIMPSON, No.202, of the Australian Army Medical Corp, that this Private was mentioned in a Despatch from General Sir Ian Hamilton, dated 22nd September 1915, and published in the Supplement to the 'London Gazette' dated 5th November 1915, for gallant and distinguished service in the Field.*
>
> *I am to express to you the King's high appreciation of these services and to add that His Majesty trusts that their public acknowledgement may be of some consolation in your bereavement.*
>
> > *I have the honour to be,*
> > *Your obedient Servant,*
>
> *M S Graham, Lieutenant Colonel, Assistant Military Secretary.*"

Sarah must have read the letter with mixed emotions, both pride and sorrow, and these emotions would well up again in 1920, when she received Jack's medals, the 1914/15 Star, the British War Medal and the Victory Medal with Oak Leaf for being 'Mentioned in Dispatches'. She later received the bronze death plaque, nicknamed the 'Death Penny', together with a commendation from King George V.

Sarah Simpson also received a Death Plaque, or Dead Man's Penny, together with a Memorial Scroll

KY Collection

At the beginning of January 1920, a package with three medals was delivered to Sarah Simpson. The trio named to Private John Simpson comprised a 1914 – 1915 Star, a British War Medal and an Allied Victory Medal with an oak leaf signifying a 'Mention in Despatches'. A similar trio colloquially known as 'Pip, Squeak and Wilfred' is shown above. Jack's medals rest in the Australian War Memorial, Canberra, donated by his sister Annie.

Image KY Collection

Then on 24th March 1921, the Commonwealth Office in the Strand notified Base Records Office that they had received a Statutory Declaration from Jack's mother *"to the effect that the correct name of the soldier who served in the A.I.F. as 202 Pte. John Simpson, 3rd Field Ambulance, was John Simpson KIRKPATRICK"*.

On 11th May 1921, Headquarters 5th District Base, Military Headquarters, Perth, Western Australia, issued a memo stating *"The records have been amended to read 'Stated to be KIRKPATRICK, John Simpson"* After six years, the Geordie lad from South Shields had at last been given his true identity.

Sarah had proved in the past to be resilient and resourceful. Although temperamental, impetuous, quick tempered and expelled from her own family, she as a teenage single mum had kept and brought up her first son Alfred on her own, contrary to all the conventions of the period. She had not only lost four sons, but also two daughters, baby Sarah in Leith and Julia in South Shields.

Bertram Street, South Shields. Number 14 was home to Sarah Simpson Kirkpatrick for about 20 years, 1905–1925, her longest time in one house. Sarah's last two letters to Jack in 1914 were returned to Bertram Street from the Seaman's Mission in Melbourne; Annie's last letters to her brother in 1915 were also returned to Bertram Street .marked "Killed in Action".
Images: KY Collection

Number 14 Bertram Street, South Shields no longer exists and was lost under new developments. Numbers 50 upwards still survive. The back lane off Bertram Street in 2014 would have been recognised by Jack.

Image KY Collection

Sarah and Annie continued to live together at 14 Bertram Street. One of Jack's letters infers that Sarah may have taken her daughter Maggie Balneaves and her three children back into the family home after Will Balneaves emigrated to Australia in 1912. There was certainly friction between Annie, Maggie and Sarah according to Jack's letters. In March 1916, the source of friction was removed. Maggie, her children – Martha aged 14 years, John aged 13 years and George aged 10 years, left London on the 1st of the month aboard the WAIPARA, bound for Brisbane, Queensland. After a separation of four years, Will Balneaves was soon to be re-united with his family.

In a letter to Annie on the 17th January 1915, Jack teased her about

> *"turning down your sailor boy….. after such glowing accounts in your last letter….. and he actually drunk beer, well he must be a brute, but take my advice Annie and don't take another sailor….., but if you must…. take my advice again and have a fireman. For they are a much quieter sort of animal and when properly trained will feed from the hand. But never mind kid, I wish you all sorts of good luck with your new boy."*

254

Although she idolised her big brother, Annie either ignored or forgot his advice. Three years after Jack's death, Annie married a mariner, and he was a sailor, not a fireman. On 3rd August 1918, while the 'war to end all wars' continued, Annie aged 23 years, married Francis Allen Parkin, aged 24 years, a bachelor and Able Seaman in his Majesty's Royal Navy. Francis Parkin's address was 173 Marsden Street, South Shields. Annie was still at 14 Bertram Street and the marriage was celebrated in the Parish Church of St Mary, South Shields.

Francis Parkin was born into a mining family in the village of Lynesack, south west Durham, one of the earliest areas in the county to be mined for coal. The 1901 census shows Francis, aged 6 living with his father, mother, one elder sister, three elder brothers and two younger sisters. In 1902, Joseph Parkin, aged 51, head of the family died of stomach cancer. His widow Charlotte was not untypical of the period. She had given birth to 11 children, two of whom had died in infancy. When her husband died, one daughter was already married but with eight children still at home, only two of whom were working, Charlotte faced serious hardship. Sometime between the census dates of 1901 and 1911, widow Charlotte Parkin moved with her family to South Shields where employment prospects for her sons were better in the new deep pits along the Durham coastal belt. Her youngest son Francis, however was destined not to go down the mines. Instead when he left school, he was enrolled at the Naval Training Establishment, H.M.S. Ganges at Shotley near Ipswich in Suffolk.

Training methods were harsh but Ganges had a reputation for turning out highly professional, self-reliant ratings. On attaining the age of 18, Francis was enlisted on the 25th July 1912 for an engagement of 12 years and was posted to HMS AFRICA as an ordinary seaman. When war broke out on the 4th August 1914, he was serving aboard HMS ANTRIM, a 10,850 ton cruiser. At the time of his wedding in 1918, he was on leave from Gibraltar.

H.M.S. Africa. One of the ships in which Annie's first husband, Francis Parkin, served during the Great War.

Image KY Collection

In 1910 just before Francis Parkin joined the HMS Africa, the Royal Navy made its first experimental launch of an aircraft from a warship. A ramp was built over the fore gun turret and bow.

Image KY Collection

In 1918, at the eleventh hour of the eleventh day of the eleventh month, the guns fell silent. The Great War was over. People rejoiced in every corner of the Empire from Sydney to South Shields. Prime Minister Lloyd George promised to make Britain a land fit for heroes.

In 1919, Annie gave birth to a daughter named Joan Simpson Parkin on the 24th May at 14 Bertram Street. Francis still served in the Royal Navy and was aboard the EMPRESS OF INDIA at the time.

County Borough of . .

SOUTH SHIELDS.

Peace Celebrations,

SATURDAY, 19th JULY, 1919.

OFFICIAL PROGRAMME.

Issued by the Peace Celebrations Committee of the Town Council.

Price, 3d.

R. Robinson & Co., Limited, Newcastle-on-Tyne.

Peace Celebrations. The Treaty of Versailles was signed on the 28th June 1919. South Shields celebrated on Saturday 19th July with a Victory Parade, bands in the park, music, dancing and fireworks.

Shields lost over 2,000 men who were remembered on page 20 of the programme, with the solemn verse below, including Jack and the son of Widow Peebles whose husband created the Marine Parks. Her son was killed at the Battle of the Somme.

Image KY collection

'Out of the long, long night the dawn comes stealing;
Glimmers the light to show the day is near,
But what our hearts when all the bells are pealing,
And you, dear lad, not here!'

In 1921, on 25th September Annie was still living at 14 Bertram Street with her mother, when she gave birth to her second child, a son named John Simpson Parkin.

In 1924, misfortune continued to hover over 14 Bertram Street. South Tyneside Library in South Shields holds a file of miscellaneous papers concerning the Kirkpatrick family, amongst which is a handwritten note, unsigned and undated. It states: *"Autumn 1921 – Autumn 1924 - Sarah and Francis – daughter's husband – latter not working from time moved in until autumn 1924"*. The authenticity of this cannot be verified but by Christmas 1924, Francis Parkin was in the merchant navy serving as bos'un on a collier steamer, the JOHN HARRISON. On Boxing Day 1924, the JOHN HARRISON, commanded by Master John W. Beeching, sailed from the Tyne on the ebb tide with a cargo of coal for Amsterdam. The journey time was normally 40 hours. After three days the ship was reported overdue, her last sighting being off 'Flamboro' Head' the day she sailed. The Master came from North Shields and ten of the fourteen crew came from South Shields. The bad news spread rapidly through the streets of the Tyne Dock ward, but as each day passed with no news, hearts at 14 Bertram Street, grew heavier and heavier.

S.S. John Harrison built 1924. This ship left the Tyne with a cargo of coal for Amsterdam on the 24th December 1924. She was lost in the North Sea with all hands, including the bos'un, Annie's husband Francis Parkin.
Image-Builder's model sold at Bonham's Saleroom 2009.

The Shield's Gazette of the 14th January 1925 carried a headline "*MISSING STEAMER – John Harrison's Lifeboat Washed Ashore*". The lifeboat was washed up on Fahr Island off the coast of Schleswig Holstein, a

258

considerable way to the North East of the JOHN HARRISON's intended course. "*all hope for her safety had already been abandoned*", reported the Gazette. The deaths of all fifteen crew were recorded in the REGISTER OF DECEASED SEAMEN for February 1925, all fifteen presumed to have drowned in the North Sea on December 27th. The two women who had loved Jack, his mother and his youngest sister, were now both widows; they had to dry their tears and get on with raising two fatherless children, Joan aged 5 and John aged 3.

By 1926, it was clear that Lloyd George's noble aspiration to make Britain a '*land fit for heroes*' after the Great War had failed. Britain faced a long term economic decline. She lost her place as the world's leading industrial power as other countries progressed through their own industrial revolutions. The four basic industries: coal, shipbuilding, textiles and steel were in serious decline and the battle for survival between the Trade Unions and the Employers culminated in the General Strike of 1926. Unemployment at just over 1 million in 1921 reached 1.5 million in 1926 and continued to increase through the 1920s and 1930s until the advent of World War II (or perhaps part II of the Great War).

Jack Simpson Kirkpatrick, if he had come home to England after the war, would have been more disillusioned than ever with what he had once called a '*louse bound country*'.

Jack's brother in law Sam Christie, a ship's plater and Jack's sister Sarah decided to avail themselves of the Australian Government's incentives to escape from the 'louse bound country'. During 1925, the Australian Government and the Colonial Office had agreed on a plan to attract 450,000 settlers from Britain, including 34,000 families). It was common practice for the breadwinner in the family to go ahead. Sam accompanied by his daughter Edna aged 12 and son John aged 10 departed from London on the 30th October 1925 on board the ORMUZ bound for Brisbane. Sarah Christie with her two youngest children Samuel aged 8 and Nancy aged 6 followed eight months later sailing from London on the 12th June 1926 on the MORETON BAY also bound for Brisbane. Sarah of course had her elder sister, Peggy Balneaves already living in Queensland. Sarah Simpson in South Shields had lost another daughter and four grandchildren, although not to bereavement. She knew it was unlikely she would see them again.

On the first January, 1928, Marguerite Balneaves, Peggy to the family, died in Queensland aged only 45 years. Although the relationship between mother and daughter had not always been harmonious, Peggy's death must have come as a blow. A mother does not expect her daughter to pre-decease her.

On the 17th October 1931, in the Parish Church of St Hilda, South Shields, the marriage was solemnized between Adam Maddison Pearson, aged 34, a bachelor and by profession – a cartman (as was his father) and Annie Simpson Parkin, aged 35, widow who by then had moved from Bertram Street to Dale Street, South Shields.

Dale Street, South Shields. In 1931 Annie married Adam Maddison Pearson and moved to 91 Dale Street, South Shields with her mother and children. Sarah Simpson Kirkpatrick died at this address on the 19th February 1933.

Image South Tyneside Images 0000120

On 10th September 1932, William Thompson Balneaves, a widower, married Louisa Caroline Heiser in Queensland, Australia.

On the 19th February 1933, at 91 Dale Street, South Shields, Sarah Simpson, otherwise Kirkpatrick, aged 77 died of Senile Decay. Her father was recorded as James Simpson, an Engine Fitter. The death was registered by Annie Pearson who was present at the death. Annie and her sisters it seems became aware in adulthood that their mother and father were not married. However there is no indication anywhere that the daughters knew anything of Sarah and Robert Kirkpatrick's life before arrival in South Shields in 1886. Sarah left a will bequeathing her estate amounting to £328 18/11d to her daughter Annie. This is equivalent to over 6 years of the war pension Sarah received from the Australian Government. In death Jack had achieved his main aim in life of supporting his mother in comfortable circumstances.

The Simpson-Kirkpatrick gravestone at Harton Cemetery, South Shields, probably erected by Annie. The deaths of her beloved brother Jack 1915 and her sister Martha in 1900 are recorded, but not her brother James who died in 1892 the year Annie was born. Did she not know of him? Who placed the artificial flowers in 2014?

Image Sept. 2014 KY Collection

Transcription of the Simpson Kirkpatrick Gravestone

IN LOVING MEMORY OF
ROBERT KIRKPATRICK
DIED OCT. 10TH 1908
AGED 73 YEARS
SARAH S. KIRKPATRICK
WIFE OF THE ABOVE
DIED FEB.9TH 1933
AGED 77 YEARS
MARTHA SIMPSON
DAUGHTER OF THE ABOVE
DIED OCT. 4TH 1900
AGED 11 YEARS
JOHN SIMPSON KIRKPATRICK
A.I.F. SON OF THE ABOVE
KILLED IN ACTION AT GALLIPOLI
MAY 19TH 1915 IN HIS 23RD YEAR
"HE GAVE HIS LIFE THAT OTHERS MAY LIVE"

KNOWN AT GALLIPOLI AS
THE MAN WITH THE DONKEY

Sarah Simpson Kirkpatrick, to whom her son Jack, was exceptionally devoted. Aged 17, he could call her 'owld lass' and get away with it.

Image from www.anzacday.org. au courtesy of the late J.S.Parkin

World War II lasted from 1939 until 1945. Annie's son John Simpson Parkin was 18 at the outbreak of war and eligible for conscription. Whether he served in the war is unknown at present.

On the 14th January 1954, Sarah, Jack's remaining sister in Australia died in Queensland; her mother's name being given correctly as 'Simpson'.

In 1956, Sir Irving Benson, an Australian Methodist Minister, and author of 'The Man with the Donkey', visited South Shields and met up with Annie Pearson, who very generously handed over to him the letters which Jack wrote to his mother between the years 1910 and 1915. These letters were given on the condition that they would be passed on to the Australian War Memorial in Canberra to be preserved for posterity. Benson after holding the letters for almost ten years did pass them on to the Australian War Memorial where they are available for research.

On the 7th May 1964, Annie's husband, Adam Maddison Pearson, aged 66 years died at the family home – 20 Nelson Street, Brightlingsea, Essex. The death was registered by John S Parkin, step son of 194 Panfield Lane, Braintree, Essex. When and why the family moved from South Shields to Essex is unknown.

On March 16th 1965, Annie Pearson visited Australia House in London for the purpose of handing over her brother's medals, identity disc and death plaque for onward transmission to the Australian War Memorial in Canberra and on the 21st April, the Prime Minister of Australia, Sir Robert Menzies released a statement to the Press.

> *"Private Simpson's War Relics*
>
> *The war relics of Private john Simpson Kirkpatrick – "The Man with the Donkey", have been presented to the Australian War Museum.*
>
> *They are the gift of his sister, Mrs Annie Simpson Pearson of Brightlingsea, Essex, who has said that they should remain the property of her late brother's beloved Australia.*
>
> *They comprise Private Simpson's identity disc, his service medals and ribbons, his Oak Leaf and scroll for his Mention is Despatches and a bronze medal presented after his death by King George V.*
>
> *The story of "The Man with the Donkey" is well known throughout Australia and Private Simpson has been honoured by the erection of a statue near the Shrine of Remembrance in Melbourne. A replica of this statue is on display in the Anzac Gallery of the war museum in Canberra and his relics will be placed with it. "*

On April 25th, Annie, accompanied by her married daughter Joan Claridge from Lawford Heath, Rugby, Warwickshire, attended a ceremony at Australia House, commemorating the 50th anniversary of the Gallipoli Landings. The Australian Prime Minister, Sir Robert Menzies sent Annie a personal letter enclosing a folder of the special stamps issued for the 50th anniversary asking her to accept this as a gift from the Commonwealth Government. The design on the stamps depicted her brother and his donkey.

Two years later, on the 16th May 1967, Annie Pearson was invited once more to Australia House in London to receive the ANZAC Medallion issued to survivors and next of kin in commemoration of the Gallipoli Campaign. This medal was also struck with the image of Jack Simpson and donkey bearing a wounded soldier. Before a number of invited guests, Annie was presented with her cased medallion by none other than His Excellency, the Governor General of Australia, Lord Casey, himself a Gallipoli veteran. Annie's medallion was the only one presented in person – all others were posted to the recipients.

On the 29th April 1975, Annie Simpson Pearson, aged 79, the last member of the family to have shared life's stage with No. 202 Private John Simpson, also known as Kirkpatrick, died at 14 Godwin Road, Hastings, Sussex.

R.I.P

Primary Sources

U.K. Births, Marriages and Deaths Index- Kirkpatrick, Parkin and Pearson
U.K. Census 1901, 1911, Lynesack and South Shields
Service Record of Francis A Parkin, ref ADM 188-1132/1177, National Archives, Kew.
Register of Burials, Harton Cemetery, South Shields
Probates and Wills, England 1933
Probates and Wills, England 1975

Secondary Sources

South Shields Gazette, January 14th 1925
H.M.S. Ganges Museum, Royal Naval Training Establishment (www.hmsganges.museum.org.uk)

APPENDICES:
THE OTHER FAMILY MEMBERS
APPENDIX I

Robert Kilpatrick - Jack's Grandfather

It should be noted that the family name was originally spelt with an 'l' and not 'rk'. In early 19th century records, the name changes 'to and fro' between these spellings.

Jack's paternal grandparents were born during the long lasting Napoleonic Wars. Margaret Lowe, familiar name Maggie, was born 20th January 1806 in Leith, just three months after Nelson's critical defeat of the combined French and Spanish Fleets at Trafalgar. Her father John Low was a cooper in Leith; her mother was Isabell, maiden name, Carmichael. Robert Kilpatrick was born 13th February 1809 in Leith, just a month after Sir John Moore's death at the battle of Corunna, in Spain. The date and place of Robert's Kilpatrick's birth are as stated by him in his application for a Master's certificate. No record of his birth has been found in Leith's Old Parish Records (OPR). The details of Margaret's birth are in OPR 692/02, South Leith for 1806.

Robert Kilpatrick went to sea probably around the age of 12 or 13, but records for seaman's service were not required by law before 1835 when Parliament passed a Merchant Shipping Act. This legislation established a Register Office of Merchant seaman and required masters of ships to file Agreements and Crew Lists with the new Office. The new Act enabled the Registrar to create an index of seamen available to augment the Royal Navy in event of war. For ship masters and owners, it was an irksome piece of bureaucracy and they complied reluctantly often making the filing of the returns more important than their accuracy.

The marriage of Robert Kilpatrick, seaman, and Margaret Lowe, daughter of the late John Low, cooper took place in Leith on 25th June 1830, the Reverend James Grant officiating (OPR 692 – 0200 Leith), and their union was soon blessed with a daughter Isabella, born 27th July 1831. Two years later on the 18th June 1833, a second daughter Elizabeth was born in Leith to Robert Kilpatrick, seaman, and Margaret Low (OPR 692/002 for Leith South).

On 26th November 1837 Robert and Margaret, now living at Queen Street, Leith had a 'lawful son' named Robert Kilpatrick on 6th December (OPR Births 692/002 0190 0213 Leith South). Robert senior was still a 'seaman'. Robert junior would one day become the father of Jack, the 'Man with the Donkey'.

Port of Leith 1827. When Robert Kilpatrick went to sea as a boy aged 12, the Shore at Leith looked like this. Steam power was employed in paddle tugs only. Ocean going journeys by steam were a decade into the future.

Image KY Collection

By the time of the 1841 census, the family had moved to York Street, Aberdeen, a major port and ship building centre on the north east coast of Scotland. Only three members of the family, under the name Kilpatrick are listed, Margaret aged 30, Elizabeth age 7 and Robert aged 3. Robert senior was probably at sea when the census was taken. Isabella, born 1831 is also missing, presumably having died in childhood. Deaths in Scotland are virtually impossible to find before statutory records commenced in 1855. It was not customary to record deaths in Scotland's Old Parish Records. Still in Aberdeen five months later, the Kilpatricks presented another daughter for baptism. On 21st October the Reverend Alexander Spence baptised their daughter, by name Margaret Low.

266

By 1844, the Kilpatricks were once more resident in Queen Street, Leith where Margaret gave birth to a second son on the 15th April. His baptism was delayed until 17th June, perhaps awaiting the return from a voyage of his father (OPR 692/Leith). The following day Robert Kilpatrick weighed anchor once more, sailing as Mate in a Leith Snow (a small sailing ship), the JANET MUIR, 213 tons, first for Newcastle thence onward to Calcutta. He would not be home again until 29th April the following year – a journey of nine months.

The census for 1851 reveals dramatic changes in the Kilpatrick family since the previous census. Both Roberts senior and junior are absent, both now at sea. Mother Margaret, aged 40 still heads the family at 14 Queen Street, Leith. Three new children are tied to her apron strings, daughter Margaret and son John whose births are reported above, but there is also a daughter Elizabeth, aged only 1 year. A daughter Elizabeth aged 7 was listed in the 1841 census, but must have died sometime in the previous decade. A new baby girl born in 1849 has inherited the name of her dead sister, a not uncommon custom of the time.

Robert Kilpatrick's career progresses

On the 24th December 1850, Robert Kilpatrick applied to the REGISTRAR GENERAL OF SEAMEN for his Master's Certificate, submitting therewith PARTICULARS OF SERVICE:

Vessel's name	Port belonging to	Tons	Capacity	In what trade	Date of Service	
					From	To
Anne Mitchell	Leith	65	Master	Coasting and Foreign	16.08.42	08.01.43
Janet Muir	Leith	213	Mate	Foreign	18.06.44	29.04.45
Eagle	Leith	157	Mate	Foreign	20.05.45	15.10.45
Tagus	Leith	101	Mate	Foreign	20.10.45	13.04.46
Conside	Newcastle	300	Mate	Foreign	01.06.46	10.01.47
Tarter	Sunderland	205	Mate	Foreign	18.05.47	20.08.47
Isabella Leith	Aberdeen	193	Mate	Foreign	21.08.47	01.09.47
Elizabeth	Hull	13	Mate	Foreign	20.09.50	24.12.50

This record is not continuous, giving only the service in which Robert acted as Master or Mate. The average journey in the 'foreign trade' was 5 months, the longest that of the JANET MUIR which reached Calcutta, was 9½ months. No Crew Agreements have been found so far, for the ships listed above.

Robert Kilpatrick's application was successful. On the 13th day of February 1851, by order of the Board of Trade, the Registrar General of Seamen, issued a 'MASTER'S CERTIFICATE OF SERVICE, NO. 42796' in the name of Robert Kilpatrick, born at Leith, County of Edinburgh, on the 13 February 1809, he having been employed in the Capacities of Mate or Master – 7 years, in the British Merchant Service in the Coasting and Foreign Trade. (Certificate 42796 in National Maritime Museum (NMM), Greenwich). In the absence of a birth record in the Old Parish Records for Leith, this certificate gives the precise date and place of Robert's birth.

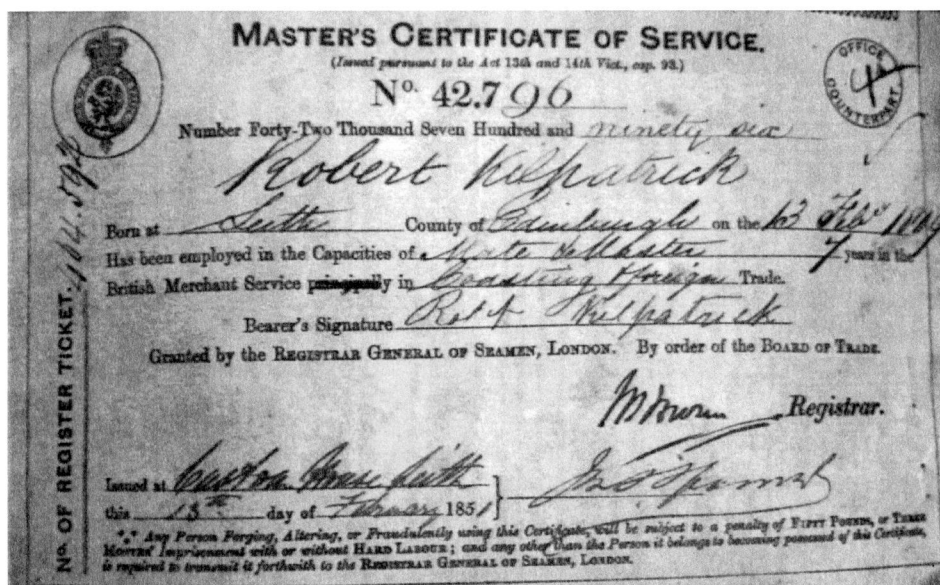

Master's Certificate of Service was granted to Robert Kilpatrick on the 13th February 1851. The certificate importantly gives the place and date of birth for Robert, Leith, 13th February 1809.

Image courtesy of National Maritime Museum, Greenwich

Possession of a Master's Certificate was, however, no guarantee of more remunerative work for Robert Kilpatrick. His service over the next four years has been partially traced, and Crew Agreements have been found for only three of his ships, namely:

Vessel's name	Port belonging to	Tons	Capacity	In what trade	Date of Service	
					From	To
Regent	Leith	106	?	?	July 52	Dec 52
Valeria	Yarmouth	113	Mate	Coasting	01.01.53	13.03.53
St Fort	Leith	95	Mate	Foreign	02.04.53	02.06.53
Haidee	?	?	?	Foreign	?	?
Martin Luther	Liverpool	1,241	2nd Mate	Foreign	18.12.54	19.07.55
Pollock	?	?	?	Foreign	?	?

The Crew Agreement for the VALERIA, a small sail ship out of Yarmouth is particularly interesting. She was small only 113 tons, and crewed by a Master, Mate, 2 Seamen and 2 Ordinary Seamen. Both Robert Kilpatricks, father and son, singed on 1st January 1853 at Leith. Robert senior, aged 44 as Mate, and Robert junior aged 16 as Ordinary Seaman. Both also gave their previous ship as REGENT, another small sail ship of 106 tons, built 1852 at Bo'ness, near Leith. On 24th November, the REGENT was reported off Gravesend, returning from St Petersburg, probably on way to Leith. The Crew Agreement for the VALERIA shows that father and son were discharged by 'their own wish' at Newcastle on 13 March 1853. Robert senior returned to Leith and on 2nd April took employment as Mate on another Leith ship. Young Robert's next move is tantalisingly obscure. The next sight of him in maritime records comes in December 1856 in Melbourne, emerging apparently from three years in Australia's gold rush and still only 19 years of age.

The second Crew Agreement for this period of Robert Kilpatrick's career shows him as Mate on board another small coasting vessel, the ST. FORT, burthen 95 tons and crew of Master, Mate and three seamen.

By 18th December 1854 Robert had changed tack completely. On that date, he was in Hong Kong where he joined a ship named the MARTIN LUTHER, a much larger ship of 1,241 tons burthen registered in Liverpool. His progress from home waters to the China Seas was made on board a ship called HAIDEE, as yet unidentified. The MARTIN LUTHER needed a 2nd Mate, so Robert found himself a smaller fish in a bigger pool. Six months later, the MARTIN LUTHER had reached Havana in the Caribbean. An entry in the ship's log, entered 17th June, Havana (Havannah) throws a new light on Robert Kilpatrick's character:

"Denis Leonard, Seaman and Robert Kilpatrick, 2nd Mate were intoxicated on board the ship and creating great disorder among the rest of the crew, and using threatening Language towards James

Fullerton, Chief Mate, at 10.00pm. Called on board the Guard Ship and sent the said Denis Leonard and Robert Kilpatrick in charge, to the Calaboose, at 11 am on the 18th both them out and set them at Liberty, Denis Leonard with orders to return to the ship.

A.A.McKeachie
James Fullerton, Mate"

A month later, Robert was discharged, 19th July at Havana. His journey back to Leith has not been traced.

The Martin Luther. Robert Kilpatrick served on this ship from December 1854 to July 1855 as 2nd Mate. He was discharged in Havanna after being drunk and disorderly and spending a night in the calaboose. Two years later she was wrecked in the English Channel; 498 emigrants bound for Quebec were rescued, but 5 crewmen drowned. A lucky escape for Robert perhaps.
Image KY Collection

In 1857, Robert Kilpatrick reached the age of 48, a critical point in his life. His career was in the doldrums. In spite of holding a Master's Certificate he was working in the coasting trade, mainly in small sail ships as 'Mate'. His venture into the Foreign Trade on the MARTIN LUTHER out of Liverpool had been as 2nd Mate, and the episode of drunkenness may have damaged his reputation in that port. He was not a man to rest on his oars however, and he decided to embark on a new course. He applied to Trinity House in Leith for a Pilot's License. The ledger of Trinity House shows he made a payment of £1.1/-(a guinea) on the 1st January 1858, the first annual fee for his Pilot's License (NASGD 226-9-10) showing that the Master and Elder Brethren at Trinity House must have been satisfied not only concerning his experience and skills, but also his character. Before the 1913 Pilotage Act, licensed Pilots were self-employed. (NAS GD 226) They owned their own pilot cutters, small fast sail boats often built to their own design. Competition for business was fierce. When a potential customer came into sight, the pilots raced each other to be the first to speak with the Master and to strike a bargain. After a fee had been agreed, the pilot boarded and his cutter was either towed behind the ship, or left in the hands of a junior to be sailed back to port.

Leith pilots were licensed to operate between St. Andrews on the North Coast of the Forth and Eyemouth on the South. The Isle of May, at the entrance to the Forth was used as a lookout station by the pilots who were granted use of a room in the lighthouse by the Northern Lighthouse Commissioners. The pilots however appear to have been far from the best of tenants. The quarterly minutes of the Trinity House Managers, held 2nd November 1871, recorded the gist of a letter received:

> "The Commissioners of the Northern Lighthouses have complained to the Managers that Pilots have destroyed the fittings of room given for their use on the Island of May. The Commissioners have resolved that if the room remains in present disgraceful state, they will withdraw the privilege altogether. From enquiry made, I find Leith Harbour Pilots are also implicated. Perhaps you may think it well that your Pilots should be informed." (NAS GD 26-11-14)

The Managers of Trinity House acknowledged the exceptional skills of some pilots who were licensed as 'North Sea Pilots'. These men, at the top of their professional tree, were licensed to pilot ships beyond the purlieu of the Forth and to conduct southbound vessels as far as Orfordness on the Suffolk coast, 13 miles north east of the major port of Felixstowe. At that point, pilotage was handed over to a Thames Pilot. The Leith pilots remained on board as far as London where they could find an assignment on a northern bound vessel. A list of Pilots licensed by Trinity House, Leith in 1865 shows 101 licensees. Only 16 of these held the prestigious title of 'North Sea Pilot', and one of these was Robert Kilpatrick. (NAS GD 226-14-5) These were prosperous times for Robert and he could hold his head high in Leith's shipping community. He could even open an account with the Clydesdale Bank, to take care of his surplus earnings. The seaman, who just a few years earlier, seemed destined to spend his days on small sailing ships, could now command respect on the bridge of some of the world's most modern steamers.

The Pilot's fee was commensurate with his responsibilities. The Master of a vessel virtually handed over temporarily the safety of the ship, the cargo, the passengers and crew to his pilot who had to have the requisite experience, knowledge, navigational skills and above all, perhaps, self-confidence. Robert Kilpatrick had all these qualities evidently, but his job was still hazardous, and had its reverses. On October 30th 1865, Robert received a letter from the Secretary to the Trinity House Managers *"desiring him to appear on Wednesday 1st November at ½ past 1 o'clock and (ominously) to bring his license with him."*

The P&O Steamship NIPHON. On 26th September 1865, the NIPHON , a brand new ship on delivery from the Forth to her owners P&O Southampton, grounded in thick fog of Flamborough Head. Robert Kilpatrick, pilot in charge, was deemed partly to blame by the Masters of Trinity House, Leith, and his Pilot License was suspended for three months.
Image www.qac.culture.gov.uk. Artist unknown.

On 26th September 1865, the NIPHON, a brand new ship purchased by the P & O Line left Granton for delivery to Southampton. A barque rigged screw steamer, registered tonnage 529, with a two cylinder engine delivering 140 HP, she had been launched at Kinghorn and completed at Kirkcaldy. For the first leg of her delivery voyage, Robert Kilpatrick had been hired as pilot. The voyage was uneventful as far as Scarborough, distant 9 or 10 miles west according to Kilpatrick's calculations, a reading not disputed by the Master and the bridge officers. A report states:

"At 11am on the 27th, when 'the weather became very thick, he set a course in accordance with the readings at Scarborough. At 11.30, he eased the Engines but took no cast of the lead. At 11.45, he stopped

*the Engines altogether; took no cast of the lead! About ten minutes
after that, he found the ship gently striking on a rocky bottom."*

The Nautical Committee of the P & O Steam Navigation Company made four
points in their complaint to the Masters of Trinity House. In their opinion:

1. The accident was caused by an error in judging the distance off Scarborough.
2. By omitting to take a cast of the lead when in fog.
3. There was no reason for supposing the Compasses to be in error.
4. From a subsequent examination of the ship in dry dock, it was considered that had the weather not been fine and the water smooth, the ship would have become a total wreck.

The Captain of the NIPHON, Charles J Perrins stated in his report:

*"With reference to my being satisfied with the conduct of Pilot
Kilpatrick, I can only say that he was quite sober the whole time he
was on board and seemed attentive to the Navigation of the ship."*

In a letter covering the reports submitted to Trinity House, the Secretary of
the P & O Board mentioned that the Pilot, being without funds when in
London was granted an advance of £5 against his pilotage fee. He also
stated his Directors would feel obliged by the opinion of the Trinity Masters
as to whether the balance should be paid or withheld. (NAS GD 226-1-16)

A Special Meeting was convened at Trinity House, Leith on 29th November
1865 to consider the complaints made against two pilots, Robert Kilpatrick
and Hugh McWhinnie. Robert in pleading his case, was adamant that
compass variation was the cause of the accident. He was asked to leave the
room while the Masters, eleven in all, came to a conclusion. They decided
he had been culpable of not taking casts of the lead. His punishment was
suspension of his license for three months. His colleague McWhinnie, facing
a complaint from the Captain of a French Frigate, the PANDORE was dealt
with more severely. His license was cancelled completely and the fact
published in the North British Advertiser. (NAS GD 226-1-16)

On the 11th November 1870, at Summerfield house, Leith, Margaret
Kirkpatrick, wife of Robert Kirkpatrick, North Sea Pilot, died of apoplexy. She

was 61 years old. Robert and Margaret were living at that address with their married daughter, Margaret Brown. When the 1871 census was taken three months later, the household consisted of:

Name	Relation to Head	Age	Occupation	Where born
Thomas C Brown	Head	31	Watchmaker	Glasgow
Margaret K Brown	Wife	29		Aberdeen
Robert Kirkpatrick	Father in law	63	Seaman	Aberdeen
Catherine Brash	Servant	16	General Servant	Leith

The Browns were apparently childless. Robert's birthplace is given as Aberdeen, surely an error, as his Master's Certificate and crew agreements consistently give his birthplace as Leith. Robert would survive his wife Margaret by less than a year.

The LEITH BURGHS PILOT, a weekly newspaper, in the edition dated October 21 1871, published the following report.

> *"Pilot* Lost *at Sea: On Saturday afternoon last, the steam yacht WASP of Dunkirk, left Leith for that port, having Robert Kilpatrick, a Leith deep sea pilot on board to direct the vessel's course. About twelve o'clock at night, when the vessel was off the Isle of May, the cry "Pilot overboard" was raised. The WASP's engines were immediately stopped, several pieces of timber thrown overboard and lights shown, but nothing could be seen or heard of the unfortunate man. A search was kept up for two hours. The WASP was then anchored under the lee of the island all night. During which one of her anchors was lost and the vessel damaged. She returned to Leith on Sunday afternoon. Mr Kilpatrick was long and favourably known in Leith. He was a widower well advanced in life. It is not known how the accident happened, but it is supposed that Mr Kilpatrick had stumbled, and been pitched over the low bulwarks by the heavy swell which was on the sea at the time."*

Isle of May, River Forth. On a stormy night in October 1871, Robert Kilpatrick, while piloting a steam yacht, WASP of Dunkirk, was lost overboard near the Isle of May, at the entrance to the River Forth. Unusually his death was not registered. The circumstances of his death were traced in the Trinity House records and in a local newspaper.

Image KY Collection 2011

Is there a hint of mystery in this epitaph for the grandfather on the 'Man with the Donkey'? Why was he walking about the deck of the ship, not the bridge? Robert Kilpatrick was sufficiently successful that he left a will. (SCO 70/1/55 Edinburgh Sherriff Court Inventories)

> *"Inventory of the personal estate wherever situated of Robert Kirkpatrick, Queen's Pilot, Leith who was drowned on the 14th day of October 1871.*
>
> **Scotland:**
>
> | | |
> |---|---|
> | *Cash in house* | *£ 25. 0.0* |
> | *Value of furniture and effects* | *£ 5.10.0* |
> | *Deposit in the Clydesdale Bank, including interest accrued* | *£100.19.11* |
> | | *£140.19.11* |
>
> *Signed by Margaret Brown (married daughter). Executor*
> *Signed by James Watt, J.P."*

There were no specific bequests, so the money was left at the disposal of Margaret Brown.

Robert Kilpatrick's records are unique genealogically.   His birth is **not** recorded in the Old Parish Records, and his death is **not** recorded in the Statutory Death Register. As a result there is no way of finding the names of his parents.

Primary Sources

OPR 168/0A Births, Aberdeen
Old Parish Records, Scotland's People
U.K. Births, Marriages and Deaths Index
U.K. Census 1841, 1851, 1861, 1871
Crew Lists and Agreements, National Archives, Kew
Master's Certificate for Robert Kilpatrick, National Maritime Museum, Greenwich
Trinity House Records for Leith Pilots, NAS GD 226-9-10
Probates and Wills 1871, Scotland

APPENDIX II

Jack's Kirkpatrick Uncle and Aunts

When Jack Kirkpatrick completed his first voyage in 1909 as a merchant seaman, his ship the HEIGHINGTON discharged her crew in Leith on 20th December 1909. If Jack had only known, he could have visited his Dad's younger brother John who lived with his second wife Mary, and three daughters at 20 Trinity Crescent. Jack's cousins Margaret aged 14, Mary aged 12 and Eva aged 11, would have taken girlish pleasure in meeting their handsome seafaring cousin still only 17, but looking more like the 19 year old he claimed to be. Jack would have found a kindred spirit in his Uncle John, a retired seaman aged 65. John's maritime career took an unusual turn. After serving as a boatswain on a Light vessel the PHAROS, he was appointed Master of the NORTH CARR LIGHTSHIP, stationed 7 miles from the Isle of May, guarding the most eastern point of the Fife Coast. John's command was unusual. He was Master of a ship that went nowhere and indeed had no means of propulsion. The lightship was towed to its station and anchored in 22 fathoms of water. The crew of six, plus a master were provisioned and relieved by an attendant vessel kept at Crail harbour. Families of crewmen were obliged to live in Crail on the north side of the River Forth.

North Carr Light Ship with Master John Kirkpatrick on the step.
Image Courtesy of the Northern Lighthouse Board

If Jack had gone to 7 Salamander Street, Leith in search of his aunt, Margaret (Kirkpatrick) Brown, he would have been disappointed. Margaret had died 31st December 1908, ten months before her brother Robert in South Shields. Present at Aunt Margaret's death, was another aunt, Elizabeth (Kirkpatrick) Goudie, but if Jack had wanted to visit her, he would have had to take a train to Glasgow, and if he had done so, he could have visited three Simpson aunts and an uncle as well. But he did not take the train to Glasgow. Instead Jack wrote a letter to his mother from Leith on December 13th 1909, saying *"I was ashore in Leith Wark* and all over the shop, but it was terribly cold, there was a severe frost on and this morning it is snowing."*

Patently he knew nothing of his relatives and perhaps next to nothing of his mother and father's life in Leith. What were Sarah's thoughts when she read that her son was walking the streets of Leith that she knew so well?

*The 'King's Wark' is still in Leith, a cosy 17th century inn with plenty of character and serving excellent seafood in the 21st century.

Primary Sources

Statutory Registers, Birth Marriages and Deaths, Scotland
UK census returns
Northern Lighthouse Board Records

APPENDIX III

Sarah Simpson's Brothers
– Jack's Uncles

When James and Ann Simpson brought their family from Malaga to settle in Govan it comprised seven daughters and three sons and with such a large family they must have had expectations of becoming grandparents many times over, perhaps, with grandsons to carry on the family name. If they did cherish such hopes they were doomed to disappointment. The three sons, all born in Malaga, were James, born 30th May 1849, Sebastian born 7th August 1851, and Samuel born 2nd February 1857. In the 1871 census for Govan only Sebastian was living in the family home at 93 Gloucester Street.

SEBASTIAN SIMPSON

Sebastian, evidently following in his father's footsteps as an engineer, was listed in the 1871 census as 'Engine Fitter (at Works)'. Age 20 he was near to finishing his apprenticeship. Sometime in the next year, maybe after his 21st birthday in August 1872 he decided to further his career at sea in the merchant navy. His first ship was called the MABEL, but no Crew Agreement or details of the voyage have been found for this vessel.

His next ship was the LIBERIA a 927 ton steamship based in Liverpool, managed by Elder Dempster and working in the West African service. The LIBERIA and Sebastian were heading for a region known in the 19th century as 'the white man's graveyard', a region where Malaria and Yellow Fever were endemic. The Crew Agreement for the voyage shows Sebastian Simpson, age 22, born Malaga, previous ship MABEL, enlisted on the 5th April 1873 as 4th Engineer for a wage of £9 a month. The LIBERIA had the accolade of Royal Mail Steamer, that is, she had a lucrative contract to carry Government Mail as well as passengers and cargo. In the course of the voyage she called at 31 ports, exposing the crew to the prevailing health hazards.

The Ship's Log which has survived along with the Crew Agreement shows the voyage was not uneventful. On the 28th April the LIBERIA was in collision with a barque, the JEANNE ET MATHILDE of Havre, which was wrecked. The LIBERIA lowered three boats and rescued all of the crew except one man who had jumped overboard. Three surf boats only were saved from the barque.

The Log also shows that Sebastian and four other crew men died on the voyage, four of fever and one of phthisis. The entry for Sebastian reads as follows:

"May 13[th,] 5.15 pm: Fernando Po.   Sebastian Simpson, Fourth Engineer, died. Cause of death, Fever. Medical treatment adopted as usual by the Ship's Surgeon.
May 13th. 8.45 pm: Off Fernando Po. Committed the remains of the late Sebastian Simpson to the Deep.

Robert Lowry, Master
John Fairburn Sanderson, Mate
John A. Ray, L.R.S.C.P.S"
(writing not legible)

Isabella-Bai auf Fernando Po.

Isabella Bay, Fernando Po. On 13th May 1872, Sebastian Simpson aged 22, 4th Engineer on board the LIBERIA, died of fever at 5.15pm. Three and a half hours later at 8.45pm, his body was buried at sea, off the island of Fernando Po.

Image KY Collection

Without obituary the life and career of a promising young man came to an abrupt and premature end. The Master and the Mate made an inventory of

Sebastian's effects and recorded this in the Log. The list of Sebastian's personal effects immediately gives us a glimpse of a very real young man.

> **_Inventory of the effects of the late Sebastian Simpson._**
> _One Carpet Bag Sundries – One small Bag Papers – One Album Photographs – One Note Book – One Round Mat – One Salineometer in Case – Four Books – Twenty Shirts - Thirteen pairs Pants – Three Singlets – Six pairs Drawers – Six Jackets – Twenty Six Pairs Socks – Two White Fronts – Two Towels – Five Neckties – Five Caps – Seven Handkerchiefs – Three Cloth Vests – Three Cloth Coats – Three Keys – One Clothes Brush – Three Pair Shoes – One Pair Slippers – Three Belts - £5-14-0 – two rings._

If only that photograph album had survived!

Along with the Log, an official Board of Trade Form, ACCOUNT OF WAGES, has been filed. This shows:

Wages due: 1 month, 9 days.	£12 – 0 – 0
Deductions:	
Advance.	£9 – 0 - 0
Shipping Fees	3 - 0
Tobacco	7 – 6
Pursers a/c	£1 – 13 – 4
Total Deductions	**£11 – 3 – 10**
Balance Due	**£0 – 6 – 2**

From this we can see that young Sebastian was already a pipe smoker.

The LIBERIA returned to Liverpool on 17th June. The crew were discharged that day, the cargo of cocoa beans was auctioned off the following week, and on 28th June the wages of the deceased seamen were handed over to the Marine Superintendent who entered the details in his register. The effects were received on 30th June, the total of Sebastian's estate amounting to £6 – 5 – 8d. (ref. BT 153/13). The devastating news of Sebastian's death must have been relayed to the family within a couple of days of the ship's arrival. The following cursory announcement appeared in the Deaths column of the Glasgow Herald dated 21st June 1873:

"At Fernando Po, on the 13th ult, SEBASTIAN SIMPSON, age 22, engineer S.S. Liberia. – Friends please accept this intimation."

The heartbreak would be repeated when the crate with Sebastian's effects reached 93 Waterloo Place. His mother must have choked with tears when she unpacked the 20 shirts, 26 pairs of socks, 6 pairs drawers and all the other clothes which she had packed lovingly to send him on a new career. The grief may also have had a damaging effect on his father's mental balance. This was another blow on top of the quarrel which tore 17 year old daughter Sarah out of the family home that same year.

Note:

Fernando Po, an island off Africa's west coast, modern name Bioku, was a Spanish colony with a strong British presence. Queen Victoria's interests in Fernando Po were represented by a British Consul, Mr Charles Livingstone, brother of the famous Scottish missionary Doctor David Livingstone and by a senior naval officer with a small team of clerks, storekeepers and admin staff. The Royal Navy used it as a base to hunt slave traders.

SAMUEL SIMPSON

On the morning of the 25th August 1870, shortly after 9.30 am, the sail-ship LOCHLEVEN CASTLE loosed her moorings at a Glasgow wharf, and a tug started to ease her into mid-stream. A 13 year old boy stood at the rail and waved goodbye to his mother and father on the quayside. The boy was Samuel Simpson, youngest of three sons born to Ann and James Simpson, 93 Gloucester Street, Govan, Glasgow. Young Samuel had reported on board with the rest of the crew before 9.30 am as required by the ship's crew agreement. His father had helped him on board with his sea chest and handed him over to the Master, John MacDiarmid, of 44 Gloucester Street, a neighbour who probably knew Samuel and his family already. James Simpson had signed the Indentures and paid a premium to apprentice his son as a trainee officer in the mercantile service. The Indenture had been registered on 27th February 1868 when Samuel was only eleven, too young to leave school, so he had to spend the next two years in the classroom before he would cast off from his mother's apron strings.

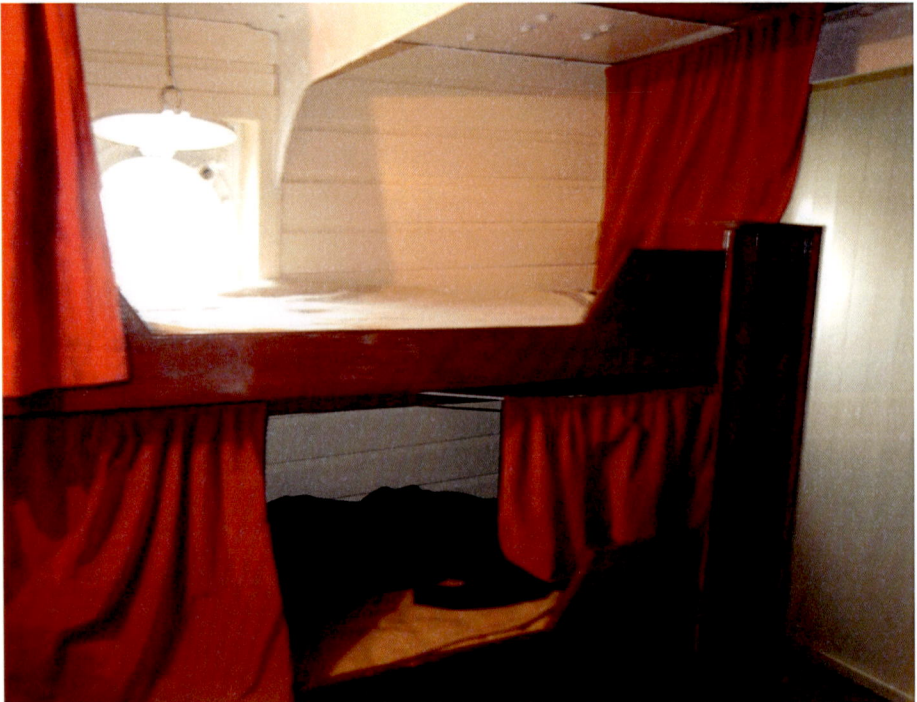

Samuel Simpson. Apprentice's cabin aboard a 19th Century sailing ship. Indentured lads worked with the crew but slept separately, and ate with the officers. Apprentice Samuel lived in such cramped quarters for three years.
Image 'On board the GLENLEE, Glasgow', K Yuill Collection

As the LOCHLEVEN CASTLE opened a gap between hull and the quay, Samuel was already distancing himself from home, a house dominated by females. He left behind seven sisters, and only one brother, Sebastian, six years his elder. His eldest brother James was fourteen years older than him, a big age gap, and had already left home to work as an engine fitter in Greenock on the lower reaches of the River Clyde. Any pangs of homesickness were soon lost in the thrill of sailing down the Clyde, amongst ships of all sizes, ferries, tugs, steamers, but best of all to his mind, the majestic sailing ships. For two years Samuel had watched the ships on the river; he had read stories of the sea; this was the day he had dreamed of and for him the LOCHLEVEN CASTLE was as beautiful as any, sailing to exotic destinations on the other side of the world.

The reality was of course, very different. The LOCHLEVEN CASTLE was a cargo ship whose sole purpose was to earn a profit for her owners, Thomas Skinner and Company of Glasgow. Weighing in at 602 tons, hull made of iron, length 180.2 feet, width 28.1 feet, and draft 18.2 feet, she could carry approximately 1,000 tons of cargo anywhere in the world without having to touch land. On shipping rates, she was competitive with the new-fangled steamers which were more costly to build, needed a greater number of hands to operate, and had to stop en-route to take on coal. LOCHLEVEN CASTLE sailed with a crew of only 20; a Master, 1st Mate, 2nd Mate, carpenter, steward, cook, 7 able seamen, 3 ordinary seamen, a boy and 3 apprentices; and she needed only the wind in her sails for propulsion, a source of power which was free but unpredictable. With sufficient provisions and water on-board she could reach ports on the other side of the globe without halting.

Samuel Simpson's fellow apprentices were William Douglas, aged 20 and David Lawrence, aged 17. The apprentices on a merchant ship occupied an ambiguous position on board a merchant ship. They were quartered in the tween deck, neither officers nor hands; they ate the same food as the seamen; they had to perform the same tasks as the hands, but had also to learn the job of an officer, tallying cargos loaded and discharged, the laws of commerce, and most importantly, sailing and navigation skills. The apprentice was cheap labour, but the Master was obliged to teach him seamanship, navigation, trigonometry, sightings, mercantile law, and to feed him. At the end of a 4 year indenture, for which his father paid £25 or £30, Samuel should have acquired enough knowledge of seamanship and navigation to pass the Board of Trade examination for a 2nd Mate's certificate.

Life for a 13 year old apprentice was no smooth passage. A seafarer who progressed from apprentice to master, Alexander Bone, a contemporary of Samuel Simpson, published his memoirs in 1932.('Bowsprit Ashore') He gives a vivid account of his time as an apprentice, an account which can be little different from the experiences of Samuel. The following quotes are from his book:

> "I had two worries, sleep and food – I could never get enough of either. That boy could go to sleep with his head in the lee scuppers in a gale wind", I heard this remark of the 2nd Mate's as I hurried down the poop ladder on the way to the half-deck and my bunk. I had gone to sleep on the companionway stairs while waiting to strike eight bells, and the 2nd Mate had found me there with the clock showing five minutes past twelve. He had cuffed and kicked me which I didn't mind much – I was used to it!"

This was a time when corporal punishment was an acceptable part of everyday life. School masters caned pupils, or in Scotland used a leather belt; the army and navy were not quite at the point of giving up flogging; and magistrates could still prescribe the birch for minor offenders.

The deck hands on board ship were divided into two watches, port and starboard, each taking a four hour turn to sail the ship, steering, lookout, setting and trimming the sails. The four hour watches ran from midnight to 4 am, 4am to 8am, 8am to 12 noon, noon to 4pm. The next period was split into two dog-watches, 4pm to 6pm, 6pm to 8pm, then back to 4 hours from 8pm until midnight. The dog watches enabled the crew to have the main meal of the day served either side of the six o'clock. This pattern of working meant no one had rest or sleep for more than four hours at a time. Some crew members, known as 'idlers', worked days: the carpenter, the sailmaker, the steward and the cook. The apprentices however, were allocated to a watch, commanded by the First or Second Mate.

Samuel Simpson's first job was time-keeping. The progression of time during the watch was marked by the ringing of the ship's bell. At the end of the first half hour, one bell was struck, at the end of the first hour, two bells, and so on until the end of the watch when eight bells signalled the time for the watches to change over. Samuel had to sit by the bell watching a half-hour sand glass, turning it as needed and striking the appropriate number of bells. This was not a strenuous task during daytime. At night he also had to trim the navigation and binnacle lights, and with little bustle to hold his attention, it must have been so tempting to close the eyes, "boys will sleep, boys must sleep", said a captain's wife.

As time progressed, Samuel had to 'learn the ropes' and the sails. He would soon be expected to climb the masts or out onto the bowsprit to handle the canvas. His training on watch below comprised of trigonometry and navigation, taking sightings from the sun or stars. This side of an apprentice's education depended very much on the proclivities of the master and mates. There was no prescribed syllabus.

The LOCHLEVEN CASTLE left the Clyde carrying a mixed cargo and she would not touch land again until she reached her intended destination, Singapore. Unwittingly, she was also carrying a passenger. Two days out from Glasgow a stowaway was discovered, who gave his name as George Fitzgerald, aged 15, from Glasgow. It was too late to put him ashore so he was put to work to earn his keep. Eventually, the Master put him on the articles (payroll) as a 'Boy' at the rate of 5 shillings per month, 'because of his good behaviour'. Samuel Simpson had a fellow trainee starting at the same point on the learning curve of seamanship.

The Crew Agreement sets out the Scale of Provisions allowed for each man daily. It also states "the Crew agree to conduct themselves in an orderly, faithful, honest and sober manner", and to emphasise the point, the last clause added to the agreement says clearly "No spirits allowed". For seamen who invariably had a liking for strong drink, the prospect of a 5 month voyage with no alcohol was grim.

On the 27th October 1870, sixty six days out, the carpenter reported to the Chief Mate that the battens on the fore hatch had been tampered with. When the Chief Mate inspected the cargo it was found 'seven barrels of Porter (a stout) were quite empty'. The Master summoned the crew aft and threatened to clap the ringleader in irons. The broaching of the cargo had started shortly after leaving Glasgow apparently. The Master's threats however did not deter the thirsty thieves. The ship's log records on 7th November, further broaching of the cargo had occurred, the thieves gaining entry through a ventilator, and by breaking through a bulkhead from the cable locker. In consequence James Blair, Thomas Todd, David Elder and John Negreene were clapped in irons, following evidence given on oath by boy stowaway, George Fitzgerald. Blair as heard to say, "the first man to turn Queen's Evidence, he would throw overboard?" Blair and Todd were also reported to say they would give the 2nd Mate and the Carpenter a drubbing for finding they had opened the fore hatch.

The apprentices were not involved in these proceedings, but young Samuel Simpson was certainly learning fast about his shipmates and their failings, and about the problems he might face some day as a Master running his ship. The ship at this point was 39.54° South; 32.44° East, that is she had rounded the Cape of Good Hope, South Africa and was running eastwards towards Australia. The next entry of consequence in the log told of quite a different problem for the ship and her crew.

The LOCHLEVEN CASTLE had left the 'cold discomfort of the forties', and by the 30th November, St Andrew's Day, the ship had reached a position of 19° South, 86° East, in the middle of the Indian Ocean between the African and Australian continents, but the Scots on the ship were not celebrating their patron saint's day. They were fighting for their lives. The account of events in the log book is quite laconic.

> "In a hurricane of Wind, lost the Fore topmast and Main top gallant Mast. I called on deck the Prisoners to assist in clearing away the Waste. During the time the Waste was being cleared away and the ship refitted, say 8 days, the men behaved so well and were so attentive to orders, I promised not to prosecute them, providing they would behave themselves for the remainder of the voyage, and that the (losses) having to do with the Broaching of the Beer would be an equal share of what was charged to the Ship for Short Delivery of Beer. They consented.
>
> (signed) J, McDairmid, Master, Thomas Kneelong, Mate."

A first year apprentice Albert Bestic, in a similar stormy situation, but different ship said, *"We were enclosed in a little mad universe of our own – nothing but fury, tumult and the ship".*

The experience of the hurricane must have been frightening for the seasoned hands. It must have been absolutely terrifying for a first time voyager like 13 year old Samuel Simpson. He survived the ordeal nonetheless and emerged the stronger for it. A sailing ship carried enough spare timber, cordage and canvas to carry out a refit at sea. The LOCHLEVEN CASTLE carried on through the Strait of Sunda, reaching Singapore on the 11th January 1871, without having to make an intermediate stop for repairs.

Singapore Docks, the destination for Samuel's first voyage.

At Singapore, as soon as the ship was made fast, with all sails furled, the crew, excepting the officers and apprentices, drew an advance of pay and headed for the bars, boarding houses and brothels to quench their five month thirst for drink and female companionship. The mates remained on board to supervise the loading and unloading of cargo, work performed by the local stevedores – not by merchant seaman. The mates had to maintain an accurate tally of the goods unloaded or loaded, and who better to assist with the paperwork than bright young apprentices who could read, write and count. Moreover the apprentices had little money with which to go on a spree. The aforementioned Alex Bone, apprentice on the KILLORAN, recollected being paid 6 pence a week. His trips ashore were with the Master to procure meat from the butcher, or provisions from the wholesaler, or ships necessaries from the chandler. The Master who controlled the purse strings, and shared the profits from the voyage, also had to call on his Shipping Agent for orders for his next cargo, a piece of business often conducted apparently over dinner and a dram in the clubhouse or hotel.

The LOCHLEVEN CASTLE's stay in Singapore was short, only nine days. On the 20th January, the British Consul returned the ship's Articles to the Master. In spite of the friction between the Master and crew on the outward journey, all hands reported on board ship at the appointed time. The vessel set off north eastwards through the Strait of Malacca and the Andaman Sea. 30 days later, the ship's Articles were deposited with the Shipping Master at Akyab in Burma (modern Sittwe) a centre of rice production. There were no desertions. The ship pushed out into the Bay of Bengal and thence sailed for home stopping only at St Helena for a supply of cabbages, watercress, potatoes, fruit and fish (thereby staving off scurvy) and sent letters to be posted for home.

The logbook entries show the return journey, 142 days was less eventful, although they reveal an unexpected side of the Master's job. On 17th March, David Lamont was promoted to 3rd Mate on completion of his indenture. He received the same pay as an Able Seaman, but enjoyed the benefit of 'cabin food'. On the 18th July, the Master once more made an entry concerning James Blair, but not for theft or drunkenness this time.

> *"45°North 20°West. James Blair off ill with Stricture and Rupture, he has been ill several times during the voyage but always got better by keeping his bowels open and administering a Soothing Mixture. Today I was obliged to use the Catheter which relieved him".*

A further entry reads:

> *"25th July 1871, in St George's Channel. James Blair is still off duty with Rupture but getting better, he walks with difficulty and wishes to be taken to hospital on the ship's arrival in Liverpool.*

The Master and officers, armed with a Board of Trade Medical Handbook, had to perform the role of doctor, nurse and pharmacist, and apprentices like Samuel Simpson would be given the opportunity to practice these skills as the need arose.

The LOCHLEVEN CASTLE reached Liverpool on 27th July 1871 discharging her cargo of rice, and terminating the crew's Foreign Trade Agreement. She then sailed for the Broomielaw, Glasgow carrying a load of Salt, arriving on the 14th August 1871. It was a changed Samuel who knocked on the door of 93 Gloucester Street, now 14 years old, tanned, taller, broader and more worldly wise.

Samuel made five voyages altogether in the LOCHLEVEN CASTLE. The Articles for the first voyage recounted above, contained the personnel log which has been used to give an insight to life on board a sailing ship in the second half of the 19th century. Samuel's second voyage, leaving Glasgow 7th October 1871, returning to Liverpool 11th August 1872, followed the same trade routes once more to Singapore.

The third voyage broadened Samuel's horizons. After two trips to the Far East, he was heading west to the Americas. The LOCHLEVEN CASTLE had new managing owners, Hargrove and Company, Liverpool, and a new Master, Henry Barlow. Samuel's indenture was transferred with the ship. He was now senior apprentice aged 14, with a green, first voyager below him, Charles McIntosh, aged 13 from Glasgow. The LOCHLEVEN CASTLE sailed from Liverpool 18th October 1872, bound for Valparaiso, the principal port in Chile, on the west coast of South America. The commodities traded were normally coal out and guano back. The latter is the result of bird droppings deposited over centuries and is a rich source of nitrate, a fertiliser in great demand in 19th century Europe and elsewhere, when agriculture was struggling to increase the production of food and cereals needed to feed rapidly increasing populations. 'Where there's muck, there's money' goes an old saying and there was much money to be made out of the trade in guano. Spain went to war with her former colony Chile, for possession of it.

Valparaiso was notorious for another trade. Old shellbacks remembered well the 'Shakespeare' and the 'Crossed Flags'. Boarding houses run respectively by a hard Irishman called Byrne and a West Indian coloured man, both ruthless crimpers and shanghaiers. Their victims, if lucky, woke with a headache on board a vessel bound for London or Liverpool; if unlucky, on board a sealer heading for the Arctic or a whaler bound for Antarctica.

WAR BETWEEN SPAIN AND CHILI.

THE PORT OF VALPARAISO, CHILI, SOUTH AMERICA.

THE PLAZA DE LA INTENDENCIA AT VALPARAISO, WHERE WAR WITH SPAIN WAS PROCLAIMED.—SEE PAGE 2.

Valparaiso. Samuel's third voyage took him to Chile, first to Valparaiso, the main port and commercial capital, a route his nephew Jack would take 38 years later.

Image KY Collection

IQUIQUE—VIEW TAKEN FROM THE SEA.

THE SOUTH AMERICAN WAR—TOWN AND HARBOUR OF IQUIQUE, PERU
SCENE OF THE LATE NAVAL ENGAGEMENT

Iquique. After discharging at Valparaiso, Sam's ship proceeded to Iquique to collect a cargo of guano – a place described by a contemporary as "a stinking town of wooden houses and godowns. Nothing but sand; no amusements, plenty of vice and gambling".

292

Inevitably the LOCHLEVEN CASTLE lost 9 hands while in Valparaiso; 4 deserted, 4 discharged by mutual consent and one remained behind due to illness.   By dint of trawling the crimping houses, bars and jail, 10 men were signed on by the First Mate, but at the time of sailing, three men 'failed to join'! LOCHLEVEN CASTLE's homeward passage terminated at Liverpool on 2nd July 1873.

When Samuel returned to Glasgow he was greeted with the sad news that his brother Sebastian, on only his second voyage as a fourth engineer had died of fever and was buried at sea near the island of Fernando Po, off the coast of West Africa.

Samuel's fourth voyage, still aboard the LOCHLEVEN CASTLE commenced at Liverpool, 4th August 1873, destined once more for the nitrate coast of Chile, but this time to Iquique, some 3°of latitude further north than Valparaiso. A first voyage apprentice, Albert Bestic, seeing the Chilean coast for the first time described it as follows:

> *"A waste of forbidding mountains with not a house in sight. Where were my Pacific Islands with blue lagoons and waving palm trees and dusky maidens dancing the hula-hula beneath the coconut groves? Instead the gods offered me Mollendos."*

No doubt Samuel Simpson suffered the same disappointment when he arrived at Iquique. Another contemporary, Thomas Fraser, a very precocious captain at the age of 23, also arrived at Iquique in 1874 in a sailing ship. He declared:

> *"Iquique was a stinking town of wooden houses and godowns. Nothing but sand; no amusements, plenty of vice and gambling".*

Before proceeding to Iquique, the LOCHLEVEN CASTLE called at Valparaiso to discharge cargo, arriving there about the 10th December 1873. The outcome was similar to the previous voyage – six men were tempted to desert for the pleasures of shore life, and again replacements had to be found from the bars and boarding houses. Captain Henry Barlow also had to find a replacement for his Chief Mate, Robert Laurence who left by mutual consent. Captain Barlow it appears was of a quarrelsome nature. On the previous voyage he logged complaints against the First Mate because the ship's boat was not waiting for him at the jetty after a late night ashore. On the current voyage, he logged complaints against the sailmaker who had not made straps to secure the Captain's chicken coops as promptly as ordered. The feud continued when 'Sails' refused to climb the rigging to carry out repairs to a sail in situ.

At Iquique, the LOCHLEVEN CASTLE had to anchor two miles off the shore. The cargo of guano was brought to the ship by stevedores in sacks aboard lighters. The ship's crew, including Samuel and the other apprentice had to stow the sacks in the hold, a task that took 2 to 3 weeks. The stench of ammonia in the confined space of the hold made this work nauseous and objectionable- a far cry from the dreams of romantic, tropical islands. The LOCHLEVEN CASTLE delivered her malodourous cargo to Havre in France on June 23rd 1874, no doubt making a handsome profit for her owners and Captain Barlow.

Samuel's 5th voyage on the LOCHLEVEN CASTLE would be his last on that ship. It also marked the expiry of his Indenture on the 3rd August 1874. The following day he was entered on the articles as a fully-fledged able seaman at a pay of £3-10/- a month. Aged 17, he moved his sea chest out of the half deck into the forecastle to join the hands in the forecastle, some of the toughest characters afloat. His mother and sisters would not have approved of his new companions. Voyage 5 took Samuel back to the Far East. Lloyds reported the LOCHLEVEN CASTLE at Singapore 27th November 1874 and at Yokohama on the 12th January 1875. Able Seaman Simpson with £3-10/- a month in his pocket could afford to enjoy the diversions offered ashore. The voyage terminated in Liverpool 21st May 1875.

Samuel stayed at home for only a month. Perhaps home was no longer comfortable for him. His brother Sebastian had died at sea; his two sisters to whom he had been closest in age, Ann and Sarah had quit under a storm cloud; his father was increasingly aloof and brooding; and his eldest sisters were a world apart from his roughneck companions in the forecastle, in their education, manners and social aspirations. Maybe Samuel was by now more at home in the forecastle. He left home and shipped out again on the 25th June returning to his old employers Skinner and Company of Glasgow, on the ROSLIN CASTLE, a sailing ship of similar tonnage to the LOCHLEVEN CASTLE. He signed on as an able seaman at £3-10/- a month. At the expiry of his indenture he could have taken the Board of Trade exam for a 2nd Mate's certificate, but had not done so. The ROSLIN CASTLE was destined for Chilean ports already familiar to Samuel, Valparaiso and Iquique. The treacherous seas round Cape Horn, and the obnoxious fumes from a hold loaded with guano, did not deter Samuel from signing on.

Valparaiso was reached on 10th November. The ROSLIN CASTLE remained there until 17th December when she sailed for Iquique, dropping anchor there on the 27th December. She was anchored off this desolate little town until March 9th 1876. Loading guano was slow and laborious, the guano being delivered in sacks, had to be hoisted aboard and stored in the hold by the crew. The ROSLIN CASTLE suffered no desertions in Iquique, losing only one able seaman, 19 year old William Lawson from Glasgow by mutual consent. He was replaced by a Londoner, Thomas O'Connor. The ROSLIN CASTLE terminated her voyage in Hamburg on July 10th 1876, where the crew were discharged. How Samuel Simpson returned to Glasgow is unknown, but a scratch crew were probably retained to sail the ship back to her home port. Samuel received the balance due of his wages, a substantial sum, £25-9-2d. Evidently there had been few distractions in Iquique on which he could spend his pay.

When Samuel reached home, he walked into a nightmare. His father had lost his sanity completely. Paranoid, he was threatening violence against his wife Ann and his daughters; he was threatening arson; he was threatening suicide and he had a revolver in his desk. Ann Simpson had initiated court proceedings to have her husband committed to an asylum. Meanwhile 19 year old Samuel, the only other man in the household, had to protect his mother and his five sisters from his father's threats. Luckily his life at sea had toughened him both physically and mentally. Samuel's watch was relieved when his elder brother James, a ship's engineer arrived home at the eleventh hour to take charge of the situation. Samuel had reached the point where he was ready to take the examination for his Second Mate's certificate, and was called on the 17th August 1876. That same day, two independent doctors called at 93 Gloucester Street, to examine his father as part of the committal process. Given the turmoil at home it is not surprising that Samuel failed at his first attempt. Two days later, the Court authorised the receipt of James Simpson senior, at the Royal Glasgow Asylum for Lunatics at Gartnavel. Three weeks later on the 6th September, at the local Marine Board, Glasgow, Samuel retook and passed in all subjects; navigation, seamanship and commercial code signals.

2nd Mate's Certificate. Samuel gained his Second Mate Certificate on 9th September 1876 but did not obtain a position immediately. He sailed from Glasgow, 3rd October on the LOCH LEVEN as an Able Seaman, bound for Melbourne.
Image Courtesy of the National Maritime Museum, Greenwich

Sometime in September, the two maritime brothers parted company – for the last time. James returned to Liverpool where he passed his First Engineer's examinations on 25th September 1876.

Samuel shipped out on the 3rd October from Glasgow on the LOCH LOMOND, a sailing ship, bound for Melbourne with Master, Mr T Meiklejohn. He was not able to benefit from his new 2nd Mate's certificate, however, and signed on as an Able Seaman for a wage of £3.10/- a month. The LOCH LOMOND, a handsome sail ship of 1249 gross tons was Samuel's biggest ship so far and was carrying 30 passengers, 17 of them in first class, and a mixed cargo ranging from pig iron and machinery to 1500 cases of whisky and 1650 casks of bottled ale. On arrival at Melbourne on 9th January 1877 Samuel deserted along with eight of his fellow crewmen. It was not uncommon for merchant seamen to desert an unhappy ship. His nephew Jack (Simpson) would do so in 1910. The reason for discontent on board the LOCH LOMOND may have been the Captain's predilection for alcohol. On arrival of the ship a number of the passengers lodged a complaint of drunkenness against Captain Meiklejohn. The Melbourne Argus of 23rd January reported the result of a meeting of the Steam Navigation Board who found the charges "fully sustained" and suspended the captain's master's certificate for 18 months. Captain Meiklejohn travelled home in disgrace, a passenger on board his own ship.

Hobson's Bay Railway Pier, Melbourne c1880. Samuel Simpson's first view of Melbourne perhaps. Sailing ships still in the majority.
Image Courtesy of the National Gallery, Victoria PH601992

Samuel spent the next three months moonlighting around Melbourne before signing on as an able seaman aboard a new ship the EAGLE WING on 11th April 1877, a Brigantine of 175 tons, with Master Henry Blake. The superintendent of the Merchant Marine Office in Melbourne sanctioned Samuel's engagement (amongst others) which suggests Samuel had disproved the charge of desertion. The crew agreement was unusual in that an extra clause was inserted against the name of Samuel and five other seamen:

> *"To be discharged on return to Melbourne, or within six months from this date, if the ship does not return to Melbourne. 11/4/77."*

297

The EAGLE WING traded as far as Wellington but at the end of six months had not returned to Melbourne but had arrived instead in the Lacepede Islands, 20 km west of the Dampier Peninsula, 150 km north of Broome. Today the four sandy bays are a bird sanctuary, uninhabited and visited only occasionally by local cruise ships. Before 1876, the islands had been home for centuries for millions of sea birds who obligingly left deposits of guano several feet thick. By 1876, guano had become a prized commodity as a source of phosphate for agricultural fertiliser, so valuable that nations came close to war to obtain it. In 1866, hostilities broke out when Spain tried to take possession of guano islands off the coast of her former colonies Chile and Peru.

THE HURRICANE AT LACEPEDE ISLAND: THE SHIPS ON SHORE AFTER THE STORM

Hurricane at Lacepede Island, Western Australia. A few months after this storm, Samuel arrived here aboard the EAGLE WING, to take on board a cargo of guano.

Sam left the ship and spent 8 months on the islands before signing on as 2nd Mate on the EASTERN CHIEF, bound for Fremantle, then onto Hamburg.

In 1876 an American adventurer raised the U.S. flag on the Lacepedes, but after a flurry of diplomatic activity between Western Australia, London and Washington the U.S. President Ulysses Grant graciously repudiated the claim. Western Australia then sent an administrator, Richard Wynne, to regulate the mining of guano and to collect the royalties payable to the Western Australian government. For a period of four years these tiny islands became a hive of activity with up to 165 men excavating the guano, bagging it in hessian sacks, and with a dozen ships in the anchorage at any one time loading from make shift jetties or small boats. The main destination for the guano was Hamburg.

When the EAGLE WING arrived in the Lacepedes in October 1877, Captain Blake wished to take his ship to Mauritius, but Samuel Simpson and the other five crewmen who had signed on for six months only, or for discharge in Melbourne refused to sail. The dispute was referred to Richard Wynne, the Government Representative who with the advice of two other ships' masters present in the anchorage, decided in favour of Samuel and his ship mates. As a result Samuel was paid off with arrears of pay amounting to £22-7-0, a considerable sum. On a near desert island there was not much for Sam to spend his money on though reports from Wynne tell of a ready supply of alcohol. Sam's money however had to last him eight months before he found a berth on a sail ship the EASTERN CHIEF bound for Fremantle.

Crew Quarters on a 19th century sailing ship. Samuel returned to Hamburg on the EASTERN CHIEF, via the Lacepedes again, October 1878 – April 1879. He reverted to the lower rank of able seaman, living in the forecastle with the other crewmen.
Image 'On board the GLENLEE, Glasgow', K Yuill Collection

Mate's cabin on a 19th century sailing ship. For his final voyage, Samuel enjoyed the luxury if a cabin to himself. He seems to have switched easily between the focs'le and the officers' quarters.

Image 'On board the GLENLEE, Glasgow , K Yuill Collection

He signed on as Second Mate, elevating him from the forecastle to the officers' quarters for the first time, and was discharged on arrival at Fremantle 19th August 1878, but immediately signed on for the return journey to Europe though on the lower rank of able seaman. The EASTERN CHIEF was back in the Lacepedes in September where she took on a cargo of guano before making the voyage round the Cape of Good Hope and back to Hamburg. There the crew were discharged on the 8th April 1879. After a month Sam found a berth on a ship returning to the United Kingdom, the SCYTHIA, a Liverpool registered ship, which engaged him as second mate. After his adventures around the globe, Sam still only 23 arrived back in Cardiff on 30th May 1879. Did he then look up his Hosgood relatives? Was it only then he learned of the death of his younger sister Julia?

Samuel's association with the SCYTHIA was evidently mutually satisfactory as he assented to return for her next trip. Sam rejoined the SCYTHIA in Cardiff on 16th June 1879 sailing once more as Second Mate undeterred by the fact that she was destined for the west coast of South America.

300

The SCYTHIA left Cardiff 18th June 1879 carrying a cargo of coal for Chile.
On board was a crew of twenty, including 2nd Mate Samuel Simpson.
Image courtesy of the State Archives, South Australia.

The last crew members came on board 17th June and the Scythia sailed on the 18th. The ship and her crew then vanished into the vastness of the oceans. After eleven months with no sightings or reports of the SCYTHIA, the authorities accepted the ship was lost with all hands – 16 officers and crew, plus 4 apprentices. The deaths were recorded in the Marine Register, the date assumed to be the day after the ship sailed. The cause of death on Samuel's certificate reads, "Supposed Drowned".

In April 1880, a Board of Trade Inquiry was convened in St George's Hall, Liverpool to look into the loss of the SCYTHIA. The ship had left Cardiff on the 18th June 1879, loaded with 1,257 tons of ocean steam coal, bound for Payta in northern Peru. Since the Pilot left her off Ilfracombe in Devon, she had never been heard of. The Inquiry concentrated on three matters; the state of the vessel, the stowage of the cargo and the ventilation of the holds, given the explosive nature of coal. The ship was iron hulled built in 1868 for the Australian passenger trade, but later converted as a cargo carrier and was well maintained. The Captain William Nicol had made several voyages similar to this one laden with coal and was well aware of the precautions needed. On conversion, the ventilation cowls needed for the passenger carrying role, had been left in place, providing more ventilation than usual in a cargo ship. The Glasgow Herald of Wednesday 28th April 1880 reported:

> "The Court had no materials on which to form a conclusion as to the supposed loss of the vessel."

The Court did not speculate of course, but the Scythia may, like many others have foundered in the notoriously stormy seas off Cape Horn.

It would take a long time for the sad news to reach Pollok Street, Glasgow and may have been transmitted to the family via the Mission to Seamen, a religious Charity which maintained hostels in all the major ports around the world. The Simpsons did form a strong link with the charity and the final residue of the Simpson family wealth was bequeathed many years later to the Glasgow branch of the Seamen's Mission. However when the news reached his mother Ann, it came as another hammer blow to one whose spirit had already suffered more than it should.

JAMES SIMPSON JUNIOR

James Simpson, the eldest of the three Simpson brothers, was born in Malaga on the 30th May 1849, at the Angel Ironworks according to the consular records. He was the third child of James Simpson, manager of the Angel Ironworks and his wife Ann Hosgood Simpson. James became a seafarer, but unlike his brothers he would die of natural causes, although he was not destined to enjoy the longevity of his sisters, Jane, Martha and Helen.

His early years, and early education are obscure. Malaga had an English speaking population of around 300 in the mid-19th century but no reference has been found to an English school. There were English boarding schools available at Gibraltar, half a day sail away. However, alternatively, his parents may have hired private tutors for their ever growing family. It is almost inevitable that James, as eldest son, would be expected to follow in his father's footsteps as an engineer, and young James duly went to work at the Angel Ironworks - at the age of 13 if a formal apprenticeship was arranged. Fortuitously James not only learned his skills as an engineer, but also a fluency in the Spanish language which opened wider opportunities for him in his future career.

When the fortunes of the Simpson family crashed circa 1867, forcing them to forsake the good life in Spain for the colder clime of Glasgow, James was 18 years of age, and his training still incomplete. He may have served out his time in one of the many yards or engineering works in Govan, while living in the family home in Gloucester Street, but by April 1871, census time, he had moved out. The enumerators found him living at 18 Cathcart Road, Greenock, as a boarder in the home of William Dodd, a ship's carpenter, aged 22, his vocation being an 'Engine Fitter'.

Greenock on the lower reaches of the River Clyde lies half an hour, west of Glasgow by rail, and James could not have chosen a better place to further his training as a marine engineer. The oldest shipbuilding company in the world – Scott's, had been launching ships there since 1711. By the time James Simpson arrived in Greenock there were several more companies involved in shipbuilding, engine manufacture and ship repair; namely Browns, William Lithgow, Fergusons, Kincaid, Rankin and others. Moreover the Clyde yards were on a high of prosperity, especially Scott's of Greenock, as a consequence of the American Civil War, 1861 – 1865. The Confederate States, desperate for fast ships to run the Federal blockade of their ports, were prepared to pay high prices for fast ships with shallow draughts. The demands of war accelerated ship developments and the builders on the Clyde were happy to oblige. John Elder perfected the compound engine, Napier's improved boilers operating at higher temperatures and higher pressures, and Scott's of Greenock entered into partnership with a Confederate agent, Thomas Begbie to produce blockade runners. Ostensibly, these were built for neutral companies and non-belligerent purposes. Greenock became a hive of spies and counter spies, watching railway stations, shipyards and shipping movements. When the Civil War ended, the Southern States were bankrupt, but the Clyde Shipbuilders had made fortunes and more importantly, the ship builders, naval architects and designers had established a technological supremacy over the rest of the world, lasting for almost eight decades. James Simpson had arrived in a shipbuilding centre buzzing with work and optimism.

Custom House Quay, Greenock. In April 1871, the census listed James Simpson working as an 'Engine Fitter' in Greenock on the River Clyde, the birthplace of Scottish Shipbuilding and Marine Engineering following the Union with England in 1707. It also became a major port trading with the West Indies in sugar and tobacco.

Image KY Collection

The call of the sea finally got to James on 23rd January 1872 when he signed on the Glasgow steamer ANDES as 3rd Engineer, for a wage of £7.0.0.a month. He made no allotment from his wage at this time. The ANDES registered tonnage 950 was built in 1870 and carried a crew of 45, all ranks. Ship owners of the period were still distrustful of engines so steamers built in 1870 still carried spars and sails, partly for emergencies, partly to eke out the fuel costs and to extend the range. In comparison with sailing ships, steamers were costly, needed twice the number of crew, had expensive fuel costs and were limited to routes served by coaling stations, but they were faster and could reliably maintain time tables. The opening of the Suez Canal, 1865, dramatically reduced travel times to India, the 'Jewel in Queen Victoria's crown', and to other corners of her eastern empire. Ironically, the cheapest way to supply coal to the coaling stations around the globe was by sailing ship, thus giving a boost to the demand for sailing ships.

By contrast with his brother Samuel, James spent his working life below deck – not for him the sea breezes, the starry night skies and the distant horizon. His domain was below deck – hot, steamy and his main instruments were the ship's telegraph and the steam pressure gauge rather than the compass.

James's career at sea starting with the ANDES in January 1872 lasted approximately 25 years but there are many gaps in his record of service. When taking his 2nd and 1st Engineer exams, James had to list his ships and dates on his applications, and these are held with copies of his certificates in the National Maritime Museum, Greenwich. Once a seafarer was established as an engineer, the Board of Trade kept a Register of his service, ship by ship. This Register is held at National Archives, Kew, but the Board of Trade clerks could not keep up with the clerical effort needed. Moreover the data was only available for British Registered vessels. If, as happened with James, the engineer worked on foreign registered ships, no data were available to the Board of Trade and large gaps appeared in the Register. Faced with an ever increasing volume of work, the Board closed the Register at the end of 1888. Given names and dates for British registered ships, it should be possible to trace a man's service in Crew Agreements. Most are held at Maritime History Archives, Newfoundland, some at National Maritime Museum, Greenwich, some in the National Archives, Kew and some in County Archives; but quite a number have disappeared without trace. Happily the crew agreement for James's first ship, the ANDES has survived, and with it the Personnel log. The latter document survived in only a few instances. The ship carrying cargo and passengers sailed for the Brazils and

305

South America on the 5th January '72, but got off to a bad start. One fireman failed to join, and the bos'un, Donald McCaffer 'suffered injuries falling down the hold'. The Master, Adam Wilson had to anchor at Greenock, to ship a new Bos'un, Alex Drysdale and a replacement fireman. The ANDES troubles were not however over. By Friday 2nd February she was hundreds of miles off course, lying at Gironde where the River Garonne flows into the Bay of Biscay. The Master handed over command to the 1st Mate, Thomas S. McDougall and left the ship. No reason was given in the log. Illness may have been the cause, but the Master Adam Wilson, was a young man, only 32 years of age.

On March 3rd, the ANDES reached its destination. Buenos Ayres (original spelling). The new captain was having the usual disciplinary problems. While in the River Plate, William Coleman, an able seaman was found drunk on watch, having filched a bottle of absinthe from the cargo hold. At Rio de Janeiro, 14th April, fireman Peter Webb refused to work for 'either the Master or Chief Engineer'? At Bahia, on May 1st, the carpenter William Wemyss challenged the steward J. Campbell to a fight.

INDUSTRIAL ARGENTINA

The Madero Docks at Buenos Aires, extending for three miles along the city front

The destination for James first voyage as a marine engineer.

Image KY Collection

The ANDES recrossed the Atlantic stopping off briefly at Corunna, North West Spain, before proceeding to Antwerp, arriving there Friday 14th June and staying until the 16th. During the three days, John Nixon, mess room steward and Peter Mullin a trimmer, were sent to prison, drunk and unfit for work. James Findlay an able seaman and John Sandison an ordinary seaman, were not on board in time for work so two men were hired in their place. On Saturday John McCafferty, a fireman was drunk and unfit for work, sent to prison and a man was hired in his place. On Sunday 16th June, six seamen refused to wash the decks when ordered to do so by the Chief Officer– six men being hired in their place at two francs each. The costs incurred by the Prison, the Constables and by the hire of temporary labour were charged against the offenders' wages. The imprisoned men all returned to the ship before they left Antwerp. The voyage of the ANDES terminated at Glasgow. The Master of the ship was obliged to issue each man with a discharge certificate and 'Report of Character' under two headings: 'For General Conduct' and 'For Ability in Seamanship'. The Master had three options under each heading, VG – very good; G – Good; and 'Decline to Comment'. Five of the crew were marked G for conduct, all were marked VG for Seamanship. In no case did the Master 'Decline to Comment'. Perhaps the misdemeanours of the crew were regarded as not unusual. Third Engineer James Simpson was marked VG in both Conduct and Seamanship.

For his second and third voyages, James chose to sail in two much smaller Glasgow registered steamers, the GOVAN, 311 tons and the GRANGE, 289 tons, compared with his first ship the ANDES 950 tons. The GOVAN left Glasgow 30th July 1872 heading for Genoa and the Island of Elba in the Western Mediterranean Sea. She carried only two engineers, a chief and an assistant chief, James Simpson. This extra responsibility earned James an additional £1 a month. The GOVAN returned to Glasgow where James was discharged on 9th September. On 3rd October, James joined the GRANGE as Second Engineer, although his wage dropped a £1 again, perhaps because he did not hold a 2nd Engineer's Certificate. His new ship also traded with France, Spain, Portugal and the western Mediterranean. He was about to experience a brief bout of nostalgia and his first taste of disaster at sea. On 10th November, the GRANGE docked in Malaga, staying until the 14th, James' home for the first eighteen years of his life. Did he look up old friends? Did he walk round the bay to the site of his old home? If he did so he would have found the Angel Ironworks abandoned and derelict. Nearby however, was a new bullring, built in 1871 on the slag from the ironworks.

Did he cross the road and visit the English Cemetery where his infant brother and sister were buried?

Malaga Harbour Tramp Steamer. On his third voyage, James found himself back in Malaga, four years after the family returned to Glasgow. The Angel Ironworks and his home for 18 years were still standing, but empty. Did he meet up with old friends, perhaps a Spanish engineer called Alfred Martin, the father of his nephew?   *Image KY Collection*

The GRANGE retuned to Glasgow on the 20th December 1872 where James spent Christmas at home, no doubt updating the family on the state of affairs in Malaga.

Princess Dock, Glasgow. James' first three ships, ANDES, GOVAN and GRANGE, were registered in Glasgow and he sailed from Glasgow. From August '73 to November '77, he sailed in Spanish ships RITA and NANA registered in Bilbao. No records have been found for these ships.

Image KY Collection

On 31st January 1873, he rejoined the GRANGE, sailing this time for Nantes in France via Cardiff presumably to pick up a cargo of Welsh steam coal. At 7.30pm on February 9th, the GRANGE anchored in Charpentier Bay in the mouth of the River Loire, while the ship with lights on sent up signal rockets, requesting a pilot. In the engine room the fireman and duty engineer were able to take things easy, keeping the boilers simmering and the steam at operating pressure. At 1am on the 10th, the telegraph from the bridge rang, signalling for the engines to proceed at half speed. The engineer set the engines in motion. At 2.30am the engine room crew were jolted off their feet and the telegraph was frantically signalling "Reverse – Full". In the words on the Master's log entry the:

> "Vessel took the ground and remained fast in spite of every effort to get the vessel afloat with the assistance of a tug and her own engines."

Captain Alex Murray attributed,

> "the casualty to the darkness of the night and having failed to see the Illes Martin Buoy and the strong eddy tide preventing the vessel from answering her helm, and the Pilot being of course".

No lives were lost happily. Henry Sutton, British Vice Consul in St. Nazaire certified in the log that all the crew had received their wages up to the 17th April 1873 and that provision was made for maintaining them and sending them back to the United Kingdom.

James' application to take his Engineer's exam, tell us he joined his next ship - RITA on the 2nd August 1873, meaning he was very likely at home with the family in Govan when the news arrived of his brother Sebastian's death at Fernando Po. Between his shipwreck at St. Nazaire and his return to sea, James was at home for three months and would be well aware of the tensions at 93 Gloucester Street, as his mothers and sisters smarted over their sister Sarah's behaviour and as his father's sanity became more volatile. He was probably relieved to go back to sea.

His exam application shows the RITA was a Spanish ship registered in Bilbao, not a problem for James who spent the first four years of his engineering apprenticeship in the Angel Ironworks Malaga. It is a problem for the researcher however. Nothing is known of the RITA as foreign ships are not listed in Lloyd's Register of Shipping, nor were Spanish vessels obliged to Register Crew Agreements with Marine Superintendents at British Ports, therefore we know nothing about James' rank or pay, and nearly nothing of the ship's movements during James' time on board. James served 4 years on the RITA and another Spanish vessel, the NANA, during which time we can pinpoint his whereabouts on only three occasions. On 6th November 1873, James Passed his exam for Second Engineer in Liverpool; on the 19th August 1876, his name appeared on the petition to Glasgow Sheriff Court to have his father committed to a mental asylum; and on 26th September 1876, he passed his exam for First Engineer, again in Liverpool.

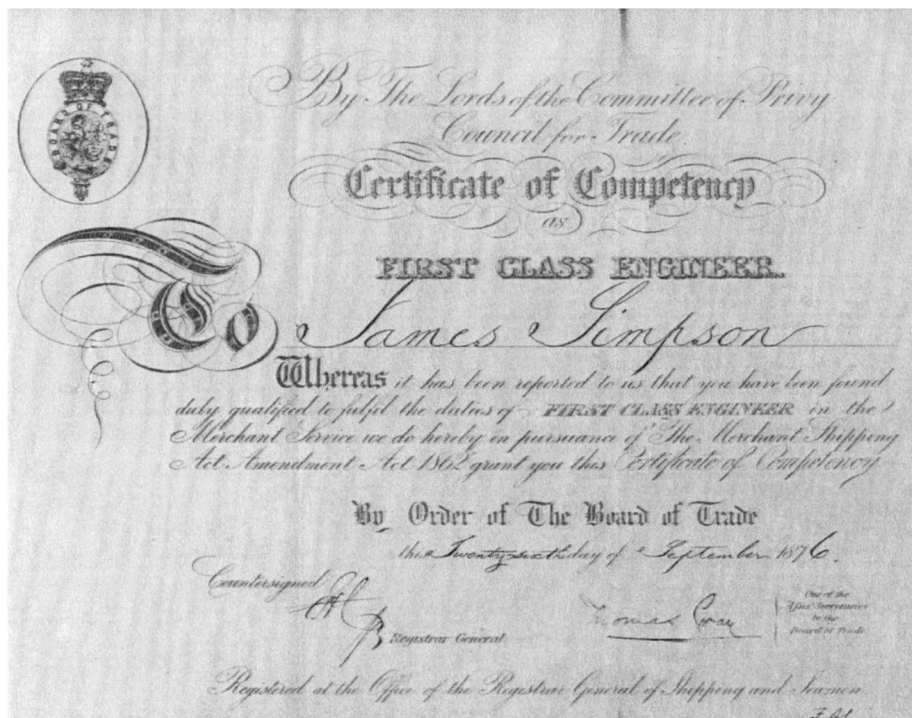

Certificate of Competency, First Class Engineer. James returned to Liverpool , thence to Glasgow in August 1876, just in time to sign the papers committing his unfortunate father to Gartnavel Mental Asylum. While on shore, he passed his First Class Engineer Examination in Liverpool on the 26th September 1876, then sailed 10th November for the Far East, once more.

Image courtesy of National Maritime Museum, Greenwich

Various newspapers (on the British Library website) reported movements of the RITA under the heading of Shipping Intelligence:

> *Liverpool Mercury: 9th February 1874, Rita from Galveston*
> *Glasgow Herald: 27th November 1875, Rita 1010T, Spain to Greenock, Esparto*
> *Liverpool Mercury: 8th April 1876, Rita sailed for Havana*
> *Manchester Courier: 20th December 1876, Rita(s) from Valencia, arr. Liverpool*
> *Western Briton Advertiser: 10th September 1877, Rita 1010T in Graving Dock, Liverpool*
> *Glasgow Herald: 22nd August 1877, Nana from Gothenburg, arr. Southampton*

The RITA traded in the Atlantic, apparently a regular caller to Liverpool and the NANA traded between Europe and various British ports. James quit the Spanish ship in 1877.

His next ship took him in a different direction completely – to the Far East, where he spent the next year and a half with only one return journey between. On 12th November 1877, he signed on the SS CYPHRENES, a Dundee registered ship of 1,995 gross registered tons. James, although holding a 1st Class Engineer's certificate, signed on as 2nd Engineer, for a wage of £13 per month. Very interestingly, he made an allotment of half his wage £6.10/-, presumably to his mother. The crew signed on "*for a voyage from London to Penang, Singapore, Hong Kong and Singapore via the Suez Canal.*" The Suez Canal was one of the greatest civil engineering projects in the 19th century. Built for the Suez Canal Company by a French Engineer, Ferdinand de Lesseps, it opened to traffic in 1869. In 1875 the Khedive of Egypt, facing serious financial embarrassment offered his shares to the British Government. The British Prime Minister, Benjamin Disraeli hastily raised £4 million from his contacts in the City of London and Britain suddenly became a major shareholder along with France, the two nations holding the controlling interest from then until 1956.

The Suez Canal made a major contribution to Britain's prosperity through ever increasing trade with India, and the Orient. To protect her interests, Queen Victoria's government made a pact with the Khedive of Egypt, Ismail Pasha, allowing British forces to be stationed in the Canal Zone, ostensibly securing the neutrality of the passage but of course protecting British interests at the same time.

The combination of steam ships and the shortened route reduced the voyage time to India from three months to six weeks, a great blessing for the constant flow of trade, troops, engineers, civil servants, merchants, teachers etc., and their families. The canal and its facilities must have been of great interest to an engineer such as James Simpson who had a broad training. After clearing the canal at Suez, he was to see many new sights and civilisations. The CYPHRENES' first port of call was Jeddah in Arabia, but she bypassed India, then called at Penang, Singapore, Hong Kong, Saigon, Cochin, Shanghai, back to Hong Kong, Singapore, Saigon, Cochin, and Singapore again. Judging by the 'to and fro' shipping movements, the CYPHRENES was working as a tramp steamer. She returned to London on 25th August 1878.

Suez Canal. From 1877 to 1888, James spent much of his time sailing to and from the Far East, via the Suez Canal which knocked 3 weeks off the journey time round the Cape of Good Hope. His nephew Jack, with the AIF in 1914 was the only other member of the sea faring family to use the canal, 1914.

Image KY Collection

James enjoyed about 6 weeks leave before sailing once more from London on October 11th, in the same ship, in the same capacity – 2nd Engineer, on the same wage of £13 per month and making the same allotment of £6.10/-. After a similar voyage to the first, CYPHRENES returned to London on May 20th 1879. James' younger brother Samuel arrived back in Liverpool aboard the SCYTHIA from Hamburg on May 30th that same year. Samuel had two weeks break before sailing again on the 18th June. Maybe the two brothers shared a brief period at home together and exchanged some friendly banter about the merits of sail and steam over a pint or two before parting – for the last time!

James remained at home until 27th November 1879. He then settled for a spell in the 'HOME TRADE', joining Glasgow tramp steamer – the ARDANACH, working between UK ports, Glasgow, Liverpool, Newport, London and ports in Spain, Italy and Greece. James signed on as First Engineer, at £12 per month, one pound less than Second Engineer on the CYPHRENES. This time he made no allotment, perhaps as he was not absent from home for prolonged spells. He paid a final visit to his old haunt Malaga on 24th – 29th October 1880, before quitting ARDANACH. James had Christmas and New Year at home before making a trip to Norway and Sweden in January 1881 as First Engineer on another Glasgow Steamer SANDA.

The cool climate of North West Europe was losing its appeal for James. On 27th January 1881 he joined a new ship OAKLANDS and was soon heading for Suez and the lure of the Orient.

VIEW OF THE BUND, SHANGHAI.

The Bund, Shanghai, China's main trading port. An anchorage familiar to James Simpson; he was there with the OAKLANDS in 881, and the WAVERLEY 1883-84
Image London illustrated News 1894, KY Collection

313

THREE CHINESE CRUISERS IN ONE GRAVING DOCK.

H.M.S. "ORION" IN DOCK AT SINGAPORE.

The Docks at Singapore. James passed through Singapore several times during his spell in the Far East. It was the hub for trade passing between the Far East and Europe. (Today it is still the hub for East-West trade and has the biggest container terminal in the world).
Image KY Collection

For the next six years he worked in the Far East, for much of the time on ships registered in the Far East. No crew agreements have been found for the period January '81 to March'88, with the exception of one, the CHARLES TOWNSEND HOOK, registered in Liverpool on which James served briefly, April – May 1884.

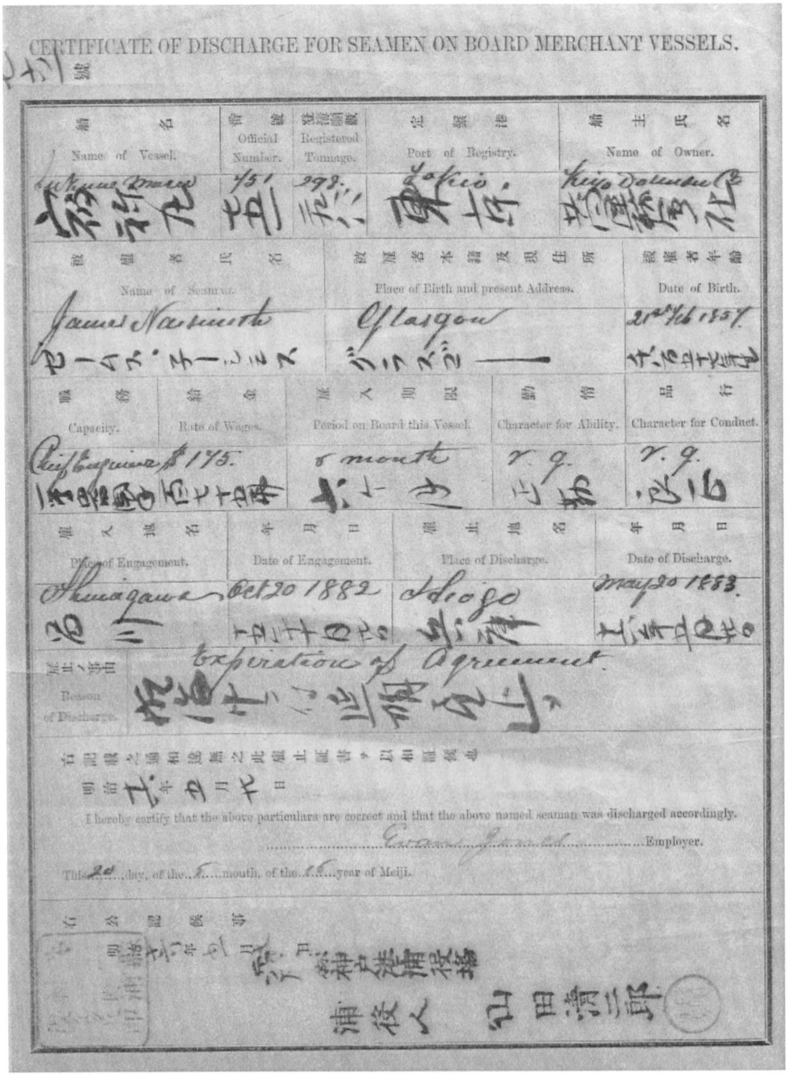

CERTIFICATE OF DISCHARGE FOR SEAMEN ON BOARD MERCHANT VESSELS.

Name of Vessel.	Official Number.	Registered Tonnage.	Port of Registry.	Name of Owner.
	451	998	Tokio	

Name of Seaman.	Place of Birth and present Address.	Date of Birth.
James Naismith	Glasgow	21st Feb 1857

Capacity.	Rate of Wages.	Period on Board this Vessel.	Character for Ability.	Character for Conduct.
Chief Engineer	$175.	7 month	v. g.	v. g.

Place of Engagement.	Date of Engagement.	Place of Discharge.	Date of Discharge.
Shinagawa	Oct 20 1882	Hiogo	May 20 1883

Reason of Discharge. Expiration of Agreement.

I hereby certify that the above particulars are correct and that the above named seaman was discharged accordingly.

.....Employer.

This 20 day, of the 5 month, of the 16 year of Meiji.

Certificate of Discharge for Seamen on Board Merchant Vessels. Some of James' ships were registered in the Far East and no crew agreements have been found. This discharge certificate, a rare find, is for a Glasgow Engineer James Naismith, a contemporary of James, and is dated 'May 20 1883'. James wound have collected a few of these.

Image KY Collection

Coaling at Hong Kong. As steam ships increased in size and number in the second half of the 19th century, so did the need for coaling stations. Ironically the cheapest way of delivering coal was by sailing ship, thus prolonging the life of sail. Only shovels, baskets and plenty of coolies were needed to fill the bunkers. James joined the CHAS. TOWNSEND HOOK at Hong Kong on 1st April 1884.

Image KY Collection

The Register of Certificated Engineers held at Kew (BT139/7) contains some cryptic comments. James was discharged from the OAKLANDS in Shanghai on the 6th July 1881 and was sentenced to loss of pay for being absent without leave.

> 1882: No entry in Register
> 1883: WAVERLEY, Shanghai 19th October 1883 – 12th February 1884
> 1884: CHARLES TOWNSEND HOOK, Hong Kong 1st April 1884 – 19th May 1884. Crew agreement shows he joined as 2nd Engineer and the ship visited Bangkok, Siam.
> 1885 – 1887: No entry in Register
> 1888: BOILEAU, Bombay 2nd May 1888 – 10th June 1888

The crew agreement for the BOILEAU, registered port Cardiff, shows James signed on as 2nd Engineer, in Bombay on the 2nd May with a wage of £9.10/-, and was discharged in Dublin 30th June 1888. After clearing the Suez Canal,

316

the BOILEAU called at Genoa in Italy, and then backtracked to Odessa on Russia's Black Sea coast before heading to Dublin.

When James enlisted on the BOILEAU at the beginning of May it was likely he had received word of the death of his mother Ann Simpson (nee Hosgood) on 22nd October 1887, and he was making his way home to help sort out the family affairs. His father was still alive but incurably insane in Gartnavel Hospital. Ann Simpson had been the last surviving trustee nominated by James Simpson senior's will, so new legal arrangements were needed to safeguard James and his estate. James Simpson junior was at home for seven and a half months during which it seems to have been decided that Jane James Simpson, eldest surviving daughter would take over the administration of her father's estate, rather than James junior, son and heir and natural successor. This makes sense if James still intended to follow his career at sea. At the age of 40 he was still a bachelor and footloose.

The family home at 116 Pollok Street was given up. The three sisters moved to Bath Street in Central Glasgow. James returned to sea on 18th February 1889, sailing as 2nd Engineer on the ABYDOS, a substantial steamer of 1,339 net registered tonnage. James' wage was £9 per month and he made no allotment. In his 16 years at sea, wage rates for certificated engineers declined rather than improved – was supply exceeding demand?

The ABYDOS sailed via London to La Guayra, Venezuela, returning to Swansea on 20th May 1889 where the crew was discharged. For James there was no longer a family home to return to, so where did he go? He did not join another ship until 5th August, an elapsed time of 11 weeks, and that ship sailed from South Shields. It seems very likely that he stayed at least part of the 11 weeks with his sister Sarah who was living in the Tyne Dock district of South Shields. His next ship RION, a bulk oil carrier of 2196 gross tons was launched 17th June 1889 from the slipway of Palmer's Yard at Willington Quay, across the river from Tyne Dock. Her first crew, including 2nd Engineer James Simpson signed on 5/6th August and the builders completed the ship, handing her over to new owners on the 8th August.

There is circumstantial evidence that James and Sarah were close to each other at this time. James' wage on the RION was £11 a month, from which he immediately made an allotment of half, £5.10/-, but to whom? He was a 40 year old bachelor. His only other kin were three sisters in Glasgow who were moderately well off and he had not made any allotments since his mother's death. At the time James sailed, Sarah Simpson was aware she was two months pregnant, and when she gave birth to a son on 7th March the following year, she named him James. One senses that James Simpson, a hardened marine engineer had more in common with Sarah and Robert Kirkpatrick in South Shields, than with his condescending sisters Jane, Martha and Helen in Bath Street, Glasgow.

1. The Engine Room.—2. Taking the Time on the Measured Mile.—3. The Electric Light in the Stoke-Hole.

Handover of a New Ship. On 6th August 1889, James signed on as 2nd Engineer on board the RION, registered in Newcastle and built at Palmer's Yard. The ship was undergoing sea trials and was handed over to her new owners, Stephens & Mawson on 8th August. This image in not the RION, but is of a similar ship of the same period. Note the fireman and greaser in the engine room, jobs that nephew Jack Kirkpatrick would perform on board the KOORINGA in Australian waters in 1912-13.

Image KY Collection

318

The RION, a new type of ship, an oil tanker made her first two trips to the port of Batum at the eastern end of the Black Sea. James completed the two trips then took his discharge. His subsequent maritime career is unknown, though appears to continue beyond 1891 when he does not feature in the UK census.

Image
www.belygorod.ru;
Artist Lev Lagario
1827-1905

James' main interests in the RION were the Palmer built 3 cylinder compound engines, nominal 216 horse power, driving a single screw. The machinery drove her all the way to Batoum (Batum) at the eastern end of the Black Sea. Hitherto oil fields had been exporting oil in tin cases for years, but bulk carriers were a novelty. Oil was not yet in demand as a fuel, but was needed in ever increasing quantities as a lubricant for the wheels of the industrial revolution. On the return journey, the RION stopped at Belfast to discharge 25 tons of oil for the shipbuilder, Harland and Wolff. She terminated her maiden voyage at Newport on 26th September 1889.

RION commenced her second voyage from Newport on 7th September 1889 still with 2nd Engineer James Simpson on board and still making the same allotment from his wage. The ship reached Batoum 15th October, completed loading and sailed on the 19th October, terminating the voyage at London on 8th November 1889. James Simpson took his discharge at that time, collecting the balance of his wages, £9.12.9½. This crew agreement was the last found for James Simpson. A seaman's service can be traced retrospectively as he has to state his 'previous ship' when signing on, but frustratingly, there is no way of tracking forward in time from an agreement.

It seems James Simpson was still serving at sea when the 1891 census was taken – his name does not appear. Ten years on in 1901, he has 'swallowed the anchor' and was settled in a one room flat at 48 Houston Street, Govan as a lodger; aged 51, still single and working as an engine fitter. Ten years further on in 1911, James is living at 266 Crookston Street, Kingston, Govan. His age is given as 62; he is living alone, and his occupation is still engine fitter. These last two addresses are in working class, industrial districts, as different as chalk and cheese, from the up-market middle class suburb of Newlands where James' three sisters lived, even although they were only three miles apart.

Crookston Street, Govan, Glasgow. On 26th May 1915, at 20 minutes past 3pm, James Simpson was found dead in his chair at 266 Crookston Street, Glasgow, in the heart of a working class district. His death was reported by his sister Jane James Simpson, 9 Woodburn Road, Newlands, Glasgow, one of the new spacious leafy, middle class suburbs. One week earlier, a nephew he never knew, died in Shrapnel Gully, Anzac cove, Gallipoli: a pity they never met.

Image courtesy of the Mitchell Library, Glasgow

On May 26th, 1915 at 3.20pm, James Simpson was found dead in a chair at 266 Crookston Street, Glasgow, just seven days after his nephew John Simpson Kirkpatrick was killed by a Turkish shrapnel ball on a dusty hillside at Gallipoli. The suddenness of James' death necessitated a post mortem which confirmed death by natural causes, 'cardiac disease'. The last two males of the Simpson Kirkpatrick dynasty were gone leaving no male heir to continue the line. Jane James Simpson, of 9 Woodburn Road, Newlands, Glasgow was the informant who reported the death to the Registrar. One wonders if Sarah Simpson, grieving for her last surviving son, was ever informed of her brother's death.

James Simpson died without leaving any estate or will. He does not appear to have received a share of his father's wealth, now concentrated in the hands of his three sisters, Jane, Martha and Helen. The impression comes through that James and his three surviving sisters were on different sides of the rift which split the family apart sometime in 1872-73.

Primary Sources

Scottish Death Index – Govan 1915
Scotland Census 1871, 1901, 1911
Sundry Crew Agreement s and Log Books, Maritime History Archive, Newfoundland
Register of Deceased Seamen BT 153/13, National Archives, Kew
Engineers and Mates Certificates, National Maritime Museum, Greenwich

Secondary Sources

"King Canvas", *Captain A A Bestic, 1958, New York*
"Captain Frasers Voyages", *Marjory Gee, 1979, New York*
"Bowsprit Ashore" *Alexander Bone, 1932 London*
"Brassbounders of the ROSEMOUNT" *Shalimar, 1944, Oxford*
"Escape to the Sea" *Tom Sullivan 2008, edited by Mike Starke, Caithness*
"Round the World Flying", *Edited by Carol McNeill, 2008, Kirkcaldy*
"The Ship Captain's Medical Guide". *Leach and Spooner, 14th Edition 1906*
"My ancestor was a merchant seaman" *Chris T and Michael J Watts, 2002, Society of Genealogists, London*
Lloyds Registers of Shipping
"A History of Guano Mining on the Lacepede Islands"
(www.kimberleysociety.org)
The Argus, Melbourne, Victoria, 23rd January 1877, 11th January 1877

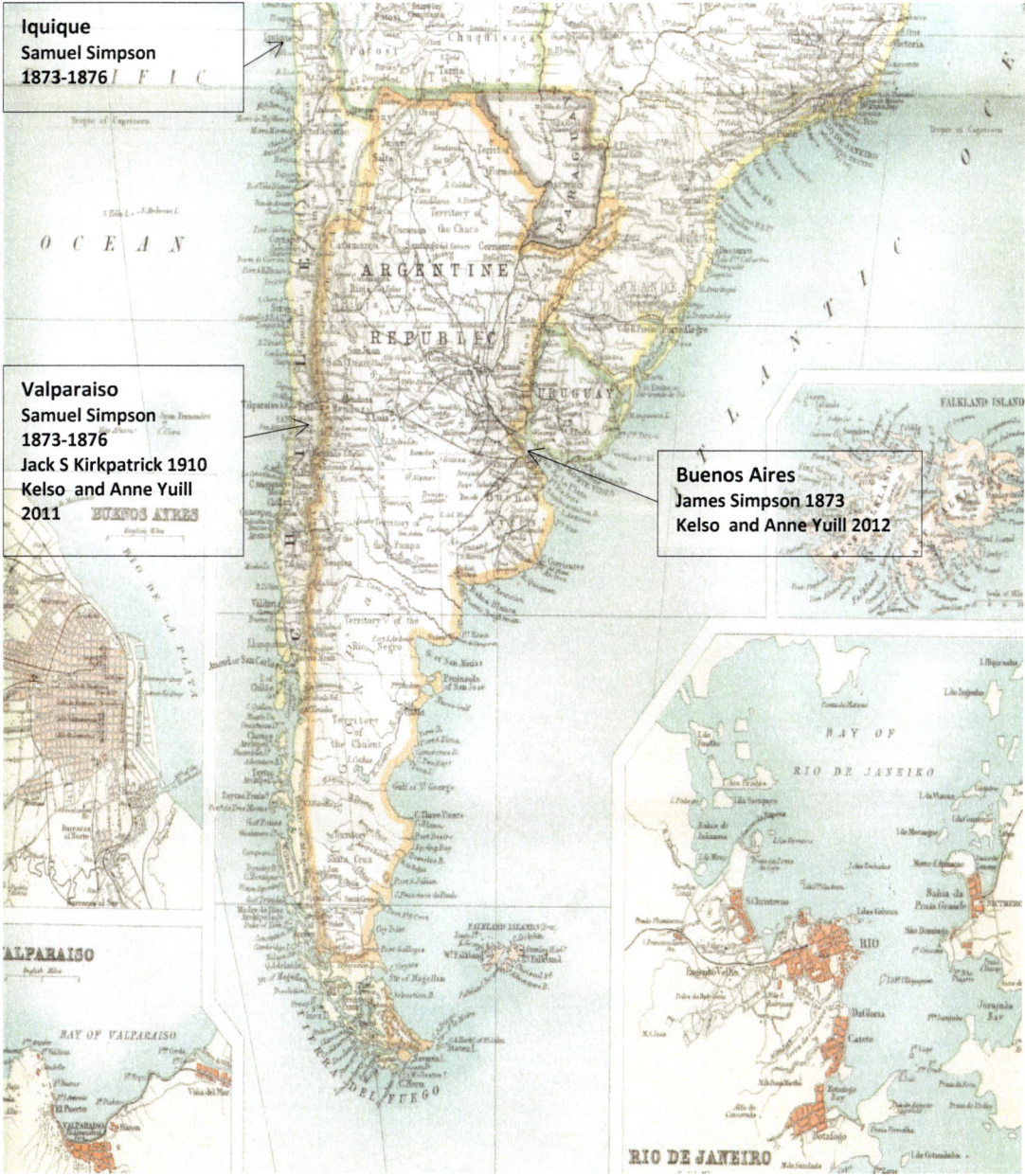

Iquique
Samuel Simpson
1873-1876

Valparaiso
Samuel Simpson
1873-1876
Jack S Kirkpatrick 1910
Kelso and Anne Yuill
2011

Buenos Aires
James Simpson 1873
Kelso and Anne Yuill 2012

Physical map of **South America** from 20 degrees longitude southwards on map by John Bartholomew & Co. 1895.

APPENDIX IV

Sarah Simpson's Sisters – Jack's Aunts

When Jack was born in July 1892, he had three aunts and an uncle living in Glasgow. His maternal grandfather was also still alive, albeit confined within the walls of Gartnavel Asylum. His maternal grandmother, Ann Hosgood Simpson had died 5 years before his birth. Ann Simpson had been the last surviving trustee nominated in her husband's will, therefore the family solicitors had to arrange transfer of authority to manage and administer James's affairs to a new trustee. The natural choice was his son and heir James Simpson junior. However James junior was a marine engineer working mostly in the Far East in the merchant service, and in no position to fulfil the role of trustee.

Power of attorney was instead granted to James's eldest surviving daughter, Jane James Simpson who was named after her Welsh grandmother, a spinster aged 39 years. Jane James was left in possession of the family home at 116 Pollock Street, Glasgow shared with her two spinster sisters, Martha aged 29 and Helen aged 22. Both younger sisters were school teachers. Not only did Jane James have possession of the family home; she had full control of her father's goods, chattels and wealth. Thus a terrible irony was worked out. When James Simpson was committed to Gartnavel Asylum in 1876, he told the examining doctors: *"…his daughters were vipers, wanting his heart's blood, and threatened to kick them downstairs."* The doctor added *"He has hatred to his wife and nearly all his family."*

Jane enjoyed the retribution. Within four years, the house in industrial Govan had been exchanged for an apartment in one of central Glasgow's most expensive streets. The census for 1891 shows Jane, Martha and Helen living at 216 Bath Street. Jane aged 43 was a saleswoman, perhaps in one of nearby Sauchiehall Street's fashionable shops, and Martha aged 32, and Helen aged 25 were still teachers. To look after the three ladies, they had two living-in servants, a cook/domestic and a housemaid. They were again enjoying a standard of living denied them since the heady days when the family prospered in Malaga's sunshine.

216B Bath Street, Glasgow. After the death of their mother in 1886, Jane James, Martha and Helen Simpson moved from industrial Govan to Bath Street, one of the most fashionable streets in Central Glasgow. Strangely in 2007, 216 Bath Street was a vacant lot amidst the buildings that had stood for over a century, but remains a very valuable commercial site.
Image KY Collection

Sauchiehall Street, Glasgow, circa 1900. As Glasgow flourished, high class stores prospered. Argyle Street, Buchannan Street and Sauchiehall Street became popular with shoppers, their trips facilitated by an expanding rail and tram network. The Simpsons lived about 100 yards from Sauchiehall Street and Jane James, a dressmaker cum saleswoman, probably worked in one of the department stores there
Image KY Collection

Martha and Helen, as teachers worked under employment conditions which were highly discriminatory against women. Any female teacher who chose marriage was obliged to give up her career. For ladies to whom teaching was a vocation rather than a job of work, this Victorian anachronism was truly invidious. This anomalous situation persisted into the 1930s, but ended with the outbreak of World War II in 1939.

Jane's role as guardian of her father's estate ended on 20th June 1897, when death released him from his madness. On the 19th September, Glasgow Sheriff Court recognised Jane James Simpson as her father's Executrix and next of kin. Jane made a declaration to the court that she had *"entered or was about to enter upon possession and management of the deceased's estate as Executrix aforesaid."* When the inventory of James's estate was lodged in the court for probate purposes, it showed precisely one asset, a life insurance policy dated 19th December 1848, with the Scottish Equitable Life Assurance Society, ref P5759.

Value of Policy	£203 – 0 – 0
Bonus additions accrued	£247 – 14 - 0
	£450 – 14 – 0
Offset against this were debts	
Amounting to	£390 - 0 - 0
Net value of James Simpson's Estate	£ 60 - 6 - 6
Amount of Estate Duty	NIL

Obviously Jane had 'already entered upon possession' of her father's estate, very likely on the advice of the family's solicitors and accountants in order to avoid estate duty.

How did Jane, as Executrix, distribute her father's estate? In short, the Simpson family wealth was kept by the three spinster sisters, Jane, Martha and Helen. Their later wills show no attempt was made to share with sister Sarah in South Shields, or sister Ann who disappeared after the 1871 census, nor even their brother James who had returned to live in working class lodgings in Govan and with whom Jane still had contact. The three sister's ring fenced their assets and would live together until parted by death.

The Mitchell Library in Glasgow holds the archives for Glasgow's education system. The records of teacher's service show Martha began teaching in April 1880 at Copeland Road School, followed by a spell at Albert Road

School before returning to Copeland Road again. Her final appointment was Bellahouston School, starting in February 1891. Helen began her teaching career as infant mistress at Hills Trust School in August 1891 moving to Balshagray School in April 1906, and then to Strathbungo School in January 1912 where she remained until retirement.

Hill's Trust School, Govan. Helen, the youngest sister, started her teaching career here in 1891, also as an infant teacher, a position held in other Govan schools until retirement in 1926. Image courtesy of the Mitchell Library, Glasgow

The Archives also include the School Inspectors' Reports and Annual Reports published by the Govan Parish School Board. An Inspector visiting Bellahouston School on March 23rd 1896 filed the following report on the Infant's Department headed by Martha Simpson.

Bellahouston Infant's School, Govan. Martha Simpson, after appointments in two other Govan Schools, was appointed Head of Infant's Department at Bellahouston in 1891, a position held until retirement in 1923.
Image courtesy of the Mitchell Library, Glasgow.

"The Infants are in excellent hands. Reading is well phrased and Arithmetic and Writing are taught in a very satisfactory manner. Object lessons are imparted in animated style, and most successful attention is paid to Kindergarten work and to musical drill. Happiness and healthy activity appear to be prevailing features of the schoolroom."

Clearly Martha was a gifted teacher, a natural with infants and happy in her vocation. The Govan Parish School Board Report for 1897 shows that Martha aged 39 years received a salary of £100 per annum. Helen was probably in receipt of a similar salary. By comparison, a 2nd Mate on a merchant ship in the Coasting Trade could earn about £95 a year and a 1st Mate about £135, assuming 50 weeks of work. For Robert Kirkpatrick, 1897 was a bad year however and he lost about six month's work. Sarah Simpson had to keep her family that year on an income of about £60.

Martha Simpson was not one to rest on her laurels. She was forward thinking and keen to try out new teaching methods for the benefit of her scholars. In August 1904, the Infant Division of Bellahouston School received another glowing report from the Inspector and he added a footnote.

"The phonic method of teaching reading has been introduced in the Infant Department and is being taught by Miss Simpson with marked skill, and results that are already very gratifying."

Phonics was a pioneering system of teaching infants to read, developed by a London school teacher, Helen (Nellie) Dale who published her methods in a series of books starting in 1898. Martha must have been one of the first Infant Teachers in Scotland to embrace the new teaching system, and as the two teaching sisters lived together it is a reasonable assumption that Helen would also be an advocate of the new method. What would the two teachers have thought of their nieces and nephew in South Shields? In 1904, Jack aged 12, was completing his formal education. They would have been amused by his precociousness, reasonably happy with his reading skills, frowned at his spelling, and been alarmed at his total disregard for punctuation. Annie on the other hand would have pleased them. She was already acquiring the literacy that would win her a job as a 'Lady Clerk'. But there was still no sisterly communication between Glasgow and South Shields.

Strathmore Garden's, Kelvinside. As Glasgow expanded, the middle classes moved outwards. The sisters moved a mile westwards to the above street in 1902.

Image KY Collection

The comfort of a middle class tenement house in Edwardian Glasgow has been preserved by the National Trust for Scotland at the Tenement House, Buccleugh Street, Glasgow. The three spinster sisters lived in very similar surroundings to those illustrated below.

Note cupboard bed in corner of parlour.

Image Trip Advisor

Bedroom with iron bedstead and jug and basin for morning wash.

Image Christian Science Monitor

Kitchen with black lead stove and hot and cold running water

Image KY Collection

The three sisters had lived in their town house in Bath Street for about ten years when Queen Victoria died in 1901. In that decade Glasgow's population mushroomed on the wealth created by imperial and industrial expansion. The character of Bath Street was changing. As commerce and trade elbowed their way in, the middle classes were moving out, migrating westwards to the elegant new boulevards, crescents, terraces and parks being created along Great Western Road. The status conscious Simpson sisters went with the flow, moving to 11 Strathmore Gardens, Hillhead, only about a mile from their old home, but a long way from the clamour of trams, carriages, carts and shoppers in the city centre. The property still stands, and in estate agent's parlance, is still a very desirable property in a much sought after area. The street has been renamed to Great George Street.

The three ladies did not remain at Strathmore Gardens for very long and were on the move once more in August 1907, probably on the retirement of Jane James then nearing sixty years of age. Moreover, Strathmore Gardens was on the wrong side of the river for Martha and Helen who were teaching in schools on the south side of the River Clyde.

9 Woodburn Road, Newlands. In 1907, the sisters exchanged tenement living for one of the new stone built villas in a garden suburb to the south west of the city centre, but still within easy commuting distance. They lived here until 1937.

Image KY Collection

In the Parish of Cathcart, to the south of Glasgow, Sir John Stirling Maxwell, Bart was selling off tracts of his Pollok Estate for housing development. On August 10th 1907, Jane James Simpson purchased a brand new house at 9

Woodburn Road for the sum of £890. The traditional tenement property was falling out of fashion with Glasgow's middle classes who could now afford spacious, stone built, two storey detached and semi-detached villas, with their own front gates and gardens. The new developments still maintained Glasgow's fondness for public parks, and Woodburn Road was only two streets away from Newlands Park where the three ladies would have taken the air on summer evenings.

Newlands Park. One of the many green spaces created by Glasgow's civic leaders for the expanding population. This park was a 15 minute stroll from the Simpson's residence.

Image KY Collection

The 1911 census showed the sisters living in a house with seven rooms having one or more windows (compared with Sarah's terraced house in South Shields which had four rooms with windows). The census shows that Jane aged 63 was a retired dressmaker, while Martha aged 52 and Helen aged 45 were teachers with the Govan School Board. The ladies no longer had living-in servants. Jane, being retired, was at home to supervise any daily help required in the house, with cooking, laundry or garden. The two teachers could easily commute to work using Glasgow's rapidly expanding electric tramway system.

The following year, 9th July 1912, Jane took the tram into Glasgow and visited the offices of Messrs Robert Dempster and Brechin, Chartered Accountants, for the purpose of making her will. The will was simple. With the exception of one small legacy, she left everything in equal shares to her sisters Martha and Helen. The Simpson wealth would benefit no other member of the family except her brother James, marine engineer, who was to be paid £25 a year for eight years after Jane's death, but his heirs and successors were excluded. Ultimately poor James received not one penny of his father's money as Jane outlived him by 31 years.

The horrors of the Great War, 1914 – 1918, passed without directly affecting the sisters. They were oblivious to the loss apparently of a nephew serving with the ANZACS at Gallipoli in May 1915, but they did suffer bereavement that same month when their brother James died suddenly in his lodgings in Govan on 26th May. Jane as usual took charge and arranged for James to be interred in the family grave at Craigton Cemetery. His name was added to the tombstone, still leaving space for at least three more names.

At the end of the war, Parliament passed the Representation of the People Act, which granted the vote to women over the age of 30 years. One wonders if the three spirited ladies had been suffragists or suffragettes prior to the war. How did they cast their first vote – Tory, Liberal or less likely, Socialist?

The education department records in the Mitchell Library show that Martha retired 20th August 1923, followed by Helen on the 22nd August 1926. All three sisters had the leisure time to spend in their garden, or in the park, and had the means to travel if they so wished.

After living 20 years at 9 Woodburn Road, Jane sold the house on 13th May 1937 to Hugh Duncan M.A. for the sum of £1,025 – giving Jane a modest capital gain of £135 over twenty years; twenty years of high unemployment and economic depression had certainly kept inflation at near zero. The large house and garden had become too much for the three elderly ladies.

Jane aged 89, Martha aged 79 and Helen aged 72 packed their bags and took the train to Bournemouth on the south coast of England, a resort much favoured by retirees and discriminating holiday makers; a resort with golden beaches, a Victorian pier, a symphony orchestra, public gardens and a more equable climate than Glasgow. They had probably spent holidays there and fallen for the attractions. The wills of Martha and Helen refer to addresses 'late of Bournemouth'.

Bournemouth pre 1939. The indomitable sisters, Jane James aged 89, Martha aged 79 and Helen aged 72 moved to Bournemouth in 1937, expecting to live out retirement in the equable climate of England's south coast. Adolf Hitler had other ideas.

Image KY Collection

THE PINE WALK, BOURNEMOUTH.   12354

The Pine Walk in Bournemouth where the three sisters would have promenaded on a fine summer's day.

Image KY Collection

Moffat, Dumfriesshire. The outbreak of WWII, forced the sisters to evacuate from England's south coast to the Southern Uplands of Scotland and the market town of Moffat.

Image KY Collection

After Bournemouth, the next location found for the sisters was in Moffat, Dumfriesshire, Scotland just after World War II. Their movements between times are conjectural and drawn from the writer's personal experiences of Bournemouth immediately post war.

On 3rd September 1939, families in living rooms from Bournemouth to Aberdeen and beyond gathered round their radios to listen to a broadcast by the British Prime Minister, Neville Chamberlain. In sombre tones he spoke these chilling words;

> *"This morning the British Ambassador in Berlin handed the German Government a Final Note , stating that unless we heard from them by 11 0'clock that they were prepared at once to withdraw their forces from Poland , a state of war would exist between us.*
>
> *I have to tell you that no such undertaking has been received and that consequently this nation is at war with Germany."*

Within days the Simpson sisters in Bournemouth, like every other person in the country were lining up in school halls to be fitted with gas masks; women were sewing blackout curtains and Operation Pied Piper was already underway. In the first three days of September nearly 3,000,000 people (school children and their teachers) were transported from towns and cities in danger from enemy bombers to places of safety in the countryside.

After the evacuation of Dunkirk in June 1940, Britain faced the threat of invasion across the English Channel by Hitler's mighty Wehrmacht army. The south coast was suddenly the front line of battle. At Bournemouth the beaches were mined, the dunes were barricaded with barbed wire, and the pier had a large section cut out to prevent its use as a landing jetty. In a famous speech, Winston Churchill, the new British Prime Minister of the day, inspired the nation with his oratory:

> *"We shall fight on beaches, we shall fight on landing grounds; we shall fight in the fields and in the streets, we shall fight in the hills. We shall never surrender!"*

The beaches were no place for frail elderly ladies however, so the sisters opted to make their stand in the hills. They retreated to Moffat, a quiet town nestling at the foot of Scotland's Southern Uplands, about seventy miles south of Glasgow. They were able to sit out the war in safety in a comfortable private hotel. Moffat had a rail link to Glasgow, reachable in little over an hour should they need to visit the city for shopping or meetings with their solicitors and accountants.

May 30th 1946, at Bankfoot Private Hotel, Moffat, Martha Simpson died of acute gastritis and cerebral thrombosis. She was 87 years old. Before the solicitors had time to complete the formalities of Martha's will, her sister Jane James aged 98 years also passed away, dying of a coronary thrombosis on September 22nd 1946. On both death certificates, parents are given as 'James Simpson, Manager Ironworks deceased, and Ann Simpson, M.S. Hosgood, deceased.' Helen, their last surviving child, now faced loneliness hard to imagine. For 80 years she had never been parted from her sisters. For 80 years they had supported each other through family dissensions; through numerous bereavements, some sudden; through the prolonged madness of their father; through two world wars; through the rise of Victoria's Empire to a peak of prosperity in Edwardian times; and through its catastrophic decline after the First World War.

The inventory of Martha's will amounted to £6,584, mostly in stocks, shares and bank accounts. Jane James's will amounted to £10,824, including £3,080 owing from Martha's estate. Apart from this last sum, the inventory also comprised mostly stocks, shares and bank accounts.

Bankfoot Private Hotel, Moffat. This was the final home of the three ladies, born in a different age and a different world. Jane and Martha died in 1946; Helen survived alone until 1958. Bankfoot is no longer a private hotel but fulfils a similar role as a residential care home for the elderly. *Image KY Collection*

Both Martha and Jane James were buried in the family grave at Craigton Cemetery in Glasgow, their names being added to the stone first erected after their mother's death in 1887. Helen continued to live at Bankfoot Private Hotel until her death on May 11th 1958, aged 92 years. In her will she made a number of bequests, mostly in cash, but a few in kind. To Miss Jessie Hay she left her musquash coat and her mother's photograph; to Reverend William Martin, secretary of the British Sailors' Society, Glasgow a hand sewn sampler. Her largest bequest £4,000 was left to Miss Annie Cameron and Miss Minnie Cameron of Bankfoot Hotel with the following poignant words:

"in recognition of their unsparing kindness and help to me and my sisters, especially to me when I was left alone, and for which kindness, I will be forever grateful beyond words."

Out of a total estate valued at £9,337 and after all bequests had been paid out, a residue of £1,574 remained. Helen directed that the residue be paid to the Glasgow branch of the British Sailors Society perhaps because of support given to the family when her brothers were lost at sea. No bequests were made to Simpson kin.

There was only just room for the monumental stonemason to carve her name, the last one, on the family grave stone in Craigton Cemetery.

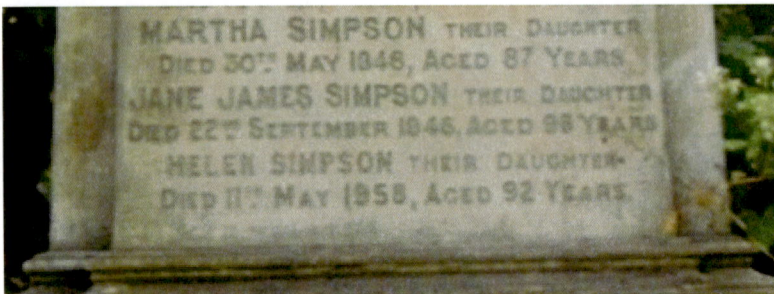

Gravestone at Craigton Cemetery, Glasgow. The coffins of all three sisters were transported from Moffat to Craigton Cemetery, Glasgow for interment. There was only just room for the monumental stonemason to incise the name of Helen, the last of a tragic family. *Image KY Collection*

Primary Sources

Scotland census 1891, 1901, 1911 Scotland's People
Death Certificate for Martha Simpson 1946 (Moffat, Dumfries)
Death Certificate for Jane James Simpson 1946 (Moffat, Dumfries)
Death Certificate for Helen Simpson 1958 (Moffat, Dumfries)
Wills of James Simpson 1897, Martha Simpson 1946, Jane Simpson 1946,
Helen Simpson 1958, National Archives, Scotland
Education Department Records of Service for Martha and Helen Simpson
Govan Parish School Board Report 1897
Reports 1896 to 1904 of H.M. Inspector of Schools, Bellahouston
Sasine Register Sheet 4833 – Purchase 9 Woodburn Road, Registers of
Scotland
Sasine Register Sheet 42125 – Sale 9 Woodburn Road, Registers of
Scotland

APPENDIX V

Family Trees

Kirkpatrick Family Tree

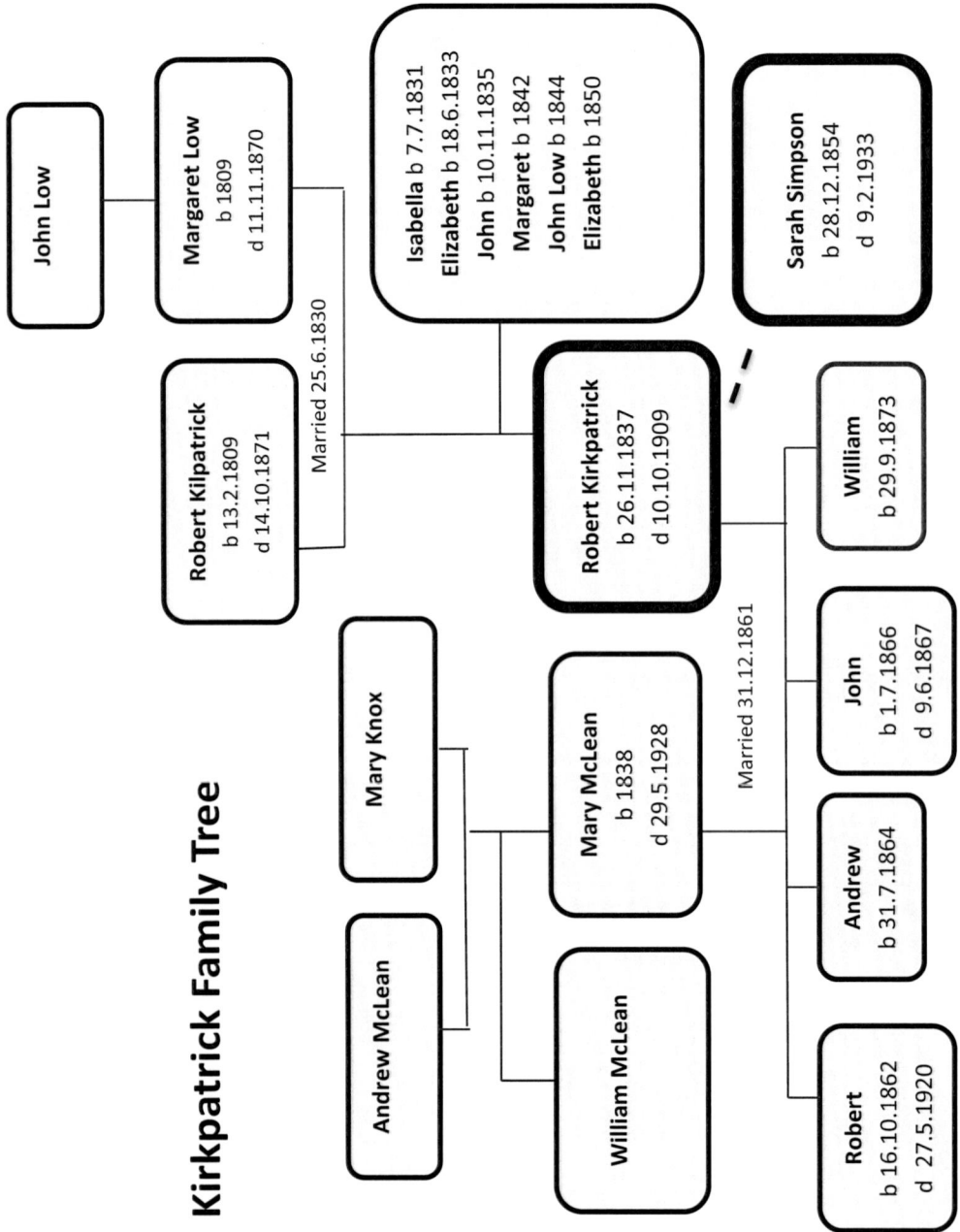

John Low	
Margaret Low b 1809 d 11.11.1870	
Robert Kilpatrick b 13.2.1809 d 14.10.1871	

Married 25.6.1830

Isabella b 7.7.1831
Elizabeth b 18.6.1833
John b 10.11.1835
Margaret b 1842
John Low b 1844
Elizabeth b 1850

Robert Kirkpatrick b 26.11.1837 d 10.10.1909

Sarah Simpson b 28.12.1854 d 9.2.1933

Mary Knox

Andrew McLean

Mary McLean b 1838 d 29.5.1928

William McLean

Married 31.12.1861

William b 29.9.1873

John b 1.7.1866 d 9.6.1867

Andrew b 31.7.1864

Robert b 16.10.1862 d 27.5.1920

339

Sarah Simpson's Family Tree

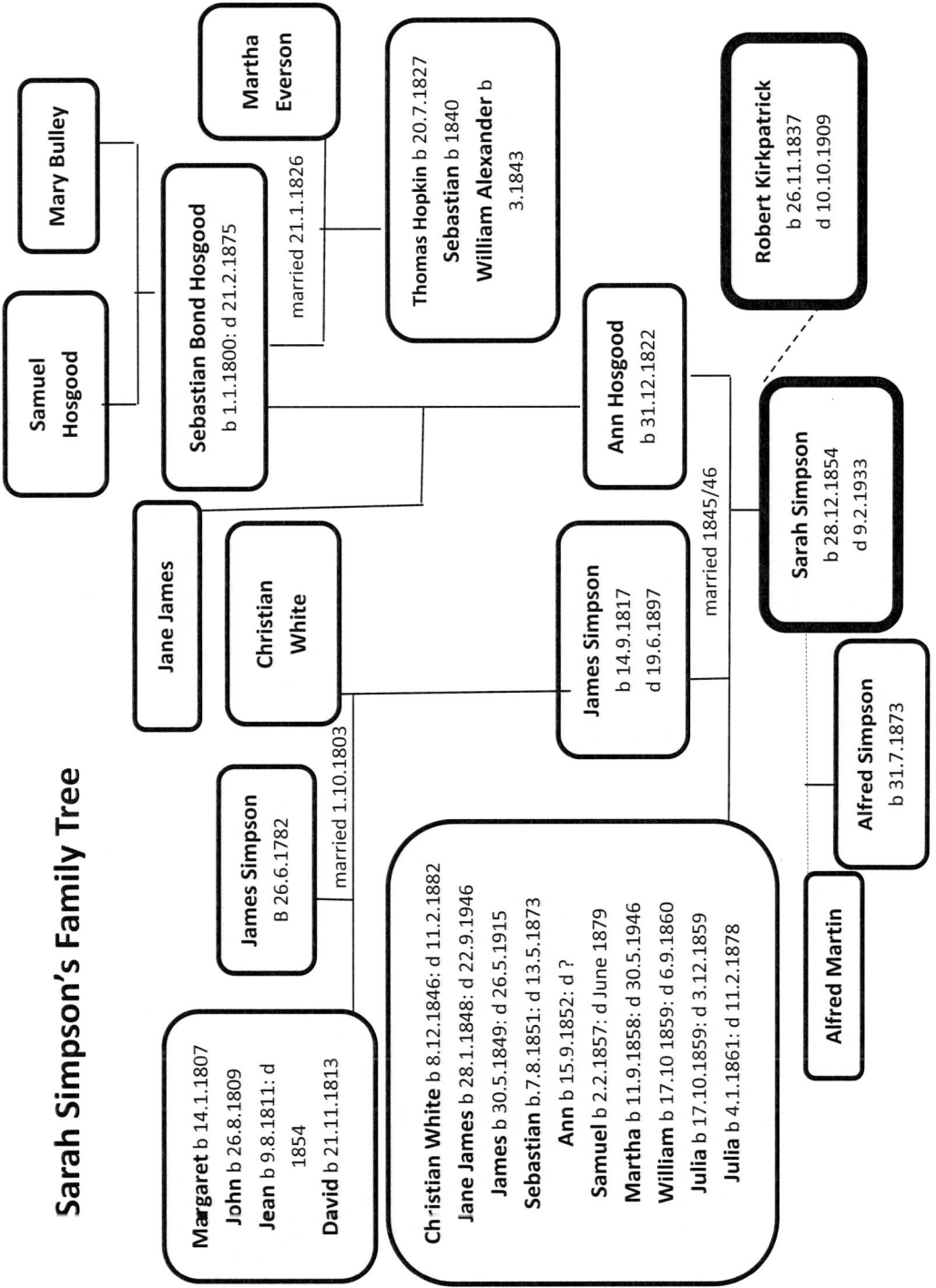

Mary Bulley

Samuel Hosgood

Martha Everson

Sebastian Bond Hosgood
b 1.1.1800: d 21.2.1875

married 21.1.1826

Thomas Hopkin b 20.7.1827
Sebastian b 1840
William Alexander b 3.1843

Robert Kirkpatrick
b 26.11.1837
d 10.10.1909

Ann Hosgood
b 31.12.1822

Jane James

Christian White

James Simpson
b 14.9.1817
d 19.6.1897

married 1845/46

Sarah Simpson
b 28.12.1854
d 9.2.1933

James Simpson
B 26.6.1782

married 1.10.1803

Alfred Simpson
b 31.7.1873

Margaret b 14.1.1807
John b 26.8.1809
Jean b 9.8.1811: d 1854
David b 21.11.1813

Christian White b 8.12.1846: d 11.2.1882
Jane James b 28.1.1848: d 22.9.1946
James b 30.5.1849: d 26.5.1915
Sebastian b.7.8.1851: d 13.5.1873
Ann b 15.9.1852: d ?
Samuel b 2.2.1857: d June 1879
Martha b 11.9.1858: d 30.5.1946
William b 17.10 1859: d 6.9.1860
Julia b 17.10.1859: d 3.12.1859
Julia b 4.1.1861: d 11.2.1878

Alfred Martin

340

Robert Kirkpatrick and Sarah Simpson's Family

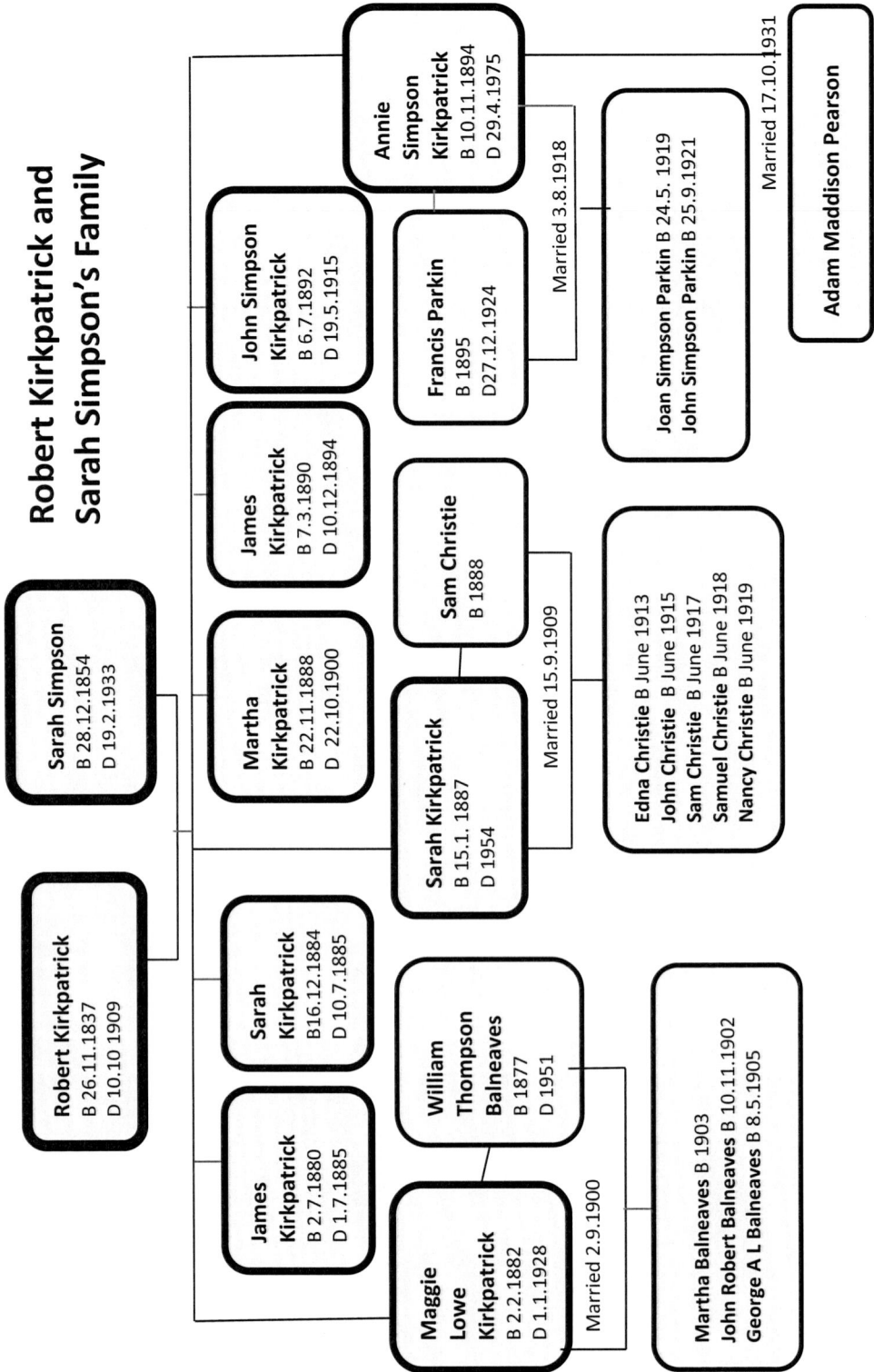

Robert Kirkpatrick
B 26.11.1837
D 10.10 1909

Sarah Simpson
B 28.12.1854
D 19.2.1933

James Kirkpatrick
B 2.7.1880
D 1.7.1885

Sarah Kirkpatrick
B16.12.1884
D 10.7.1885

Martha Kirkpatrick
B 22.11.1888
D 22.10.1900

James Kirkpatrick
B 7.3.1890
D 10.12.1894

John Simpson Kirkpatrick
B 6.7.1892
D 19.5.1915

Annie Simpson Kirkpatrick
B 10.11.1894
D 29.4.1975

Maggie Lowe Kirkpatrick
B 2.2.1882
D 1.1.1928

Married 2.9.1900

William Thompson Balneaves
B 1877
D 1951

Sarah Kirkpatrick
B 15.1. 1887
D 1954

Married 15.9.1909

Sam Christie
B 1888

Francis Parkin
B 1895
D27.12.1924

Married 3.8.1918

Adam Maddison Pearson

Married 17.10.1931

Martha Balneaves B 1903
John Robert Balneaves B 10.11.1902
George A L Balneaves B 8.5.1905

Edna Christie B June 1913
John Christie B June 1915
Sam Christie B June 1917
Samuel Christie B June 1918
Nancy Christie B June 1919

Joan Simpson Parkin B 24.5. 1919
John Simpson Parkin B 25.9.1921

INDEX

343

ABOUT THE AUTHOR

Kelso McEwan Yuill was born in 1934 in a mining village in Scotland, only nine months after Sarah Simpson Kirkpatrick died in South Shields. He left school at 18 and after National Service in the Royal Air Force, he trained to become an accountant. Kelso spent 26 years with a large multi-national company, followed by 9 years working for a Charity.

His main interests are military history, and particularly the Napoleonic Wars spurred by the interest in his great, great grandfather who had fought for the British Army in Spain, Portugal, France and at Waterloo; family history; and in the last 8 years, the story of the Simpson/Kirkpatricks.

Kelso is married to Anne and they have three sons and two daughters between them and at present 5 grandsons and 2 granddaughters, ranging in age from 9 to 22 years. They are all his special passion and raison d'etre.

The author placing a small cross at the grave of No. 202 Private John Simpson Kirkpatrick at Beach Cemetery, near Anzac Cove, Gallipoli.

346

Image KY Collection